Bringing in Finn

An
Extraordinary
Surrogacy
Story

Bringing in Finn

SARA CONNELL

SEAL PRESS

BRINGING IN FINN
An Extraordianry Surrogacy Story

Copyright © 2012 by Sara Connell

Published by
Seal Press
A Member of the Perseus Books Group
1700 Fourth Street
Berkeley, California

Library of Congress Cataloging-in-Publication Data

Connell, Sara, 1975-
  Bringing in Finn : an extraordinary surrogacy story / Sara Connell. — 1st ed.
    p. cm.
  ISBN 978-1-58005-410-2
  1. Connell, Sara, 1975- 2. Motherhood—United States—Biography. 3. Surrogate mothers—United States. 4. Mothers and daughters—United States—Biography. I. Title.
  HQ759.C7244 2012
  306.874'3—dc23

                              2012006969

Some names and places have been changed to protect the privacy of individuals involved. Also, for literary purposes, some scenes and conversations are composites.

9 8 7 6 5 4 3 2 1

Cover and interior design by Domini Dragoone
Printed in the United States of America
Distributed by Publishers Group West

To my mother, the Great Mother,
and the mother in all of us

Prologue

I couldn't breathe. I lay in bed in the labor and delivery ward of a Chicago hospital on the South Side of the city, the doctor's words smashing my heart like a wrecking ball.

"We can't save them. I'm sorry," Dr. Eagan, head of Maternal-Fetal Medicine, told us. When the attempt to sew my cervix shut had failed, Dr. Eagen had shouted, "Shit!" and thrown the stars-and-stripes do-rag he'd been wearing in the OR to the floor.

Everything in the room was an assault: the lights too bright and fluorescent, the whirring of the medical equipment too loud, the furniture dated and worn. I turned my head to the wall, unable to bear the stricken faces of my husband, Bill, my obstetrician, my sister, and now my mother, who had jumped on a plane from Washington, D.C., to Chicago that day after receiving a panicked phone call from Bill.

I twisted on the bed, stretching my hands over my protruding belly, trying to hold on to the lives that had been growing inside me for more than five months. Going into the procedure, Dr. Eagan had told us we had only an 8 percent chance of success. But we'd been hopeful. Babies at twenty-four weeks sometimes survived. We were weeks, if not days, from viability. Someone had to be in the 8 percent.

"We'll take you back to the OR tonight," my OB said. She looked at the wall behind me as she spoke. "You'll be out for the duration."

For five days after the operation, I lay tormented in a hospital room, desperate to find some way for this not to be real. Our burgeoning family (Bill, the twins, and I) had passed all the reassuring milestones: trimester one; genetic screening (all good!); trimester two; the twenty-week ultrasound, where we not only discovered that both babies were boys but saw them with our own eyes—moving and full of life. They did scissor kicks and somersaulted; they had heartbeats, ten fingers, ten toes. At one point, Baby Boy B, as the technician called him, had even sucked his thumb.

The day we left the hospital, a therapist from the perinatal loss department presented us with two death certificates and asked us if we wanted the bodies for a burial. I'd been packing the things Bill had brought me from home: bathrobe, toothbrush, two purple stones from our garden. As the counselor held the papers out to me, I dropped the stones and listened to the knocking sound they made as they hit the linoleum floor and rolled under the metal bed.

"There's no rush to decide," the therapist said gently. "We can keep them here for up to a month. It's probably something you want to decide once you've talked it over at home."

As Bill helped me into the wheelchair I was required to leave the hospital in, I overheard an on-call OB talking to some nurses outside the door of our room. She'd neglected to close the latch, and the door had crept open.

"When they're ready to go, take them out the back way—in the service elevator. I don't want them going out through the reception area with all the new moms and babies."

I slumped into the chair next to the hospital bed, folding the top half of my body over my legs, trying to suck in a breath. I understood the doctor meant well, but I couldn't help seeing her decree as yet another rejection: We were being taken out the back like the trash, sparing those families who came to the hospital and left with a baby, arms full of balloons and flowers and plush toys, the unsightly image of two devastated parents with shell-shocked eyes and dangling arms empty, like wraiths.

Two months later, I flew from Chicago to my parents' house in Virginia, where I'd grown up, for the wedding of a family friend. I was tired from the weeks of grieving and yearned for the comfort of the rolling hills and the woods near my family home. As soon as I arrived, I questioned my decision. The wedding was crawling with new babies and children. My stomach was still round from the pregnancy.

The aunt of the bride, who lived out of state, rushed to greet me from across the room.

"I heard you were having twins," she said, her eyes bright with excitement. "When are you due?"

I struggled to answer. Death seemed an inappropriate thing to mention at a wedding. "Stillborn" was a word that was still unutterable on my tongue.

Late that night, I stood in the hallway of my parents' house outside the bathroom, sobbing. I'd started brushing my teeth but stopped when I realized I could no longer see. The blood in my head made a *whoosh*ing sound, like fast-moving water, in my ears. Spots appeared in front of my eyes, and I wondered if I was going to faint. I dropped the toothbrush into the sink and leaned into the hallway, bracing myself against the wall beams with my arms.

My heart fluttered in the unnatural way it had since I had lost the twins. Sometimes I found it difficult to breathe, and it did not seem unrealistic to me that a person could die from this kind of pain. My raw cries sent my father to the basement, but my mother came to meet me in the hall. There had been a time, even two or three years before, when she would not have come, or when I would not have let her near me. Our reconnection had come as a surprise, with a will of its own, fueled perhaps by the same phenomenon that allows mothers to lift cars to save their infants.

She encircled me in her arms, squeezing my body as if she was trying to suck the pain out of me, as one does for snakebites. I remember vaguely the feel of this embrace, her brown skin, a freckle on the side of her neck, her short hair that had become a bit coarse from coloring. I heaved and wept. When I'd exhausted myself, she held me a foot or so from her and lifted my chin, forcing me to meet her eyes.

"You will know joy again," she said.

I cried harder. I shook my head no.

"Yes," she said, almost laughing at my obstinacy, the way one might to coax a toddler out of a tantrum. Instead of offending, her lightness wedged an opening between me and the hurt.

"There is going to be joy at the other end of this pain," she said again.

I looked into her face through the gleam of tears and still couldn't imagine it. But I stopped crying and began wiping my eyes with the edge of my nightgown. My mother pulled me to her chest again. This time our embrace was quiet. The house was still. Through the cotton of her T-shirt, I could feel the thumping of her heart. Against my chest, it sounded like hope.

Chapter 1

By the time I arrived for my appointment with Dr. Bizan, a doctor of osteopathy (DO) OBGYN I'd found in Chicago, I hadn't had a period in almost three years. I had just turned thirty, and even though Bill and I had not officially begun trying to have children yet, the fact that we might already have fertility issues weighed heavily on my mind.

When I signed in, the receptionist informed me that the doctor was running two hours behind schedule. *Two hours.* I took a seat in the waiting room and tried to calm my nerves. It seemed an inordinately long time to wait. I was already anxious.

Bill and I had just celebrated our fourth wedding anniversary. Six years older than I was, he said he felt forty stalking him. Even if *Details* and *GQ* didn't write about it, men felt the pressure of the biological clock, too, he said. "I don't want to be sixty when our child graduates from high school."

I was trained in holistic medicine and for two years had pursued a natural approach to resuming my cycle. But when I still didn't have a period, Bill became alarmed and, after twenty-four months of acupuncture and herbs and tinctures and teas, it was my turn to try something different. My hope was to find a Western doctor who was at least open to a complementary approach.

Dr. Bizan's office had an air of neglect—a somewhat disconcerting contrast with the luxurious and polished offices of Chicago's other highly ranked OBs I had visited or would visit over the next six years. Looking around at the disarray of Dr. Bizan's entryway—the fingerprint-covered glass, floorboards from the 1930s that were crumbling in places and had never been restored— I wondered if she had the expertise of a top-level doctor. But while Dr. Bizan's lack of punctuality and office aesthetics did not inspire my confidence, what I really wanted in a doctor now was someone with expertise in fertility and menstruation, an open mind, and some compassion, qualities that had been lacking in the plush, clockworklike offices of the last OB I'd visited. I'd left that appointment with Dr. Angelli in tears, after she'd chastised the alternative approach I was taking with my menstrual health, and hadn't been back to a Western MD since.

I sat in a grungy waiting room, cluttered with stacks of pharmaceutical ads and tattered magazines that looked as if they'd been dropped in water and possibly even chewed on by children who'd grown bored with the colored blocks and wooden toys that were strewn around the room.

The air was stuffy. A harried-looking woman with a protruding belly tried to interest her older child in a stack of blocks. I sat beside a younger African American woman whose belly was too large to be contained, even by her army green maternity top. A stretch of her caramel skin gaped between her shirt and pants as she fanned herself with a magazine. I'd taken a seat in the least stained chair I could find and pretended to look at an old *Cosmo*. I hadn't realized how much I wanted Dr. Bizan to be on time. I thumbed through the magazine, looking for a distraction. New sex moves, how to dress sexily, sex secrets of married couples—the usual *Cosmo* fare. I replaced the magazine on the table. Ten minutes in the waiting room would have given me time to think. One hundred and twenty minutes gave me time to obsess.

I had not had a regular menstrual period since I'd stopped taking birth control pills three years before. I'd learned that the technical name for the condition, lack or absence of a period, was amenorrhea. So I knew the when and the what, but not the cause.

My friend Caroline, who had referred me to Dr. Bizan, had told me that she was an open-minded and excellent OB. Dr. Bizan had delivered all three of Caroline's children, supported her in natural childbirth, referred her to a doula-midwife practice, and recommended that she do prenatal yoga. I saw nothing of the holistic influence in the waiting room, though. From the brand-name wooden magazine rack to the plastic clipboards advertising the latest hormone-replacement drugs, the office seemed to be sponsored by Pfizer and Eli Lilly.

I worried that she would try to dissuade me, the way Dr. Angelli had, from taking a holistic approach to menstruation. My sister, a Western-trained MD, explained that because holistic principles weren't taught in medical school, doctors could not endorse them and often explained them away as "placebo" or some kind of primitive medicine, akin to rubbing two sticks together when right here at the flip of a switch there was fire.

I continued flipping the pages of the magazine, attempting to read but failing. I was still angry at myself for having gone on the Pill so unconsciously in college. At the time, I'd suffered from intense menstrual cramps and one of the student health center doctors had told me that the Pill would regulate my cycle and alleviate the cramps. "Plus, it's great birth control," she'd said. Going on the Pill seemed like a rite of passage for a college-age woman. It seemed like the responsible thing to do. Now, I wasn't sure.

I had stayed on the Pill for nine years. When I'd gone off it, three years into my marriage, I had been so optimistic. I'd just assumed my cycle would resume. Bill and I had been living in London, having the expat experience of our lives. It was in England where I'd discovered holistic medicine and had taken every opportunity to study with pioneers in life coaching and the healing arts.

I became certified in reflexology and then as a life coach and counselor. I trained with teachers from Africa and Ireland and visited the research lab and greenhouses where flower essences and essential oils were distilled and transferred to the dark amber bottles we used at the holistic clinic where I went on to work. As manager of the clinic, I had the opportunity to apprentice with herbalists and homeopaths and a fourth-generation teacher of ayurvedic medicine from India.

Growing up in a traditional Western family, I was ignorant of alternative healing. There was no mention of meridians or quantum physics at the dinner table with Uncle Tom, the cardiologist from San Diego; or Aunt Jen and Uncle Alan, who worked in hospital administration in New England. If the subject of alternative medicine had come up among the Midwestern intellectuals on my mother's side, it would have been seen as a joke, appropriate for a cartoon in *The New Yorker*. My new field of work seemed uncharted and exotic. At the same time, I felt I'd come home.

For the first two years we lived in London, Bill supported us while I did my postgraduate programs and training. I'd met him at the advertising agency where I worked straight out of college. He remained with the company, and his work with the agency was the source of our move to London. What I first noticed about him was his lean, wiry body and dark eyebrows that gave him the look of a character out of one of the Brontë novels I used to love.

One of our first conversations was on a walk back to the office from a business lunch, during which we discovered we shared a dream to live abroad in England and to have children. The relationship progressed, and within months we put in a request with human resources for a move to the UK, one that was initially greeted with a guffaw.

"We have English-speaking people who can do the work in England," the company rep said. "The only way you'll get transferred to London is if something gets majorly screwed up and you're the only one in the agency who can fix it."

We didn't have to wait long. In June 1999, two weeks after Bill asked me to marry him, the account that he had spent the past five years growing in the United States was put on probation in London. He was, according to the executive vice presidents, the person to fix it. And so they moved us to London, into a row house on the River Thames, close enough for Bill to walk to the agency's office in South Kensington.

We embraced the experience, spending long weekends in Paris and exploring London's burgeoning culinary scene. I wrote and studied and worked part-time. I joined an artists' group and started reading my pieces in small circles. I was offered a column in a holistic-health magazine, and Bill and I celebrated with a dinner at Nobu in Mayfair. We savored the freedom, taking care, as people often reminded us, to enjoy this time, unhindered, before we had children and would need to be more *responsible*.

I made the decision to go off the Pill because of an article I read at the clinic while preparing for a women's health workshop on hormones. My friend Kaitlin, who was leading the workshop with me, discovered the work of a homeopath named Melissa Assilem, who'd written a treatise about taking a natural approach to women's health. The article expressed concern about a possible link between women who'd been on the Pill for an extended time and later fertility issues.

"Young women in our culture are now going years, if not decades, without ever having a natural menstrual cycle."

Even though I understood that the Pill controlled my menstrual cycle in some way, I had never considered exactly how it worked.

"Did you know we're not even having real periods?" Kaitlin asked after I read the article. "Did you know we haven't been ovulating?"

I had not known, and we guessed we were not the only women with a deep misunderstanding of what was happening in our bodies.

"I am going off the Pill starting tonight," Kaitlin said. I had come to the same decision. I offered to consult my gynecologist to obtain more information and went home to tell Bill I wanted to stop taking the Pill.

It was May and balmy for London. Bill made pizzas and we ate outside in the garden, from which we could make out the outline of colorful houseboats bobbing on the lapping brown water of the Thames. At low tide the river receded to expose rocky sludge and the houseboats sat wedged on the slanting gravel river floor; the air smelled mossy and damp.

"So, we just wouldn't use any birth control?" he asked. I'd been on the Pill since I'd met him, and we'd never had to explore other methods.

"We can use condoms, or foam, or spermicidal jelly," I said, giggling as I tried to recall various birth control methods I had learned about in seventh-grade sex ed.

"Actually, I'm fine if we don't use anything." He smiled at me and pulled at one of my fingers. "I know we're planning to wait until we move back to the States, but if we have a baby sooner than planned, it certainly wouldn't be a bad thing."

I looked at Bill for a moment, surprised, and then grinned. I imagined strolling through Hyde Park with a baby in a Moby wrap, snuggled to my chest. The image filled me with joy. I reached for Bill's hand and he squeezed mine firmly.

My gynecologist in London, Dr. Eagen, confirmed the information Kaitlin and I had read in Assilem's article. Dr. Eagen was Cambridge educated, a tall, reedy woman with formal manners. She was caring, though, and took extra time in consultations. When answering a question, she would place on her nose and then remove a pair of wire-framed glasses to emphasize her points.

"The Pill does suppress ovulation. The period you have is caused by the low dose of hormones in the Pill," she said, holding her glasses like a pointer in her left hand.

"So, I haven't ovulated in almost nine years?" I said, incredulous. "Could not ovulating for so long have an impact on my fertility?"

"I wouldn't worry," she said. "Most women are able to get pregnant, even after taking the Pill for many years. You are young and healthy, and you have no reason to be concerned about your fertility."

I relaxed a little in Dr. Eagen's confidence. I hadn't been worried about my fertility until I'd read the article, even though I'd already had one reproductive issue—an ovarian cyst when I was fifteen years old that had ruptured, causing my left ovary to be removed. The surgeon and every gynecologist I'd seen since affirmed that the operation would have no negative impact on my ability to have children. Of course, in the years to come, as we navigated the tangled world of fertility treatments, I often questioned whether this assessment had been accurate, if perhaps the removal of my ovary did play some role in my fertility issues. That day, though, I took the affirmation with relief and reassurance. I had no reason to doubt.

"Each ovary has enough eggs for many lifetimes," the doctor had assured me the day of the surgery. "The human body is pretty incredible. You'll even have a period every month."

And I had, or I had until I'd gone on the Pill in college and apparently started pseudomenstruating.

Melissa Assilem's article scared me. Several of Bill's peers at the ad agency were having trouble conceiving, women without any reproductive trauma at all. I'd also worked with clients at the clinic who'd undergone fertility treatments. One of them, a writer for a top UK magazine, detailed her journey in a monthly column. She wrote candidly of the fear, the painful longing to have a child, the crushing despair when an in vitro cycle was not successful. In private, she'd confided in me that her marriage was in jeopardy, that she was jealous of her friends who were having babies, that she felt like a failure and was ashamed of her inability to conceive.

I held her hands while she talked, my palms growing sweaty as she expelled her pain. My desire to be a mother was like my desire to continue breathing and maintain the use of my limbs. It sounded excruciating to want something so deeply and not know whether you'd ever be able to experience it.

I knew that I couldn't control any of these women's destinies, but I looked for ways I could give support. I let their sessions run overtime, and Kaitlin and I concocted herbal tinctures made with ingredients known to increase fertility. We poured them into amber bottles with black rubber stoppers and wrapped them in handmade paper and petals from Quasadi roses, a marriage and fertility flower from a village in Iran.

Dr. Eagen supported my decision to go off the Pill.

"It can take some time for the body to remember what it's supposed to do," she told me. "It takes some women up to ten months for their regular cycle to resume."

When I told Dr. Eagen that our expat term was up and that Bill and I would be moving back to Chicago at the end of the year, she encouraged me to find a good OB-GYN.

"Find someone you really like," she said, winking. "Someone you'll want to deliver your babies."

As we prepared for the move, I said goodbye to our friends and our life in London. It was a sorrowful parting with our friends, so many of whom had become our family in the UK. But the crushing wall of sadness I expected in making the move never came. In the previous four months, a kind of homesickness for America had come on; Bill said he felt it, too. A new vision emerged in my mind: a spacious house with a home office, a roof deck/garden, space for a child, a place to grow our family.

Seven months had passed since our conversation back in May. Per our agreement, we hadn't used any birth control. And I hadn't had a period.

Every so often I would feel the twinge of a cramp or mood changes that I hoped were indications that my period was coming. I would find the nearest bathroom in anticipation, but no blood came. The cramps were like the phantom pains of an amputated limb, or maybe psychosomatic; I wanted so much for my period to return. If I thought about its absence for too long, I became fretful until I remembered Dr. Eagen's words: that it might take close to a year for my cycle to resume.

After we'd been in Chicago two months and I'd finally unpacked the last of the moving boxes, I decided it was time to find a doctor. I didn't have any close friends in Chicago yet, so I went online to research OB-GYNs in the city and found Dr. Angelli.

Dr. Angelli was one of four female OBs in what many patients and the media considered a top-rated practice. The office was located in what people called the Playboy Building, named for the notorious magazine that had occupied its upper floors from 1966 through the '90s. Its ninety-five floors were now filled with luxury condos, doctors' offices, and an Asian-fusion restaurant on the first floor.

I arrived at the office feeling nervous, as if I were going there to take an exam instead of be examined. I arrived early and sat in the plush waiting room. After a few minutes, a nurse came to get me and showed me to an examination room. Dr. Angelli was already poised at the door, wearing pin-striped Brooks Brothers pants and a pink cashmere cardigan. She shook my hand and motioned for me to take a seat on the examining table. The room was neat, clinical. Dr. Angelli took a seat on a stool next to the table and asked me about my medical history, making notes as I spoke. When I told her the date of my last period, she stopped abruptly.

"Excuse me," she said. "How long has it been?"

"Almost ten months," I said. "My doctor in England said it can take some women a while."

"Two months is average," she said. "Three months max. Ten months is absurd—not to mention unhealthy."

I received her words as a slap.

"I have been trying to let my body resume a cycle naturally," I sputtered.

"Well, it's not working," she said.

My face burned. I wanted to explain my dedication to a holistic approach, but I stopped myself, thinking I would sound foolish, like a child describing a make-believe world.

Ignoring my obvious distress, Dr. Angelli pulled a prescription pad out of a drawer and began writing in neat, perfect script, the kind children are praised for in elementary school. She prescribed a low-dose birth control pill and told me to start immediately.

"But if I go back on the Pill, I won't have a full cycle," I said.

"I won't ovulate." My voice sounded wobbly and pleading. I was embarrassed at my vulnerability but determined to voice my concern. I wanted to ask how taking a pill that suppresses ovulation would be a good move for someone who wanted to become pregnant in the near future, but didn't think I could speak further without my voice breaking.

"You have to have a period," she said, ignoring my concern. "Then we can talk."

I started crying before I made it to the exit. The building was downtown, a block or so from Lake Michigan, and the March wind whipped through the tunnel created by the tall rows of buildings. Tears forced themselves out in a chute and blurred my vision. I pulled my coat closer as I leaned on the side of the building and called Bill.

"I feel so humiliated," I said when he answered. I felt childish for crying, for being upset by the appointment. I'd crumbled in front of a woman I'd just met, just because she was a doctor. "She doesn't understand my concerns about the Pill. She didn't talk at all about underlying causes. This is my complaint about Western medicine: Treat symptoms. Literally, 'just take a pill.'"

Bill listened patiently, then said, "There are other doctors. You can get a second opinion."

"Yeah," I said, feeling a shard of confidence return. I felt relieved. I wasn't under any orders to do what Dr. Angelli prescribed.

I wiped the corners of my eyes with the backs of my hands and told Bill I'd see him at the house. On the way to the parking garage, I passed a metal-mesh trash can. Inside I could see candy wrappers, Big Gulp cups, and half-eaten sandwiches. I pulled out the prescription Dr. Angelli had given me and threw it inside. The square of white paper fluttered in the wind for a moment and then fell into the basin. I felt lighter.

As I walked the rest of the way to the car, I remembered a colleague of Bill's who had mentioned that he was studying Chinese medicine. Acupuncture had a good record for helping with fertility; I made a note to contact him. By the time I'd turned onto Lake Shore Drive, I was humming along with the classical station on the radio. The sun peeked out from a congregation of gray clouds, and I felt warm inside the car. Winter might go on for months longer in Chicago, of course, but if I looked intently enough at the trees, I thought I could see the earliest notes of spring.

Bill's friend referred me to the College of Oriental Medicine (COM). The school was one of two large acupuncture and Chinese-medicine schools in Chicago. COM worked like a teaching hospital, offering acupuncture sessions with a supervising instructor and team of students several afternoons a week. For my first consultation, I met with Elizabeth Jane, who, at thirty-five, was the youngest female supervising instructor. She was intelligent and comely, with round brown eyes behind black-framed glasses.

I told her about not having had my period, and Elizabeth felt confident acupuncture would help my body resume a regular menstrual cycle and ovulation—reestablishing the balance of my reproductive system at a root level.

I started seeing Elizabeth once a week. Each session, she guided her students to insert a series of needles into my hands, legs, feet, low abdomen, and ovaries. I looked forward to the treatments and COM's utilitarian space; the smell of moxa, with notes of deep spice and earth, that permeated the treatment rooms and hallways. During the treatments, I liked looking at the posters of the meridian channels taped up on the painted yellow walls.

At my second treatment, Elizabeth informed me that she was going to give me loose herbs to make into a tea.

"I'll send you home with instructions," she told me. "The tea has to be made precisely. The process takes about two hours, but the loose herbs are much more potent than taking them in pill form."

Having worked with dried herbs at my clinic in London, I was thrilled by the idea of making my own tea. Elizabeth led me into the room where the herbs were stored. The room was cool, windowless and temperature-controlled, to maintain the herbs' integrity and medicinal properties. I took a tour of the large glass jars, delighting in the variety of large and small leaves, the spore-bellied mushrooms, and silken strands of lemongrass. Elizabeth carefully picked herbs from at least six different jars and folded the contents into a piece of stiff white butcher paper. She wrote my name on the package with a Sharpie and handed it to me. I carried the packet home as if it contained precious gems.

My affinity for the tea was matched proportionately by Bill's intense dislike.

"What's the problem?" I asked, when he groaned as I began to prepare the tea for week three. "You don't have to drink it."

"The smell is disgusting, and it's laborious. I cannot imagine what it must taste like."

The tea was acrid and, truthfully, hard to get down. I developed a strategy to avoid having to taste it: I poured it into my throat without letting it touch my tongue, then chased it with small sips of grapefruit or some other juice.

"It's not so bad," I said, not wanting to concede anything negative about the tea. I shoved the juice glass into the dishwasher and licked my lips, pretending the taste was delicious.

"It's supposed to be very potent," I said, continuing my defense.

Bill pantomimed throwing up, until I laughed and dropped the strainer I'd been using to distill the herbs into the pot.

"Seriously, though, this tea could help me have periods and then help us get pregnant," I said.

"With what? Rosemary's baby?"

I shook my head at him but didn't resent his complaints. Despite his protesting, I knew Bill supported my efforts. He sat with me in the kitchen, preparing food for dinner, while I got the tea ready. If he finished the cooking prep, we'd look through cookbooks for inspiration or he'd play a bootleg recording of a new band he'd discovered. Bill was a drummer in bands since high school. He was shaped by the Who, the Clash, and Rush the way I was by the Brontës, Tolstoy, and Sylvia Plath. His passion was what attracted me to him most strongly when we met; art bonded us in spirit long before we took formal vows of marriage.

Once the tea was ready, I'd pour it into a glass jar and put it on the top shelf of the refrigerator. Bill said it would be better to keep it outside. "It's not like any animals would drink it."

I told Bill if he kept up the jokes, I'd slip some of the tea into his morning coffee.

"Fat chance I wouldn't notice that smell," he said, poking me in the ribs.

When I hadn't had a period after nearly twenty-four months of acupuncture, something in Bill caught like a trip line. For two years he'd taken the support role, letting me seek the treatments that felt comfortable to me for my body.

I was thirty-two, still within the optimal fertility age, according to Web MD, but he was six years older, and attending his friend's fortieth birthday party the week before had triggered a sense of biological urgency in him.

We came together in our kitchen, where we always seemed to have our serious discussions. I sat on one of our bar stools at the island in the center of the kitchen, going through mail. Bill was prepping for dinner. He julienned carrots, shaving them precisely into ribbons of orange that fell soundlessly onto the dark wood surface of his cutting board. I was organizing bills into file folders, and the granite countertop was strewn with open envelopes and mail.

"I should have put my foot down months ago," Bill said, assuming a parental tone. "I don't even want to think about what we've spent on these treatments, not to mention the teas. It's a total scam."

"Acupuncture has helped thousands of people get pregnant," I protested. "Probably millions if you take into account the thousands of years it's been used."

"It's bullshit," he said.

"It just hasn't worked for us," I said.

My shoulders slumped and I slid down the back of the chair until my neck rested on its metal rungs. I'd only just allowed myself to admit, in the midst of Bill's tantrum, that acupuncture really hadn't worked. I had remained so convinced that it would just take a little more time, that surely my body would remember to ovulate and I would start having periods again.

I was quiet for a moment, listening to the sound of garlic frying in a pan on the stove. We agreed that I would seek out a Western medical doctor, and I began making inquiries among my friends.

Even with Caroline putting in a personal referral, the first available appointment I could secure with Dr. Bizan was three months away. I asked the receptionist to call me if anything opened up earlier. Once I'd booked the appointment and circled the date twice with a Sharpie in my calendar, I felt a cold shock of fear. For the first time, I was afraid that something might be seriously wrong with me and afraid that we would have problems becoming pregnant. I was scared enough that I was even ready to take the Pill if that was what Dr. Bizan prescribed.

"You're sure Dr. Bizan is an actual medical doctor—with a real degree?" Bill asked as I came out of the shower on the day of my appointment.

Bill had been testy since I'd told him Dr. Bizan was a DO, rather than an MD. I had just learned about DOs: Western medical doctors who are trained to treat the whole person, as opposed to being symptom-focused. I was excited to find out this kind of doctor existed.

"Yes—geez," I said, hanging my towel on the back of the bathroom door and pulling a dress over my head. "DOs are fully licensed Western medical doctors. Dr. Bizan has been Caroline's OB for three pregnancies, and she works out of St. Joseph's, a totally Western hospital. Like I said, you're welcome to come with me."

Dr. Bizan's office had called the day before with a cancellation, and I'd scrambled to reorganize my own schedule to be able to make the appointment. Bill had recently left the advertising agency and started his own creative group with a best friend. He had two meetings and a shoot scheduled that day, so we'd already agreed that I would go on my own. As I waited in that grungy, airless office, I was happy I'd come by myself. Bill hated small spaces—and waiting— and I could imagine him pacing back and forth like a caged tiger in the cluttered room.

I'd moved through the remainder of *Cosmo*, *Elle*, and a ten-month-old *InStyle*, when the nurse finally called my name.

"I'm Sara," I said, jumping up so she could see me.

"Follow me."

She ushered me into an examination room and told me Dr. Bizan would be in shortly. Another nurse came in and took my weight, blood pressure, and temperature: all normal. After she left, I looked around for something else to distract me. I felt more nervous than ever, afraid that Dr. Bizan either wouldn't be a good fit or would chastise me for going so long without consulting a doctor.

In direct contrast with the waiting room, the examination room was spare and orderly. My stomach grumbled. I glanced at the clock on the wall. It was after 3:00 PM, and I hadn't eaten lunch. I decided to lie back on the exam table and meditate. I'd studied various meditation techniques in my training in England and joined a meditation group when I moved to Chicago. Someone from the group had recently shared an article about an order of yogis from Tibet who were able to nourish themselves with their breath instead of with food. If they could fast for weeks at a time, I could wait to eat until after my appointment.

I'd found meditation impossible when I first started; I'd been unable to sit still for more than one minute at a time. I'd dedicated myself to the practice, though, believing for reasons I did not understand that it was important for me. In the years to come, I would often thank whatever intuition had guided me to meditation. "The middle of a crisis is probably not the ideal time to start a practice," one of my teachers in England said. A gift of meditation was said to be equanimity, calmness within uncomfortable situations.

The sanitary paper crackled beneath my body. I tried to find a position where my spine was straight and I could stay still. I counted my breaths. Inhale, "one." Exhale, "two."

I made it to twenty-six before a knock on the door jolted me out of the quiet. I sat up fast, blood rushing to my head. Dr. Bizan entered the room. She was trim and athletic-looking, with honey-blond hair pulled back into a low ponytail.

"I'm terribly sorry for the wait," she said, shaking my hand and then, as if deciding more was needed to apologize, moving in for a hug. "The practice has just exploded, and I've delivered twelve babies this week so far."

She took a seat in a chair next to the exam table. I liked hearing about the babies Dr. Bizan had delivered that week. The high volume perhaps explained the lack of organization in her office. I wondered if Dr. Bizan worked by herself and if she was a mother, and if she ever got a complete night of sleep.

Dr. Bizan scanned the files I'd had sent over from Dr. Angelli.

"I see here that you haven't had a regular cycle in a couple years, and that you and your husband would like to start a family," she said.

I braced myself for a reprimand, but Dr. Bizan moved right along.

"And you've tried acupuncture and herbs," she said, looking up at me from the folder. I nodded.

"That's great. A lot of my patients become pregnant incorporating alternative therapies. They can be very effective."

I relaxed further. I uncrossed my legs and laid my hands next to me on the table as Dr. Bizan continued.

"Since you've been trying for a while and have not started having a cycle on your own, I'd like you to see a reproductive endocrinologist."

I felt unnerved at the immediate referral to another doctor. Dr. Bizan continued speaking, but I felt distracted. I watched her lips move, but I heard only one out of every few words.

She handed me a business card. "I recommend Dr. Colaum. Her office is in Evanston, which is a drive, but I believe she's worth the commute."

Anxiety prickled in my chest. I thought Dr. Bizan would at least examine me and give some kind of assessment. I felt comfortable with her; I didn't want to go see someone else. I asked if Dr. Colaum would see me exclusively or if I would see her and Dr. Bizan in tandem.

"Dr. Colaum can advise you on that—after she gets a sense of what's going on," she said. "Before you see her, though, I want you to have a test for something called empty sella. Have you heard of it?"

Empty cellar? Sella? I shook my head no. Was empty sella an illness of some kind? Aside from not having a period, I felt healthy and strong in my body and hadn't had even a cold in three years.

"Empty sella is a condition affecting the pituitary gland that prevents it from signaling the ovaries to ovulate. The first drug many fertility doctors prescribe is Clomid, which is pituitary focused. And if the pituitary isn't functioning properly, Clomid won't work. The condition can be detected by MRI."

Dr. Bizan wrote an order for the test on a notepad and handed me the paper. "Go for the MRI first, and then you'll go see Dr. Colaum."

Before she left, I asked if a reproductive endocrinologist (RE) was the same as a fertility doctor. She told me it was.

"I know your focus up to this point has been menstruation and ovulation," she said. "An RE is the right doctor to help you with that, as well as assisted fertility, *if*"—I liked that she paused there, at the word "if," suggesting to me that nothing was for sure yet—"you should need it."

I said goodbye to Dr. Bizan, not sure if I would even see her again and feeling somewhat depressed by the thought. I remembered a client from the clinic in London who had undergone cycles of in vitro fertilization (IVF). Timed intercourse, artificial insemination, frozen eggs—was that where Bill and I were headed? Were we skipping right over trying to conceive naturally?

I knew Bill would take a practical approach to the appointment with Dr. Colaum. *It's just a consultation,* I imagined him saying. But I was shaken anyway, and still light-headed from not having eaten lunch.

It was after four o'clock when I reached my car.

I thought of what I would recommend that a client do in this moment. First: eat something. Second: go home. Maybe take a bath or a walk. Then talk to Bill. I would tell him about Dr. Bizan and the MRI and Dr. Colaum when he came home, and together we'd figure out what we wanted to do.

Chapter 2

I scheduled my MRI for the following month at St. Joseph Hospital, where Dr. Bizan was a resident OB. St. Joseph was a smaller hospital with a branch in Lakeview—not far from our house and Elaine's acupuncture clinic. I took the first available appointment, on a Saturday morning in April. The next day, my parents called and said they were coming to Chicago for a conference the same weekend.

When Bill asked me if I was planning on telling my mother about the MRI, my immediate response was no. Over the past four or five years, I'd developed a policy of not sharing many personal details with my family. I hadn't confided in either of my parents about not having a period, or that Bill and I might have a fertility issue. They knew, from comments we'd made, that Bill and I wanted and planned to have children, but they'd never directly asked about the status of our procreative endeavors.

Our relationship had not started out this way. I was the oldest of three girls, and my mother told me she had been ecstatic to have a baby. She had wanted sons—six boys, to be exact, like Jo March and her "little men." Still, she and my father said they took joy in the shining bundle that arrived at 1:15 PM on February 25, 1975. For the first four and a half years, my parents and I lived in a town house on Hickory Street in Alexandria, Virginia.

There is a picture of me in the back yard of our house; I am about three years old, wearing a navy corduroy dress under a blue-and-red cape my mother had made for me on an old Singer sewing machine. I am in midair, jumping off the top of a slide, arms outstretched, fingers extended, a look of uninhibited exhilaration on my face.

The picture was sent around to the grandparents and great-aunts and uncles that year and is still considered the quintessential photo of my youth. For a time, I could not bear the photo: The image seemed to capture both my spirit and the problem. The bubbling exuberance and the intense thirst for life with which I came into the world became, I felt, a source of conflict between my parents and me.

"Where do you even come from?" my mother would say regularly, mystified at some or other behavior or personality trait. Although she had been a conscious and willing participant in my being there, she seemed unable to understand how something so different from her own introverted self, which craved containment and solitude, could have come from her body, her own DNA.

That I was biologically my parents' child was clear. I was pale, with light eyes, small and athletically built, like the Irish Caseys of my paternal side. I had my mother's mouth that turned down at the corners and the dark, wavy hair of her relatives in the Languedoc region of France. So, while there was no question that I was genetically of this family, I began to wonder at times, too, if there wasn't some other way of being misplaced or adopted, metaphysically perhaps, and whether I might, indeed, have come from someplace else.

It's not that my mother and I didn't try. *The Mother's Almanac*, a tome that came out the year I was born, states: "For a child to become an interesting adult, they must have an interesting child-hood." My mother embraced this idea. She took my sisters and me on field trips and outings; we were touring the Smithsonian before we could talk. She didn't mind a mess and let us build forts in the back yard and in the house; when we wanted to play hospital with our dolls and stuffed animals, she brought out real Ace bandages and made "blood" with Karo syrup and food coloring. When I was four, she bought me blank books and journals that I filled first with poetry, drawings, and little stories. She encouraged me to memorize sections of poetry and perform them at home. When I wanted to start acting in plays, she took me to auditions and rehearsals and avidly attended performances. Day to day, though, our energy seemed mismatched. We would return from a movie and she would be ready for a nap, while I wanted not just to talk about the film, but to *be* a Jedi Knight, *be* Black Beauty, gallop-ing around like a horse, neighing and asking to be fed sugar cubes from my mother's palm.

My sisters arrived two and six years after I did, with person-alities that fit more snugly into the familial pod. As we grew, they mirrored the family bewilderment as to why I was so dramatic, so sensitive, so *much*.

Much was made about the way I would lie listless on the couch for several days after a play closed or, when I was quite young, would work myself into such a state at Christmastime that I would throw up from excitement.

On those Christmas Eves, the duty of caring for me was always left to my mother, who, after having put together the bikes or the dollhouse or whatever bounty Santa had brought us that year, would guide me to the hallway bathroom, hold my head over the toilet, and wrap me in a blanket on the couch.

"You feel things so deeply," she would say. "It's exhausting."

With my father, the issues were different. In some ways I was too much like him—the perfectionism and rigid self-discipline—and in other ways we failed to connect. Why did I have to prefer such activities as rowing and Shakespeare in the Park to something like basketball, which he liked and would have happily coached? "I feel like you don't love me as much as you love Ellen and Laura," I told him once, when I was seven.

"I love you," he said. "Just not the same."

As a child, I couldn't hear the difference between "as much" and "not the same," and I internalized my differentness as abnormality. I responded with compulsive achievement and approval seeking, eventually starving myself in my teens. When my efforts for validation appeared unsuccessful, I withdrew. I knew there was love in my family, but I wasn't always sure of acceptance.

It was a revelation to me when I moved to England in my twenties, in training to be a counselor, to read Carl Jung and Caroline Myss and to learn about the ways in which families unconsciously play out roles and archetypes. In my family I played the scapegoat— the one with the problem, archetypally; the ugly duckling. My joke nickname, even, for several years in my family, was Ug.

In England, I began to find my voice and my place. This rebirth seemed to require facing past traumas, and seeing and then changing the roles I had played. The healing work I engaged in left me feeling tenuous and raw. I limited family phone calls and visits. I feared that sharing what I was uncovering would be seen as another problem, that my new career in counseling and holistic medicine would be treated as another weird thing I was doing that no one really understood. When Bill and I flew home every year or two to visit my family, we stayed in a hotel.

"We don't understand why you won't stay at the house when you visit," my mother lamented over the phone before Christmas the second year we lived abroad. "What's wrong with our house? I don't understand."

"I know you don't, Mom," I said, choking back tears. It pained me to hear the hurt in her voice. "I think I just need some time." I didn't know for sure how or when I'd be back, but I believed the best chance we had for something real was for me to continue down the path I'd embarked on.

If I ever believed the hotel boundary was unnecessary, it proved its importance to me the only time I denied it, laughably early, only months into our time in England, when my grandfather died.

Bill was in Portugal for a client meeting, and I flew to the funeral on my own. Fragile and unsteady in the earliest stages of my own rebuilding, I descended into the swirl of grief and extended family dynamics. Two days in, I buckled under the criticisms about my appearance (still too thin), and the jokes about my new "so-called" career path. That the comments came mostly from my extended family didn't matter. I went under as if caught in a riptide.

While my grandmother grieved with her sisters, I offered to clean up the kitchen. I ate off the plates, out of the trash, and shoveled fistfuls of food into my mouth from the gift tins and casserole dishes that caring friends had brought to the house. The sounds of my grandmother's angst, the French songs she sang with her sisters, the occasional wail, matched the churn of my own inner tumult. When I reached the point where I could no longer force anything else down, I went into the bathroom and vomited over and over and over again, jamming slick fingers into the back of my throat, hard, like the barrel of a gun.

A large mirror ran wall to wall over the toilet and sink. I caught the reflection of my eyes and watched, perplexed, as if someone else were committing this act. I felt sad to dishonor my grandfather in this way, for the desecration of my grandparents' bathroom. I could hear my therapist's voice reminding me that perceived criticism from others was a *projection* of my own self-hatred; how I needed to develop my own sense of worth and validation from within. I could conjure up these ideas in my mind but had no access—as if they were inside a clear but impenetrable balloon. I'd rarely been bulimic, but I now welcomed the violence of the act, the opportunity to taste and expel the self-loathing and the rage I was feeling.

When Bill picked me up from the airport, he found me broken. My eyes were underscored with dark purple semicircles, and I still felt drugged from the binge. "This is why we stay in a hotel," he said, leading me to a taxi, where I curled into a ball in the back seat.

"Where are your parents going to stay?" Bill asked the week before my parents' scheduled trip. The visit would be their first to Chicago since we'd moved back from London, almost five years since my grandfather had passed. In the past three years, our relationship had improved. Over phone calls, we had started a gentle process of reconnection. I remembered often the guidance of my therapist in London, who reminded me, "The goal is not to change them. It's to change you."

During the two years I'd seen her, I'd made strides. I was eating normally, writing every day, and in training for my licensure in holistic medicine. Before Bill and I moved back to the States, I went to see her for a follow-up session and to say goodbye. She offered me a challenge.

"You are clear about having wanted unconditional love and acceptance from your family growing up, but have you offered the same in return?"

I thought about the ways in which I had focused on what I hadn't received, the hurts I'd experienced, my longing for certain childhood needs to be met.

"Let that be your practice now."

I told her that I would try.

The reason for my parents' upcoming trip to Chicago was a restorative-justice conference that my father wanted to attend. He had just retired from a thirty-five-year career at a government agency and was treating his first year of retirement as a sabbatical, using it to explore his next steps. My mother, who planned to continue at her job writing contracts for a technologies firm for another year or two before retiring, had decided to come along for the weekend.

"Only your father would devote an entire year to personal discovery and spiritual retreat. Other people retire and play golf," my mother told me over the phone before their visit. I imagined her in the kitchen of our family's house, putting away baking pans from a batch of lemon squares she'd baked for their book club that night. She relayed the information about my father's sabbatical with a mock tone of exasperation, but I thought I detected admiration in her voice as well. I wondered if she was in some way living the year vicariously through him, looking to see what wisdom my father might glean and for clues to how she might structure her own sabbatical year, should she ever choose to be so audacious.

The plan for the weekend was for my parents to stay at the hotel downtown where the conference was being held. My mother and I and my aunt who lived in Milwaukee would have a touristy day in Chicago exploring Millennium Park and the Art Institute, followed by lunch at one of the nicer restaurants off Michigan Avenue. Bill and I would see my parents again on Sunday afternoon, after the conference ended, for tea or a late lunch at our house before they flew home to Virginia.

My MRI at Saint Joseph was scheduled for seven o'clock the Saturday morning of my parents' visit, but the week before they were due to arrive, the hospital called and offered me the same time a week earlier. I took it, grateful I would have the test out of the way before they came.

On the morning of the MRI, I gave myself plenty of time to drive to the hospital. At six fifteen, the sun had already risen high in a clear sky. Spring, which in Chicago can come as late as May or not at all, had arrived in April that year, and the young pear trees and azalea bushes were bursting with flowers. A good number of people were already outside, watering tulip beds and tending dutifully to their small city yards.

I'd chosen to go to the MRI on my own. The hospital's confirmation letter didn't mention bringing a support person, and I didn't see any reason for both Bill and me to spend the morning inside.

"It's a good thing I'm not getting an MRI," Bill said, kissing me goodbye before I left. "I'd freak out in that thing."

A doctor friend had told us at dinner the night before that some people had to stop the test and be sedated in order to proceed. I tried not to think about it as I parked in the hospital's lot and followed signs to Radiology. I had never been to a hospital for any outpatient procedure. I felt odd walking through the sliding doors feeling healthy. I had always thought of the whole hospital as the ER—full of crisis and fear.

Taking an early-morning appointment boded well for being seen on time.

I came prepared anyway; I'd brought a book, my journal, and my iPod, onto which I'd downloaded a variety of guided meditations.

I signed in at the front desk with the receptionist, a plump, gray-haired woman named Gladys who wore her glasses on a chain around her neck. She handed me some forms and a waiver absolving the hospital of any responsibility if I experienced any ill effects from the procedure. Trying not to picture any of the catastrophic outcomes, I scanned the form quickly, not fully reading. I would come to loathe these forms. If I really allowed myself to think about any of the outcomes as actual possibilities, I never would have gone through any of the medical procedures I ended up subjecting myself to.

I took a seat, leaned my head back against the wall, and started one of the meditation sequences I found especially useful for combating anxiety. I had drifted just to the edge of sleep when someone shook my arm. A blond, pleasant-faced man in blue hospital scrubs apologized for waking me and introduced himself as Sam, the technician who would be administering my MRI.

Sam looked fit and outdoorsy. I imagined him running marathons and mountain climbing on his days off. He pointed me toward a set of wide swinging doors and told me the MRI team would take good care of me. As he walked me to the procedure room, he briefed me on the test, saying that they would give me an injection of radioactive dye and then insert me in the MRI tube for thirty to forty-five minutes.

"The machine will be very loud at some points," Sam said. "That's the part that really gets to people." I asked if people had to be sedated, as I'd heard. "Sometimes," he said. "You look pretty tough, though. I think you'll do great."

When we got into the room, I sized up the machine—a sleek, colossal thing—and hoped Sam was right. It was larger than I had envisioned, the size of a small bus, filling the room. Sam told me I couldn't have my iPod with me during the test, and I felt confident I could meditate without props, even in an MRI tunnel. The only thing that concerned me was the injection.

"It's pretty neat, actually," Sam said, showing me the needle up close once I was lying flat on the table. "We inject the dye right into your vein . . . " He waved to another technician, standing in a control booth. "The dye will move through your body and will show us what's going on in your brain."

It didn't sound neat to me, and I immediately wished I had asked Bill to come. The needle looked alarmingly long and the dye looked toxic, dark and slick, like tanker oil. Sam twisted a rubber band around the upper part of my arm and deftly inserted the needle into my vein. I felt a brief searing pain, and then coolness as the dye entered. I imagined it barreling through my capillaries and looping through the coiled grooves of my brain.

Sam fastened me to the MRI table, which was more of a tray, securing my body with straps at my chest, waist, and legs. He joined his colleague in the booth, dimmed the lights, and began pushing some buttons. The machine started to whir, and I felt the table begin to move toward the center of the machine. Sam gave me a wave, which I tried to return before remembering I was restrained. As I moved into the mouth of the tunnel, I thought of the scene from *The Exorcist* where the possessed girl is taken into a white room with crashing large machines, glaring lights, and electric shock therapy.

The rest of the test was anticlimactic. I found it boring more than anything else; the clanging noise was distracting, but not scary. I couldn't tell how much time had passed, but I'd restarted the counting meditation I knew about a hundred times and was relieved when I felt the tray finally start to move and heard Sam's voice on an intercom saying he was going to slide me back out of the tube.

"Piece of cake, right?" Sam said with a grin.

"Well . . . " I said, not really answering but thankful for his positive attitude. I felt tired now that the test was finished and wanted to leave the hospital as quickly as possible.

"We'll send the results directly to Doctor . . . " He paused, scanning my folder. "Bizan," I said. I'd been so focused on the MRI test itself, I'd forgotten I was there being tested for something. I'd purposely avoided reading anything about empty sella on the Internet. "Medical websites are pure poison," my friend Kaitlin often said.

I figured that if I didn't have empty sella, I wouldn't have spent two weeks imagining catastrophic scenarios, but if I did, I'd receive better information from a doctor than from my own "enough to be very harmful" Internet research. Also, Bill had checked a few sites and told me that the condition didn't have major overall health implications. I turned my attention back to Sam.

"It will probably be a week or so before you hear," he said, walking me to the door. I searched Sam's eyes, wondering if he knew something already. "A doctor in the department reviews the film," he said, anticipating my question. I thanked him and then hugged him impulsively. It struck me how much his kindness had meant to me. He reciprocated with a big bear hug of strong arms and confidence.

"Good luck!" he said as the doors swung open. "You're strong, remember!" I gave him a thumbs-up and a smile.

The sun reflecting off the asphalt in the parking lot was blinding. The radiology department was windowless, so I had no sense of the time. The digital clock on the dashboard read 9:25. I felt mentally exhausted but full of nervous energy. I needed to ground myself.

I realized if I took the side streets, I could probably make the Saturday-morning meditation group I'd been attending regularly since I'd moved back from England. The meditation groups and classes met on Belmont Avenue and Clark Street, a grittier part of town. I liked that the group gathered in a room on the second floor, devoid of metaphysical accoutrements, outfitted only with metal folding chairs and a blond-wood desk where previous occupants, probably there for some kind of city-mandated after-school program, had carved their names or phone numbers into the wood.

Regulars in the group took turns leading the meditation, signing up on a clipboard that was circulated at the beginning of the session each week. I made it into the room while announcements were still taking place. I waved to a couple of people I knew. One was an opera singer, another a stay-at-home mom. There were a couple of men who attended regularly, too: an attorney, a psychotherapist, and a man named Louie who lived in a halfway house. These were people I likely would not otherwise have come into contact with had we not all been drawn together by a calling to this mindfulness practice.

Mary, a chic woman in her fifties with a neat gray bob, was facilitating. She announced that the meditation was about to begin and read a passage from Eckhart Tolle about listening to the inner voice, before guiding us into silence.

I went into the meditation with low expectations. I felt vulnerable and tired from the MRI, like I was hungover. I hoped to let go of any anxiety about the test. Any other meditative benefits would be a bonus.

I dropped deep right away. I had a sensation of floating, as if carried by a river with an easy current. I felt so content that I was only vaguely aware of the time. I forgot about listening for the inner voice, the MRI, empty sella. And then, moments before Mary rang the meditation bell, I felt something swoop in, a thought that seemed almost to hover in the air in front of my closed eyes.

Open your heart to your family.

The thought came again, clearer this time, not outwardly audible and yet audible nonetheless—perhaps what Mary had read about: the inner voice. The inner voice was not a regular feature of my meditations; I could in fact recall only one or two other times I had heard it.

Mary chimed the bell. "Come back to the room, come back to your body." Her gentle voice filled the room. I struggled to hang on to the ocean, the peacefulness, the floating, but the idea came again: *Open your heart to your family.*

I felt an instinctive resistance rise up, a default response to protect myself and my heart. I pulled my arms in close to my body. "Take one more deep, cleansing breath," Mary instructed, "and when you're ready, open your eyes."

The lights in the room were disorienting. I blinked several times and the room seemed off-center, as if it had enlarged and then contracted while we had been meditating but had not been set back exactly the way it had been before.

A few people discussed going out for tea, but I declined. I gathered my bag and car keys and moved toward the door without entering into any conversations. I was unnerved by the message I had received and not entirely sure what opening my heart to my family entailed. But I had the idea it involved going beyond the respectful cordialness we'd established, with which I'd grown comfortable in the past several years.

I felt exhausted by the time I arrived home. Bill had left a note saying he'd run out to do a few errands. I climbed into the dark oak four-poster bed we shared and collapsed into the pillows.

I fell into a hard sleep and dreamed that I was in the hallway of a school and that arms and hands were reaching out to me from the classrooms. I tried but was unable to grasp them, even as I extended my arms as far as I could toward the doors. It was four o'clock in the afternoon when I woke to the sound of Bill unpacking groceries in the kitchen.

"I didn't mean to wake you," he said. "You never take naps. How was the MRI?"

I filled a pint glass with water and told Bill about the test and Sam's being so nice, and then about the meditation group and the thought that came to me at the end.

Bill picked up a knob of fresh ginger from the counter and began shaving it into a bowl.

"We're going Indian tonight," he said, gesturing to the jars of cumin, turmeric, and star anise on the cutting board. "I wanted a project."

I waited for him to continue.

"You know how I feel about messages in meditation," Bill said. "But you seem moved. Is there something specific you want to do?"

There was. The idea had come when I woke up, after the dream.

"I want to invite my parents to stay with us when they come to Chicago next week," I said.

Bill set the long Shun knife he'd been using to cut vegetables on the counter.

"If you are open to it," I said, eyeing the knife.

Bill waited a moment before answering. "You know I like your parents," he said. "I'd be happy to have them here. If," he paused, picking the knife back up, "you think *you* can be okay." He waited until I met his eyes. He wanted some assurance. Neither of us wanted to relive the past.

"I think I can," I said, interested to note that I felt as confident as my words.

"Then let's do it," Bill said.

We made the call to Alexandria together.

My dad sounded surprised at the invitation but quickly thanked me. He called my mother to the phone, and she affirmed that they would be delighted to stay with us. "We'll see you next week!" she said.

"Great!" I said, meaning it.

The weekend felt easy and pleasant, effortlessly so. The weather was eighty degrees and sunny, the lakefront and downtown heavy with people and blooming trees. Everyone wanted to be outside. My father reported that he thought the conference was excellent.

On Sunday, Bill and I gave my parents a tour of our garden, which we'd built on the deck that extended over the back of our house. Bill pointed out the five varietals of heirloom tomatoes we'd chosen for the summer, and he and my mother spoke rapturously of the best ways to enjoy them.

"Plain, or on cottage cheese, with lots of salt and pepper," my mother said.

"Sliced thick on a turkey sandwich," Bill chimed in. My father was amazed that anyone would take the time to cultivate a garden in the city. "How often do you have to water?" he asked, peering at the boxes of herbs Bill had planted along the wall that abutted the kitchen. "Twice a day; three times when it's really hot," Bill said. "I enlist Sara for watering support as needed," he said, giving me a nudge.

"I'm a good assistant," I said.

When it was time to call for their taxi, Bill suggested that perhaps we could come for a visit in late August, when the tomatoes would be at their ripest, and bring my mother a basket of her favorites. She gave him a hug.

While my father went inside to gather the last of their things, my mother sat outside on our front steps. The late-afternoon sunshine cast kaleidoscopic shapes through the leaves onto the sidewalk.

"I had an MRI test last weekend," I blurted. "I haven't had a period since I stopped taking the birth control pill. It's been three years. We're going to see a reproductive endocrinologist."

"You're trying," my mother said, "to get pregnant?"

"We haven't officially," I said. "We've been doing the getting-ready-to part."

"Oh, Sara! I'm so happy!" my mother gushed.

"I might have something called empty sella," I said. "We might need some help." I braced myself for a criticism, a condemnation.

"Science has made incredible advancements in this area," my mother said. "There's a lot of good help out there these days."

I watched her face. She looked earnest. No judgment. Just "there's a lot of help out there."

I started to laugh. The protectiveness around my heart loosened a bit, like fingers unfolding from a fist. The blood rushed in, strange but welcome.

"Being pregnant was the most thrilling thing I've ever done," my mother said. "Having children is the most wonderful experience in the world."

Chapter 3

On the Monday after my MRI, I called Dr. Colaum's office and made an appointment for a consultation, explaining that I'd been referred by Dr. Bizan. I took a Friday-morning appointment three weeks later, figuring that would give the hospital ample time to deliver the MRI results. I called Dr. Bizan's office to let them know I'd completed the MRI and made the RE appointment.

"We'll call you when your results arrive," a nurse at the office said. "Dr. Bizan will need to meet with you in person to review your MRI. If you don't hear from us in a week, call. This office gets crazy."

I called the next Monday and again the following, reminding the receptionist of my upcoming appointment with Dr. Colaum.

"I don't know if Dr. Bizan will be able to see you," the nurse said. "She's booked solid."

"Well, what do you suggest?" I asked, feeling edgy and frustrated.

"Don't tell anyone I told you this," she said, dropping her voice, "but come in tomorrow before her first appointment—eight o'clock AM—and I'll try to corral Dr. B. for you."

I arrived at the office at seven forty-five, but Dr. Bizan had been called away to deliver a baby. I asked the nurse if she could give me the results so I could take them to Dr. Colaum, but when she checked my file she found that the results had still not arrived. She advised me to call the next morning. I called the next morning, then every morning that week. No one could confirm if my MRI results had arrived or when I could get in to see Dr. Bizan.

On the Friday morning of my appointment with Dr. Colaum, I went to Dr. Bizan's office again before it opened. I sipped tea from a paper cup and watched the elevator as if on a stakeout. The building's foyer was as dilapidated as Dr. Bizan's waiting room. The elevator was small, with steel metal doors; more than three people inside would be cramped. The receptionist was the first to arrive and let me into the office. She told me to take a seat on a chair in the hallway, circumventing the waiting room. Twenty minutes later, a nurse grabbed my arm and hurried me down the hall. She said Dr. Bizan could see me for three minutes before her first appointment.

I half-ran down the hallway to room 3. Dr. Bizan was on her cell phone and motioned for me to take a seat in a chair opposite her.

She hung up and turned toward me. "I know we only have a moment, but I'm so happy we could meet this morning."

"Me too," I said. I told her that I was going to Dr. Colaum's office after our meeting.

"Well, your test results never did make it over here." Dr. Bizan paused; I fought an urge to scream. "But I was able to call someone I know at St. Joseph and have him give them to me over the phone this morning."

I unclenched my hands, which I had balled into fists.

"The MRI came back positive for empty sella," Dr. Bizan said, her eyes resting on my face. "This explains why you have not been having periods," she continued. "And it gives Dr. Colaum some direction in terms of treating you."

Dr. Bizan paused again. I nodded to indicate that I was following her, encouraging her to go on. "As I may have mentioned, there are two kinds of empty sella: primary and secondary. Yours is secondary. It is not a threat to your overall health but is important to know in terms of fertility."

I nodded, happy for that reassurance. "I have to meet my next patient now, but I can answer a couple questions if you make them quick."

I had questions but felt rushed; I had to leave in minutes to make my appointment with Dr. Colaum. I thanked Dr. Bizan for seeing me and started toward the door. As I reached for the knob, I thought of something that seemed important to ask.

"Is there a cause?" I asked, turning back to Dr. Bizan. "Something that causes empty sella?"

Dr. Bizan tilted her head to one side for a moment, thinking. "Primary empty sella is most often caused by obesity. Secondary empty sella," she said, "can be caused by surgery or"—she dropped her eyes to my file—"by trauma."

"Oh," I said.

Dr. Bizan glanced at her phone. "I really do have to go," she said apologetically.

I nodded and thanked her. "You will be in good hands with Dr. Colaum," she said, shaking my hand. "Keep me posted on your progress."

I took side streets back to my house, driving fast. It was already 9:25 AM, and Bill and I had estimated the drive to Evanston would take at least forty minutes. I rounded the corner to our house, parked my car in the garage, and ran around to the front, where Bill was waiting in his car with the engine running.

"The MRI came back positive for empty sella," I said, once we'd found the main street that would take us north to Evanston.

"Okay," Bill said, keeping his eye on the cars in front of him. "It's good that we're meeting with the specialists today, then."

"Dr. Bizan said I have secondary empty sella," I answered, feeling unable to repeat what she had cited as the cause.

I leaned against the seat and squeezed my eyes shut tightly.

"What is it, hon?" Bill asked, glancing at me and then back out the windshield.

"She said secondary empty sella is caused by trauma," I said, trying not to cry.

"That makes sense," Bill said. "Your ovarian cyst was a real trauma."

I nodded and let out a jagged breath. The surgery had been a horrific experience. I preferred not to think of it and rarely did anymore, usually only when filling out a form that asked, "Have you ever been hospitalized?" Then images of that day would streak to the surface in shards: the metallic taste of adrenaline in my mouth; the excruciating pain; the confusion on the doctors' faces as to what might be wrong, then the palpable shift in the room when they discovered the cyst and rushed me to surgery; being wheeled to the OR, my parents' worried faces bobbing up and down next to me as they ran to keep up with the gurney; an IV drip of Demerol in my arm; an oxygen tube inserted in my nose; a blue protector sheet going up like a laundry sheet—no time for any explanation about what was happening. Counting backward from ten, nine, eight, seven . . . and then blackness.

I woke up after surgery in a private room, still with no clear understanding of what had transpired. I folded myself into the bed, pulled a pillow around my ears, and tried to become as small as possible. The surgeon came by on his rounds and told me about the cyst, that it had ruptured, that it had been a messy ordeal, and that the surgery had lasted six hours. He told me that my ovary had been removed and then, kindly, before I even asked, told me that what had just happened would not impact my ability to have children. That was when he told me that the human body was miraculous, that I would still have a period every month. That each ovary had more than enough eggs—hundreds of thousands, enough for many lifetimes.

I hadn't been thinking of that trauma, however, since the moment of disclosure in Dr. Bizan's office. When she said the word, my mind offered another exhibit, exhibit A, the memory of which now swam toward me now like a great silvery fish, its belly scales flashing glints of light into the deep, dark water in which it swam.

For so long I had not even really remembered. There were signs: hysterical reactions to hearing about children abused in the news; having difficulty staying in my body during sex; leaving the theater in the middle of a film if there was a rape scene. "It's just a movie," a boyfriend once said in college. "You act like it's happening to you."

In England, with an ocean separating me from my birthplace, the memories emerged. In my first acupuncture session, I watched, in full color, my mind reveal those events that I'd known in some dungeon of my mind had transpired, but had not consciously remembered until twenty-seven needles had been stuck into body, opening pathways that now had stories to tell. The acupuncturist had been as surprised at the revelation as I was and hurriedly handed me a business card: Irena Dashani—the therapist I would work with for most of my time in the UK.

As part of my healing, I wanted to name what had taken place in that cold, cement-floored room in our basement and then later what had transpired at a friend's house with her stepfather. If I was going to go back to my family's house at all, I needed to say what had happened there. I thought if I acknowledged it, if my family could bear witness, I could let go, integrate the experience, move on.

The more I was dedicated to my self-discovery, though, the more distant I felt from my family and the more my hope that I would ever have the discussion with them diminished. An opportunity came a few years later, however, during a phone call with my father. He'd called after one of our hotel Christmas visits, saying he'd felt me slipping away like the horizon from a ship.

"I'm not okay with just watching you go," he said. "What can we do?"

I surprised both him and myself by telling him what I had uncovered in England. I said I wanted to be able to talk about my past with him and my mother.

"I don't feel as if I can talk to Mom about this," I said. A rule I'd adopted in the family and pledged allegiance to, though unspoken and without verification, had been not to bring up something that would upset her.

I heard silence on the line and the faint echo, the hollow sound sometimes present on international calls, reminding me we lived on separate continents.

"No," he said. "I don't think it would be a good idea."

But I told her anyway.

It happened during my next visit, five months later, when I was alone with my parents after returning my sister to medical school. The weather was already hot for May, and my father had cranked up the air conditioner. We drove on a monotonous stretch of highway, tall pine trees and oaks flanking both sides of the road.

"I want to share something—some things—that happened when I was growing up," I said.

My father kept his eyes on he road. He already knew the basics of what I was about to say. To my knowledge, my parents never kept anything from each other, and yet I had no idea if my father had told my mother what I was about to relate.

When I was six, two older neighborhood boys came over to play in our basement and began a game of Simon Says that turned sexual. When I protested, they forced me to touch them. Afterward, they told me I'd done something very bad, that I wasn't a virgin anymore, and if my parents found out, I'd be sent away, or killed—just like Laurie, a girl on our street who had disappeared suddenly. (I found out later that she was not dead, as they had said, but had been sent to live with her mother in another state. But by then it was too late.)

And two years later, during a sleepover, Courtney, my best friend in the third grade, and I danced in our underwear for her father, who was drunk. I went to use the master bathroom, and he was waiting for me when I came out, naked aside from a yellow bath towel wrapped around his waist. He shut the door behind him. "I'm going to show you what grown-ups do," he said, carrying me to the bed.

"He raped or molested me—I don't know which," I said from the back seat of the car, an Oldsmobile sedan my father had taken over from my grandfather when he died. I remembered only snippets from that night: the yellow towel, his arms around me, warm breath on my face, the vastness of the bed. The next clear memory I have is of being back in Courtney's bedroom, she asleep and I pushing her dresser in front of the door and being unable to stop shaking.

For several minutes, neither of my parents spoke. My father's head faced forward, eyes fixed on the road. My mother, too, had remained looking straight ahead in the front seat during my report. I don't think I could have had the conversation had we all been looking at each other, or outside a moving vehicle. I was holding my breath. I watched the back of my mother's head for signs of combustion, but she was as alive as she'd been ten minutes ago before I'd started speaking, her hair puffy from the humidity, her neck that had the same slope as mine. I could hear the tires roll on the road, the whir of the engine. The blowing sound of the air conditioner. When they finally spoke, they didn't say much. My mother said she wished it hadn't happened.

"How can you forgive something like that?" she asked, keeping her head locked forward, looking at the highway.

"They were probably abused, too," I said, sharing one of the insights I had come to in my forgiveness work.

"Not them," she said, still not moving her head. "Us."

Having the conversation was what I had wanted. I saw no need for further forgiveness. The moment she'd spoken, I'd melted into the seat. I'd spoken of these events, and she hadn't died. Neither of us had.

I felt elated afterward, struck by the lightness that accompanied my confession. My mother had stayed with me; neither parent had said it was my fault. What I did not anticipate was that the acknowledgment they gifted me with was, for a time, a one-time thing. I didn't know how strange it would feel afterward when, for a period of several years, any reference I made to the abuse would be greeted with silence, as if the conversation in the car had not taken place, my words falling like snow.

After the experience, I'd moved closer, calling more regularly, sharing more of Bill and my life in the UK. But I'd kept a buffer of space, not venturing too close, proceeding cautiously in reconnecting.

Bill and I arrived at the Reproductive Medicine Institute (RMI), Dr. Colaum's practice, at 10:01 AM. The office was located in a small, grid-shaped brick building on Ridge Road that looked like it had been built in the '70s. The lobby was small and unremarkable. The air was stuffy and hot. June had descended upon Chicago with a burst of heat that seemed to have been saved underground all winter and was now being released in a long, ferocious exhale.

The air conditioner, if there was one, appeared to be broken. While we waited for the elevator, I fanned my face with the folder of information the office had sent in advance of our appointment. We rode to the second floor and walked down a short hall to suite 205. The waiting room was cool and serene, with low lighting and furniture from the federalist period. Whoever had decorated had done so with care, and with a love of Frank Lloyd Wright, apparently; framed works of his art and architecture hung on the cream-colored walls.

We were the only people in the waiting room when we arrived. I signed in with a receptionist, a heavier-set woman who introduced herself as Lorelai. Bill picked up a brochure from the table. "Did you know this?" he whispered, pointing at the bio page for Dr. Colaum.

Dr. Colaum's brochure photo revealed a grandmotherly woman, perhaps in her early seventies, with gray-blond hair wrapped into a bun. Bill was pointing at the copy under the photo. "Dr. Carolyn Colaum, MD, is the mother of ten children." The brochure went on to detail an impressive career as a researcher and clinician of reproductive endocrinology.

"Do you think they're all hers, biologically?" Bill said, our heads leaning over the brochure.

"They are," Lorelai interjected from across the room. "She conceived and delivered each one naturally, too. It was before the days of IVF."

"That's pretty amazing," Bill said.

"I like the idea of a fertility doctor that's so fertile," I said.

"I agree," Bill said. "Seems like a good sign."

At ten after ten, a somber nurse named Rachel escorted us into a spacious office also decorated with federalist-period American furniture. Dr. Colaum was sitting at a large oak desk, in front of a wall that showcased more framed works by Frank Lloyd Wright. A large portion of the desk was covered with framed photographs of children and newborn babies.

"My grandchildren," Dr. Colaum said proudly. "I have fourteen now." I took in the bright smiles and cherubic faces of her brood and turned away. On the way into her office, we'd passed a wall filled floor to ceiling with baby announcements and holiday cards featuring what I guessed were the clinic's assisted progeny. I felt anxious as I wondered whether we would ever have a card with our own child on it to add to the collection.

Dr. Colaum's hair was pulled up in the same bun she'd worn in her head shot. She wore a large cut-glass necklace over a loose-fitting shift dress that hung to her shoes.

"It's nice to meet you," she said, extending her hand, first to Bill, then to me.

"Dr. Bizan referred you?" she asked.

"Yes," I said. "I believe her office faxed you my file."

"We didn't receive anything from their office," she replied. I grimaced.

"That happens," she said. I'll ask you whatever questions I need to know. What I want to do today is go over your history and then ask some specific questions relating to your reproductive cycle. Then I can make some recommendations."

I shifted in the chair. I was annoyed that Dr. Bizan's office had neglected to send the file. I didn't want to go over my whole medical history again, but Dr. Colaum seemed like the kind of doctor who would want to hear everything for herself anyway. She asked about my menstrual cycle pre-Pill, how many years I'd been on it, and how long I had not menstruated. I told her about the MRI and the diagnosis of secondary empty sella.

As I answered her questions, Dr. Colaum took notes with a

tortoiseshell pen, writing meticulously on a clean piece of unlined paper fastened to the inside of a folder. Peering down through crescent-shaped reading glasses on a chain, a black shawl draped over the chair behind her, she looked like a professor from Hogwarts. She gave no sign of her thoughts as she wrote.

At a certain point she stopped, leaned back in her chair, and stared past us at the back wall, or possibly the window. I dropped my eyes to her desk, not wanting to disturb her concentration. I could feel Bill's foot bouncing against the side of my chair.

"Okay," Dr. Colaum said, "here's what I think."

Bill grabbed my hand. I sat up straighter in my chair.

"First, though, do you know if you ovulate?" Dr. Colaum asked.

"Could I be, if I don't have a period?" I asked.

"It's unlikely, but possible. Have you ever used an ovulation kit, or checked your temperature and mucous membrane each month?"

My cousin had given me the name of the ovulation kit she'd used to become pregnant with each of her three boys. It worked like a pregnancy test: By urinating on a strip, the woman could figure out when she would ovulate. I'd bought one when I started acupuncture, thinking we could use it when my period started. I'd never opened it, actually had forgotten I'd bought it. I pictured where it would be now, gathering dust on a shelf in our bathroom next to a box of tampons that was also almost three years old.

I told Dr. Colaum I had not monitored my ovulation.

"Don't worry. The next step I recommend for you both is to have the full panel of fertility tests. If we're going to support you here, we test every aspect of fertility. You too, Bill. We wouldn't want Sara to have all the fun."

"Great," Bill said, looking uneasy.

"From there we'll have a clear idea of where we stand and what we might be able to do to help you."

"There's one more important question I need to ask before we go further," she said, looking up at us from the folder. "It may be obvious because you are here, but I don't want to make any assumptions."

Bill looked at me and I shrugged. I guessed it would be something about our insurance information or financial resources.

"Do you want to be parents?" Dr. Colaum asked. "Specifically, is pregnancy and having children your ultimate goal?"

I squeezed Bill's hand. "Definitely, yes," we replied simultaneously.

Once we agreed to the tests, Dr. Colaum sent us over to see Rachel, the serious nurse, who took us to a smaller consultation room down the hall. She printed out a list of the tests Dr. Colaum had ordered and a calendar to schedule our dates. She handed me a large stack of papers with a description of each of the tests, instructions for how to prepare, and what to expect afterward.

Among the list was a hysterosalpingogram, a word I had difficulty pronouncing at first glance, designed to see if my fallopian tubes were open.

"We just call it an HSG," Rachel said, sparing me. "I recommend you take some Tylenol or Advil before you come in. Some people feel uncomfortable afterward."

Over the next two weeks, Rachel scheduled us for several appointments. I was to take the female fertility panel, which included the uterine ultrasound and evaluation and blood work to test my levels of the hormones estrogen, progesterone, and prolactin. Rachel scheduled Bill for a semen analysis to determine the quality and quantity of his sperm. We signed paperwork that stated we would pay for any lab tests insurance didn't cover.

It was close to noon by the time we finished our appointment and left the office. My mind felt overloaded by the time we got back to the car. As we turned back onto Ridge Road, Bill said, "I think we should go out to lunch. I'm getting a headache."

"That was intense," I said.

We decided to drive back to the city and go out somewhere near our house.

If we go to Que Rico, we can listen to mariachi music and pretend we're on vacation in Mexico," Bill said.

"Que Rico it is," I said.

I drove to Dr. Colaum's for the HSG at noon the following Friday. I hadn't remembered to take the Tylenol that Rachel had recommended before the appointment, but I thought it was probably unnecessary. I'd been told I had a high pain threshold and believed this to be true. After my cyst had ruptured, I'd asked one of the nurses if that pain I'd been in was equivalent to what women experienced in childbirth.

"Good lord—no, sweetie. What you had was many times worse." After watching a film on natural childbirth years later, I didn't know if that was true, but I appreciated what the nurse had said at the time. It was empowering to think I'd already survived pain worse than labor.

The hysterosalpingogram worked via internal ultrasound. A bubbly nurse named Tracey escorted me into an examination room that held a hospital bed and several large machines. As I changed behind a screen, Tracey and I chatted about her work at RMI. She told me that she and her fiancé had just adopted a puppy. Dr. Colaum entered and directed Tracey to the ultrasound machine. She took what looked like a large condom from a box and pulled it onto a plastic tube attached to the machine next to the bed.

"This is a vaginal wand," Tracey explained, squirting some blue gel onto the tip. "It uses ultrasound to let us see your reproductive organs from the inside." Dr. Colaum inserted the wand and began to move it around from side to side. The gel was cool, and I could feel pressure but no discomfort.

"All looks good so far," Dr. Colaum said to Tracey, who was taking notes. "I'm coming around to the right ovary now. All looks good here." Dr Colaum moved the wand across to the other side of my vaginal wall. "Where is . . . ?"

"Sara doesn't have her left ovary—remember?" Tracey said, smiling and throwing me an apologetic look.

"Of course," Dr. Colaum said. Winking at me, she said, "I was just checking."

"Why not?" I said, trying to lighten the mood. "Do they ever grow back?" I laughed.

"You could be the first," Dr. Colaum said, continuing the joke.

"We'll do the hysterosalpingogram now," she said, pulling on a pair of latex gloves. "You'll feel a cramp as I inflate a balloon into your uterus and inject the dye. We'll pump the dye a couple of times to determine that your fallopian tubes are open and functioning. I'll do a closer examination of your uterus afterward. Then we'll be done. You can watch along with us here," she said, angling a flat computer screen toward where I lay on the table.

"Ready?" she asked. I guessed I was and nodded.

Dr. Colaum inserted the speculum and fed the tube through.

"I'm going to inflate the balloon now," she said.

Tracey moved around the table next to me, as if standing guard. Suddenly, I felt a pressure inside my low abdomen, a pause, and then a long, flat pinch. I felt like my low abdomen had folded in on itself and bitten down. Hard.

The clamping feeling continued for a moment, like a musical note being sustained.

"Fuck!"

A yell had come out of my mouth, but I prayed I had used the profanity only in my head. I could not believe I might have just said the f-word in front of Dr. Colaum, seventy-year-old grandmother of fourteen, as if struck by some momentary bout of Tourette's.

"I know," Dr. Colaum said, without apparent offense. "It can hurt."

I gripped the side of the table, bracing myself.

"That should be the worst of it," she said. "I'm going to do a few more pumps of the dye, and then we'll be done."

Tracey offered me her hand, but I declined, preferring to continue holding the table.

"It's not the first time someone's yelled in here," she said, and I gave her a weak smile. *I'll bet,* I thought.

"The good news is that your tubes are clear and open," Dr. Colaum told me, removing the catheter and speculum. "Everything looks good in your ovary. Your follicles look healthy and good, which bodes well for good eggs. You have such a nice uterus, too." Tracey nodded in agreement. I looked at the fuzzy black-and-white screen, unable to make out the shape of my uterus amid the pixilation.

"Do they vary much from person to person?" I asked.

"There's a wide variety," Dr. Colaum said. "Shape, size, position in the pelvis." Tracey nodded.

"You're done for today," Tracey said. "Take your time getting dressed, and take it easy this afternoon."

I felt relieved. Now that I was no longer in pain, I was grateful for the test, appreciative more than I had anticipated for the confirmation that all my reproductive organs were healthy, functioning, and clear. I felt embarrassed for yelling in front of Dr. Colaum, though, and hoped I would not see her on my way to reception.

If I saw Rachel on my way out, however, I was going to give her a friendly piece of patient feedback. Specifically, about her recommendation to take Tylenol before the hysterosalpingogram.

Two Tylenol, my ass. Tylenol with codeine, maybe, or Demerol.

Chapter 4

I went in for my remaining fertility tests a week later, the same day as Bill's sperm test. Once Bill provided a sample, a courier would carry it directly to the lab in a cooler, just like an organ for transplant. The lab would run tests the same day and provide a report for volume, motility (how many were swimming), and morphology (how many were a normal shape).

The morning of our joint tests involved a lot of shuttling back and forth between the lab, examination rooms, bathroom, and main waiting room. When we were finally done, we met in the waiting room and walked to the car together.

"It was a bad cliché," Bill said when we reached the lobby. "I don't know what the women's test rooms look like, but mine was a seven-by-nine-foot room with a black La-Z-Boy chair and a table. The nurse hands me a cup and leaves. There's instructions on the table telling me to collect as much of my ejaculate as possible and then fill out my name and social security number and avoid any spillage on the label. Really arousing. And you should see the material they have in there: two magazines, *Playboy* and *Maxim*, as if we're fifteen. Some more variety and better ambience would have been nice," Bill finished.

"They're not running a gentlemen's club," I said.

"Well, then, they should let partners come in. I could have been done in three minutes if you were in there with me."

"That's sweet," I said. "Don't think they'd go for it, though."

"Yeah, well, I got it done," he said. "I really don't like pressured donations, though," Bill said. "Did you know that's what they call it?" he said, revving up again. "My *donation*," he repeated as he got into the car.

I couldn't help laughing.

"Yeah, hilarious," he said. "You didn't just have to masturbate in a doctor's office."

"I'd take masturbation over the uterine crunch," I said, the memory of the previous week's test lingering.

"I don't know," Bill said. "I feel dirty." But he was grinning.

Rachel called us to schedule a review appointment with Dr. Colaum once our results came back. Bill and I shuffled meetings and client sessions to make room for the consultation. We'd made the trip enough times to know it would be a minimum of three hours door-to-door.

"The good news is that you have all the necessary parts to have a child," Dr. Colaum told us as we sat facing her desk once again. "Sara, you have great eggs, follicles, uterus, and open tubes. Bill, your sperm rate is high in both mobility and motility."

Bill had announced on the drive that his "boys" were going to be pronounced stellar. He flashed a proud smile.

"We have a number of options," Dr. Colaum continued, "in terms of assisted fertility." In the past few weeks, Bill and I had talked to a handful of people who had seen fertility specialists.

The majority of them had been prescribed Clomid, which we knew wouldn't work for us because I had empty sella. One couple had done artificial insemination, and they knew a few others who had gone through IVF. All I really knew of IVF was that it was emotionally intense and carried a shocking price tag. I hoped Dr. Colaum would recommend something more moderate.

"What I suggest we try first," Dr. Colaum said, "is what we call follicle stimulation, or stim."

No IVF. I leaned back into the chair, shifting my back on the cool leather, and allowed myself to relax a little bit.

"Is there any way we could get pregnant on our own?" Bill interrupted.

"You could—possibly. But you could also try for years before becoming pregnant, or not become pregnant at all." Dr. Colaum paused. "I don't recommend it for you."

A puff of air escaped my lips. I wasn't surprised, but it was hard to hear officially that we had little chance of natural conception.

The evening of our joint tests, Bill and I had talked about what would happen if we were told we couldn't conceive on our own. We were clear we wanted to be parents, so if we couldn't get there without fertility treatments, we were willing to do whatever we needed to do to have a family.

Dr. Colaum explained that stim involved injections of a drug called Follistim, a gonadotropin drug named for its purpose: to *stimulate* the eggs in the ovaries' *follicles*. Dr. Colaum wrote in our file as she talked. "We'll identify the optimal days for conception and tell you to have intercourse several times during that three-day period. The night before intercourse, you'll take an intramuscular injection of HCG to release the eggs from the follicle. If all goes ideally, sometime in the next week you'll be pregnant."

I had been taking notes while Dr. Colaum was talking, but

stopped when she came to "intramuscular injection." I was lost. I was sure Tracey or Rachel would be handing us yet another packet that would explain everything, so I set my pen in my lap and listened.

"One additional thing to consider," Dr. Colaum said, "is that there is a higher likelihood of multiples—twins or triplets—with stim."

Bill looked at me and shrugged. The idea of triplets sounded completely overwhelming but also fantastical. I'd heard of people having them, especially people who engaged in the kind of fertility treatments we were considering, but perhaps by the same hormone-induced backward logic that made teenagers feel immortal or that made people practice unprotected sex, I could not imagine triplets happening with us. Twins, though, sounded overwhelming but fun. If we were lucky enough to be blessed with two babies in one pregnancy, I'd take it as a gift.

Dr. Colaum made more notes in our file. As I listened to her pen scrape the page, I grieved, for a moment more, the idea of making a baby by making love—no doctors, treatments, or money involved; just Bill and me, natural and organic. But I was also excited. We were crossing a threshold—from *we'll see what happens* into actively *trying* to become pregnant.

Bill cupped my left hand, which I'd been resting on his knee. "We're in," he said. I nodded.

Our next step seemed like it would be easy. The stim kit arrived in a small box, sent directly from Braun Pharmacy, a specialist pharmacy in Lincoln Park. Tracey printed out a calendar that established August 6 as the day I'd begin treatment. The night before our start date, Bill read the instructions out loud while I pulled out the components of the kit.

The Follistim pen would become my favorite of the injection devices we'd use over the years. Even on first contact, I appreciated the ergonomic design, the cheerfulness, of the blue-and-yellow plastic pen, more like a Crayola crayon than like a medical device. The medication came in glass vials the size of small perfume bottles. The needles were tiny, too, no more than half an inch long.

"Follistim is given via a subcutaneous injection," the pamphlet informed us, meaning it needed to penetrate the skin only slightly to administer the medication. The instructions were simple: Insert vial into pen tube, clean and attach needle with alcohol swab, clean skin with alcohol swab, twist pen top to designated medication dose (150 millimeters, in my case). Inject into abdominal region, depress until medication reading is at zero again. Swipe area with alcohol swab. Take Follistim medication at the same time every day.

Bill left me a voicemail midday, while I was in a session with a client: "I'll be home to inject you tonight at seven!"

Bill offered to administer the shots for me, but the idea became less appealing as the day wore on. I worried that I'd be angry at him if the injection hurt. We'd heard some statistics about how hard fertility treatments could be on a couple, and had made a pact to stay positive and connected to each other throughout the process. When Bill arrived home with flowers and a bag of groceries to make dinner, I told him I'd be giving myself the shot.

He didn't argue.

Bill cooked dinner and I laid out the supplies. When I had everything assembled, he filled two small flutes with champagne a friend had given him the day he left the ad agency where we'd met to start his own firm, almost exactly one year after we'd moved back from England. Over two nail-biting years, he'd build the business from nothing into a legitimate creative group that now supported the full-time salaries of himself and his best friend and creative partner.

Starting our fertility journey with a gift from another successful venture seemed auspicious, like breaking a champagne bottle over the bow of a boat. "You won't be able to drink this once we're pregnant," Bill said.

"Woohoo," I replied, taking a glass. We clinked the rims, and I took a small sip before quickly replacing the glass on the countertop. I had a task to attend to, and my hand was already shaking. Summoning courage, I pulled up my shirt and swabbed a patch of skin with alcohol. Bill filled the Follistim pen to the 150-millimeter mark and handed it to me, needle side facing him, the way you would pass scissors. I held the needle, poised an inch from my body, and then stopped. I couldn't bring myself to inject. It suddenly seemed crazy to stick myself voluntarily, and equally silly to be afraid. I'd been stung by bees, by a wasp, and even once by a jellyfish. I doubted if it would hurt more than stubbing a toe, but I was paralyzed.

I held my hand there for another couple of seconds, looking at Bill, frozen in that preshot position. I wondered if diabetics felt this way before they administered their first insulin injection. It would take some getting used to. Finally, I plunged the needle into my skin and pressed the top of the pen firmly until all the medication had drained from it. Then I counted to three, as the pamphlet suggested, to ensure the medication was absorbed.

"Three!" Bill said, finishing the count with me.

I left the needle in for another few seconds—just to be sure—and then pulled out the pen and rubbed my skin with another alcohol swab. Bill peered at me, waiting. I shrugged and then began laughing. I'd hardly felt the needle, just the tiniest sting, less painful than the scratch of a fingernail. "That was easy," I said, wiping my eyes on a napkin, feeling relieved and empowered.

"One down, twelve to go," Bill said.

The nightly injections marked the countdown to our medically scheduled sex. As we approached our three-day window, Bill started dropping things and swearing a lot more in the kitchen. The day of our first scheduled "session," I was lying on our bed naked, inviting the awe that accompanied the fact that this might be the moment our first child was conceived. Bill, meanwhile, was doing his kind of animal pacing back and forth across the room, still fully clothed. I asked him what was wrong.

"I'm the one who has to perform here," Bill said.

"At least we get to have sex, right?" I said, trying to break through his anxiety. Normally, Bill would have pounced on the bed. In the entire time I'd known him, I'd never experienced him be anything but wildly enthusiastic about sex. His only complaint had ever been "not enough."

Also, in the entire time we'd been together he had never had difficulty achieving or maintaining an erection, nor had he failed to climax. He was a virile guy. Despite this, he was disturbed. "It's fine for you," he said, pulling off his shirt and boxers and throwing them into a pile on the floor. "You can just lie there and do nothing, and it could still work."

I decided not to respond to his interpretation of my role in the interaction but instead tried to coax him into the bed. "You're gonna do great, honey. It's just us and maybe, if this works out, a baby." I found out that while envisioning an egg and sperm coming together in a divine moment of creation was a big turn-on for *me,* the idea was mostly pressuring, and not even a little bit erotic, for Bill.

We resorted to some sex talk and foreplay, and despite his fears, Bill ably completed the mission.

I stuck my legs up in the air afterward, even though none of the medical websites considered the practice one that definitively or even probably aided in conception. Bill collected his clothes from the floor, looking relieved and revived, and asked if I wanted to go out to lunch.

We agreed not to talk about stim or our schedule or if we might be becoming pregnant *that very minute*. "It's our very first time," Bill said. "It would be amazing if we got pregnant right away, but statistically, it's more likely to take a little while."

Still, the next day I spritzed our sheets with essential oils that were supposed to increase the chances of conception, and I moved the wooden fertility statue, which one of my colleagues in London had sent me, next to the bed on the floor. It was a two-foot-high aboriginal goddess with a pointed head and a silver- and red-painted face. Bill shook his head when he saw it but didn't ask me to move it. We'd take whatever help we could get. "Just keep it on your side of the bed," he said. "I don't want that thing looking at me while we do it."

The second day's stim sex was better. We took our time and laughed a lot. When we finished, Bill went to the store to get groceries for dinner. I walked to the park and lay in the grass. It was a Saturday, and the mid-August sun was just the slightest bit less yolky than it had been at the height of summer, its waning intensity a whisper of the fall that would come. I rotated my body until the sun was shining straight on me and tried to imagine my body as the earth, my womb as the great womb, as lush and fertile as a rain forest, the rivers, the trees.

I tried to sense if we could be pregnant, but I didn't feel anything telling in my body. It was too early to feel anything anyway, I told myself. I imagined the process: Bill's sperm propelled by its life force, burrowing like an arrow into the center of my egg, and the new embryo life that was formed floating weightless, as if in space, down the fallopian tube and into the uterine chamber, falling, falling, floating into a soft landing in the plush, cushioned lining of the uterine wall.

I stood up, my back stiff from the hard ground. The sun had moved further toward the west, and the afternoon felt long, timeless. I guessed we were probably not pregnant, but I would have been happy to have been proven wrong. My mind was already trying to guard my heart from disappointment.

Ten days later, I got my period. I took small joy in seeing a period again, even one brought on by fertility hormones. But we were not pregnant.

"You have a great attitude," Tracey said, when she called to follow up and ask if we'd like to do another round. "I sensed that about you right away. It will make a difference. Keep positive. We're thinking the best for you guys."

I didn't feel too disappointed. It felt good to be in a process, to have an expert team, to have a plan. Bill hadn't had any illusions about getting pregnant the first time, and we were ready to try again. We'd confirmed that our insurance would cover the Follistim medication and office visits, giving us the means to continue immediately. I gave Tracey the go-ahead to call in our next order and told her I would pick up the Follistim from Braun Pharmacy myself.

The most common complaint I'd heard from people who'd gone through fertility treatments was how difficult it was to schedule the "scheduled sex." "After a while it really stops being fun," one of my clients lamented after her fourth round of stim.

Each month we had a forty-eight-hour window during which we were supposed to have sex three times. Our first time around, the

window happened to fall on a weekend. We'd purposely not scheduled anything else, and finding the time was easy. The following
month's window came on a Wednesday and Thursday. Bill had client meetings booked for months, I had already scheduled clients for
sessions, and Bill's father and stepmother were coming to town and
were staying with us.

Over a late dinner the week before his parents' visit, Bill and I
compared calendars. We'd lit a large pillar candle, and aside from
the small radius of its glow, the room was dark. The light from our
cell phones illuminated our faces in the semidarkness as we scrolled
through our schedules for the week. Once we'd overlaid our com-
mitments and the parental visit, we identified two twenty-minute
windows, in addition to late nights, which had never been our ideal
sex time.

"I guess we can do it after breakfast the first day my parents are
here—and then again before dinner the next night, as soon as you
finish your five o'clock session."

I looked at Bill and shrugged. "We'll make it work," I said.

The first morning of his parents' visit, over an awkward breakfast of muffins and fruit, Bill talked really fast and I lost the thread
of the conversation several times as Bill's stepmother told me about a
show opening soon at the Cincinnati Museum. Bill and I had let his
parents know that I had a "conference call" at 8:00 AM that I needed
to take upstairs, "because the reception was better." At seven fifty-
five, I went upstairs and then, as planned, called down to Bill to ask
if he would help me with calling in to the conference line through my
computer. We were like bad actors in a play. I had no idea what his
parents were thinking.

Bill tore into our bedroom, where I was already lying naked,
holding some organic lubricant. I'd removed the fertility goddess in
favor of a single red candle, only to burn my hand trying to light it.

We did our best to be amorous, but I felt the time pressure. So we just did what we could (quietly) until we reached our goal—like athletes racing in a sprint.

We did not become pregnant that month, either.

As we continued, the scheduled sex became more like regular sex. We planned around and for it, streamlined our travel schedules, and spent more weekends in Chicago, nesting at home. On the prescribed injection days, I gave little more thought to the nightly jabs than I did to flossing my teeth or taking out the garbage. I experienced no hormonal mood swings or noticeable side effects from the medication.

Dr. Colaum adjusted our dose of Follistim each cycle. "We're looking for your magic number," she said. "Too little, and you'll have less egg/follicle growth. Too much, and you'll hyperstimulate and we'll have to cancel the cycle. We didn't hyperstimulate the first time, but I did develop some tissue buildup, like debris in a river, which took a few weeks to clear. I felt afraid of hyperstimulation, mostly because it meant another month that we wouldn't be able to be pregnant, as well as potentially an additional month off to rest in between—a wash of that precious investment of time. My trust in Dr. Colaum and her many years of experience was what allowed me to be more optimistic than worried.

In November, during our fourth cycle, I flew to New York City for a friend's bachelorette weekend. Amanda had become my best friend in the sixth grade, when I transferred to public from Catholic school. She was consistently the smartest person in the class and a consummate athlete. The boys in our school loved her for her long, shiny, super-straight hair and sculpted calves. Her father was a skilled painter, and through her family I explored art and had my first contact with artists like Monet, Miró, and Picasso. We'd remained best friends through high school and kept in close touch during college. We'd both taken jobs in advertising right out of college and somehow, by some generous cosmic gift, we had ended up in London at the same time. Amanda had met her now fiancé while we were all living there, and when he proposed, she had called me from their flat in North London and asked me to be her maid of honor.

The bachelorette fell during the final two days of my stim injections, requiring me to bring the medication with me and to leave earlier than I'd originally anticipated on Sunday (to make it home in time for Bill and me to have sex). Dr. Colaum upped my dose of Follistim. She approved me for travel but encouraged me to listen to my body in terms of activity. "Be sure to take your injections at the same time as you would in Chicago, and keep the medication cold." Follistim required constant refrigeration—so I needed to find a discreet place to store it in flight and during our hotel stay. I wondered about flying with needles, but was able to find a note on the American Airlines website informing me that as long as I could produce a prescription for my medications, I could bring them with me on the plane.

On the Friday of the bachelorette weekend, I rubber-banded the medication, needles, and prescription labels between two ice packs and left for the airport.

I arrived early and alerted the officials at security that I was traveling with injectable medication. The guard waved me through and didn't even ask me to unpack the package or for a prescription. The flight boarded on time, but we sat for over an hour on the tarmac as the Follistim box grew wet with melting ice.

Once we took off, I wrestled with whether to bother the flight attendant for ice. I walked toward the back of the plane ready to offer a heartfelt appeal, and found the flight attendant in the galley, standing in front of the beverage cart, flipping through a magazine. I'd barely made it through the word "medication," when she held up her hand, as if to spare me from any further explanation, removed two club sodas from the ice drawer, and laid the Follistim package with care in their place. She handed me the sodas and told me she'd put some ice in a bag for me when I deplaned.

I was touched by the flight attendant's kindness. My throat tightened into a knot. I began to thank her, but she waved me back toward my seat; the extra hormones may have finally started to affect me. By the time I reached my row, I was wiping tears from my face with my hand. I pretended to be looking for something in my bag, sticking my head in as far as I could to give myself a few seconds to catch my breath. When I emerged, I made a show of blowing my nose as if I had allergies, in an attempt to assure fellow passengers that they were not flying with a crazy person.

The bachelorette party's gathering place was the Gansevoort Hotel in the Meatpacking district. We'd booked a suite for seven of us who were traveling in from out of town. The eight other guests, all New Yorkers, would join us for various events throughout the weekend. Pastis was a hive of activity across the street, with paparazzi staking out the front entrance. I experienced the jolt of energy I always felt in New York, but it gave way quickly to a wave of dizziness and fatigue. If I didn't know every minute detail of my fertility status, I might have thought I was pregnant.

I found out at the front desk that Amanda and several others had already arrived, and I made my way to the room on the fourth floor. I heard laughter coming from the room and hesitated in the hallway amid the mod carpeting and silver-framed black-and-white photographs on the walls. Another wave of fatigue rose up and passed; my mind felt fuzzy. The other women coming this weekend were mainly acquaintances, mostly single or newly married. The wet bag in my hand made me different, someone with a secret agenda. I didn't want to arouse any questions. I hadn't even told Amanda we were *trying*.

I stashed the bag with the Follistim in the minibar fridge, wedging it behind the beer cans and Orangina bottles in the back. The first night we convened at the pool bar on the roof deck, which made it easy for me to run back to the room at 8:00 PM to take my injection without anyone's noticing. But the next night presented a challenge. As eight o'clock approached, the larger group gathered in our hotel suite to hang out for a few hours before going out to a late dinner. I waited for the bathroom to become available. Four additional people had joined the party for the evening, coming in from Philadelphia and Boston. Everyone needed to shower.

By the time I got into the bathroom, the counters were covered with toiletry bags, makeup, and hairbrushes. I peered out into the bedroom before closing the bathroom door. Quickly, I set up the needle, Follistim vial, and pen on a tissue. I swabbed my skin, ratcheted the medication to my new dose, and stuck the needle into my stomach. I didn't hear the door before it swung open. Amanda's college roommate burst into the room. "I'll be right ther—" she called out to someone down the hall. And then she stopped. "Um. Oh my god. Sorry." Her face reddened as she took in the case of needles and the pen jabbed into my stomach.

I blanched, feeling as if I'd been caught shooting up.

"It's fine, really." I contemplated telling her it was insulin, for diabetes. "It's fertility medication," I said.

"You don't have to—oh, wow, really? You're trying to get pregnant?" she asked. I nodded, inwardly cringing.

I hated this. I didn't want to be asked about our progress at the wedding the next month or in the group emails that circulated over the years, usually when someone got engaged.

"That's so great," she said. I hurried to pack up the kit and store the needle in the Ziploc bag I would take back to Chicago, since I couldn't throw them away in the regular trash. (Braun had provided Bill and me with our own superhandy biohazard container for disposing of needles at home, but it was too bulky to take on the plane.)

"And you have to take shots?" she asked, as she watched me swab off my abdomen and pull down my dress, which I only then realized was hiked up around my neck. I flushed and hurried to pack up my kit.

"Do they hurt?" she asked. I wondered if she really wanted to be having this discussion or was just trying to normalize the situation for me.

"Not much," I said, although my lower-right abdomen had been feeling tender since earlier that evening. I wasn't sure what was causing the pain. It felt internal, and that made me nervous. In my mind the word "hyperstimulation" loomed. Abdominal pain was one of the symptoms listed in the packet from RMI.

"I hope it works," she said, her eyes full of goodwill.

"Thanks," I said.

I thought about asking her not to tell anyone, but decided not to ask someone I barely knew to keep a secret for me.

"You didn't tell me you're *trying!*" Amanda gushed, running up to me as soon as I reemerged. "And you're doing fertility treatments?" she asked, dropping her voice and pulling me to the side of the room.

"We're a few months in," I said. I felt exposed, and fatigued. When I added up the years of acupuncture and more recent doctor assessments, it seemed like we'd been doing treatments a lot longer than that.

The conversation around the room quieted, and I was aware of being the focus of attention. I'd married Bill at twenty-six, years before most of the rest of our peer group had entered marriages, and was perhaps the first in this circle to have entered into fertility-treatment territory. I felt obligated to say something. I made a few jokes and hoped the topic could be closed.

Satisfied, the group turned our conversation elsewhere and we went out into the night—to Morimoto's, where the bathrooms had cherry-blossom holograms and European bidets, so beautiful and warm that we lingered at the sinks, warming ourselves before reentering the frigid air-conditioning blasting through the restaurant.

By the time dinner ended, it was eleven o'clock and the group was moving on to a club. I couldn't imagine dancing at this point. The fatigue had started again, and the tenderness in my abdomen had progressed to a consistent dull pain. I was concerned enough about hyperstimulation and the similarities, although faint, to the pain from my ovarian cyst in high school that I called Dr. Colaum's after-hours service and was put through to Lisa Rinehart, Dr. Rinehart's wife. Lisa had started RMI with her husband and had none of his or Dr. Colaum's scientific reserve. She wore bold print shirts and perfume and bright nail polish, and once she got to know patients she greeted them with motherly hugs.

"Sara?" she asked. "How are you?" I dropped back from the group and waved my hand to Amanda to indicate that I would catch up. I pressed the phone into my ear and covered my other ear with my free hand, trying to hear Lisa's voice over the din. The connection was staticky and cut in and out. Lisa took me through a symptom inventory.

"Does the pain feeling sharp-shooting or consistent?"

"Consistent."

"Intense or low-grade?"

"Medium."

"Anything else?"

"Yes, the area around my lower-right abdomen feels hot," I said, pressing my palm over the skin. My ovary felt like a furnace.

"You're at the peak of your cycle," Lisa said. "Your symptoms are normal for a stim cycle. We won't know until you come in, but I don't think you've hyperstimulated. Have you taken some aspirin or Tylenol?"

I had not. I'd wanted to make sure I could feel what my body was doing. "Call if it gets any worse, honey," Lisa said. "The best thing you can do now is to take it easy."

I was glad that Lisa could not see me through the phone. I'd had to pick up my pace so as not to lose the group. I kept an eye fixed on the bobbing image of Amanda's orange dress in the crowd ahead, moving into a half-run every time I thought I was about to lose them. I didn't know what Lisa had made of the background noise (I hadn't told her I was in New York City), but I doubted walking seventeen blocks to a club to go dancing at eleven o'clock at night was what she had in mind when she said "take it easy."

The line outside the club snaked around two blocks, but someone had called ahead to get on the VIP list, so we were ushered right into the club's velvet mouth. Inside were dance floors, a lounge area, and three bars. I was sober, having had only a few sips of wine at the restaurant. Bodies pressed against me from all sides: men in suits and hipster sportswear, women in short dresses and ultra-high heels. I cupped my hand over my low abdomen and tried not to get jostled.

As we waited in line at the bar, I asked around for some aspirin. Gen, a striking woman who worked with Amanda in London, offered me a travel pack of Tylenol from her purse. "I heard Mary-Kate and Ashley Olsen were here last week," a woman next to us gushed to her friend.

"Who cares?" Gen whispered to me, nodding in their direction. She hailed a bartender with a hundred-dollar bill. "As if that's a reason to come here. Get your own life." I laughed. I gave her some money for the champagne she was buying for the bride-to-be and ordered a club soda for myself. I took the pills, swallowing the water in large, urgent gulps.

I found our group toward the left side of the dance floor and looked around for a place nearby where I could rest. "You okay?" Amanda mouthed, waving to me from the throng. I nodded yes. Gen passed around champagne glasses and we toasted Amanda's upcoming celebration. "And here's to Sara getting knocked up this week!" Amanda's college roommate added as a PS toast, yelling it out, her voice carrying over the thumping beat. I spit the last of my water onto the floor. Gen saw me and held up her glass. "Nice," she said.

The pain in my abdomen had subsided. Either the Tylenol had kicked in or my ovary had settled. I felt an impulse to dance. I laid my glass on a table in the lounge and joined the swirl of the crowd. The music was so loud, the lyrics were inaudible. All I could hear was the pulse of the bass and the rush of blood in my ears. A new song emerged, a popular summer anthem. The crowd responded and began to chant the chorus. We moved as a group, snakelike, to the center of the pulsing floor. Raising our arms, we danced for Amanda's marriage, her happiness, her future, stomping our feet, laughing, encircling her as a tribe.

Back in Chicago, I took the rest of the Follistim and the HCG hormone and Bill and I had sex. I propped my legs up on the wall over our headboard and tried to visualize being pregnant. Sunrays streamed through our wall of windows. It was the one room we'd never quite decorated as we'd worked systematically through the main house, doing improvement projects as our budget allowed. Our bedroom was therefore an eclectic hodgepodge of traditional European pieces mixed with an Asian wedding cabinet we'd found on Portobello Road and a neutral rug. A framed oil painting of a small village in the South of France hung over our bed. The sheets and duvet, tangled underneath me, were all white, my favorite. It was a happy room, spacious and not too rigidly defined. I willed myself to feel open to possibility, but still, my visualization felt halfhearted.

I didn't know if I was having a hard time envisioning pregnancy because stim hadn't worked or if I just didn't believe stim was going to work for us at all. After each cycle, when my period would alert us that Bill and I were not pregnant, I would call Dr. Colaum's office to let them know, and then Bill and I would drive to Evanston for another consultation.

The meetings in Dr. Colaum's office were already beginning to feel repetitive. Dr. Colaum would walk us through the treatment, doses, and possibilities and make a recommendation for next steps. On our fourth consultation, on a warm day in late November, Dr. Colaum leaned forward at her desk and got straight to her point.

"We can keep going with stim," she said. "You've given it a good try, but I think you may need something more." I sensed what was coming.

A year or so earlier, a few months before I'd seen Dr. Bizan and then Dr. Colaum, a friend of Bill's father had taken us to dinner and asked bluntly why we didn't have kids yet. I had yammered something about working on it, and he'd said he didn't see why anyone who didn't get pregnant within a month or two on their own wouldn't go straight to IVF.

"My wife and I had all our kids through IVF. And scheduled C-sections. I'm telling you," he said, his face boring into ours, "IVF is the best way to go."

"It may be the best way when you have seventeen million dollars," Bill said in the cab on the way home. We didn't know for sure how much his friend's family had, but they owned several homes and often flew in their own plane, so we were fairly sure cost hadn't been a consideration in their family planning. While I had purposely not asked for exact numbers on IVF yet, I'd heard rumors that one round could be somewhere around $20,000.

Additionally, IVF was complicated: a complex matrix of medications, injections, and frequent doctor visits—for "monitoring." More than that, though, I realized that I'd perceived IVF as extreme, something to turn to as a last resort. I didn't like that we were at this place. If we tried IVF and it didn't work, we had nowhere to go biologically.

"The advantage is that we'll take over your cycle, or, in your case, create a cycle and have control of every aspect of the process," Dr. Colaum was saying. "The statistics for conception are higher"—about 33 percent per cycle, Bill and I had read. "And if we get a good batch of eggs, as there's every reason to believe we will, based on the stim cycles, we can implant more than one embryo and your chances of pregnancy go up even more."

We told Dr. Colaum we would take some time to think about it.

"We've already started people for December cycles," she said. "You could do one more round of stim over the holidays and then, if you're not pregnant, we can regroup in the new year."

"We pretty much knew this was where we were headed," Bill said on the somber drive home. Most of the leaves in the city had fallen to the ground weeks before. On the stretch of the ride coming out of Dr. Colaum's office, however, a few rows of trees maintained a fiery orange mane, leaves hanging proudly on the branches on the sides of Ridge Road. The sun, in this last warm breath before winter, was hot through the windows of the car.

"I know," I said, "but I feel kind of freaked out anyway. IVF involves a lot of shots."

I thought about the day in London when Bill and I had decided

I should stop taking birth control pills, the first time I had viscerally imagined having a child. I thought about the promise Bill and I had already made—that we would do anything, whatever was necessary, to have a family. I was committed to this promise like a covenant, and yet I was balking slightly in the face of moving forward. I thought about a talk I had heard once about covenants: They can provide whatever power or courage is necessary for their fulfillment.

"I want to take a little bit of time before we start the process, just to be sure this feels right," I said.

Bill looked at me, and I tried to appear confident.

"Since we can't do IVF right away anyway," he said, "I'm up for doing one more round of stim and deciding in the new year." I agreed.

I reclined my seat and stared up at the trees that whizzed past against the pale sky. I felt comforted that Bill and I continued to agree on what to do next. The light was fading, but the sun still shone overhead. I found my coat, which I'd left in the car earlier, and laid it over me like a blanket. As we crossed from Evanston into Chicago, I thought that I was lucky. Bill and I had each other, the power of a covenant, and, according to a note Rachel had handed us on our way out of the office, a strong likelihood that our insurance would pay for a good portion of three rounds of IVF.

"Three rounds. Thirty-three percent chance each round," Bill said, almost to himself, calculating the odds.

Chapter 5

Before we made the final decision to do IVF, I wanted to take quiet time each day in meditation, to see if I could reach some clarity about our choice. Bill did not practice formal meditation. He tended to have a gut feeling about things, either immediately or over time. If he was uncertain about something, he cooked or gardened or took a walk.

"It's the same as what I do," I said once when he described his process.

"It's not meditation," he said. "It's just the way ideas come to me."

"Same thing," I repeated.

Since I'd returned from England, I'd been immersed in a writing project on female sexuality and feminine energy. I'd done extensive research on the female archetypes around the world, and in my reading I'd come upon what Carl Jung called the Cosmic Mother and primal cultures called the Great Mother—the mother archetype that showed up in most every culture and religion.

A friend in the UK who knew about the work I was doing had sent me a card the year we moved back to Chicago that featured a watercolor painting of Quin Yin, the mother goddess from China.

The image was painted in washes of pink, rich purples, and blue. One of Quin Yin's hands was raised, thumb and forefinger touching, with her palm forward in a gesture of peace. The folds of her robe and the outline around her face were etched in gold. I knew I'd saved the card somewhere in my office; I found it in a box on the lowest shelf where I kept old journals and vision boards and thank-you cards from clients. I'd protected the card in a cellophane sleeve; the pulpy watercolor paper was still a crisp white, the image beatific and serene. I carried the photograph upstairs and placed it next to my bed, leaning it against a stack of books on my nightstand.

In a way I hadn't done since I was a child, I knelt at the side of the bed. I asked the Mother for guidance. I wasn't sure what, exactly, I was praying to—I had not grown up with a female image of God—but it didn't matter. I believed that God, in whatever form, was multifaceted and that some aspect of it was female, and maternal. It was this aspect I prayed to. What I was really praying for was a *sign*.

In the two weeks that followed our November consultation with Dr. Colaum, I dutifully did extra meditation every day. But by the middle of the second week, I didn't feel any clearer about doing IVF. I had not received the kind of sign I like: I hadn't driven by a billboard with the letters "IVF" on it, nor had any stranger accosted me on the street, saying, "Sara, do IVF." I did, however, keep going back to a lecture my professor of reflexology in London had given about complementary medicine. "Our work is to use the best of what modern medicine and holistic treatments offer to bring about the most successful outcome or healing. Do not become rigid and holistic-exclusive," she'd said.

Then Kaitlin called from London to tell me about a documentary she'd just watched on IVF, in which the embryologist talked about being a channel for conception, versus "playing God."

"I'd always regarded IVF as unnatural," Kaitlin said, "but I feel differently now. I'd do it if we needed help."

I had not yet told Kaitlin, or any of my other friends, for that matter, that we were considering IVF, yet she'd provided a new context, one I needed. If Kaitlin, who practiced holistic medicine almost religiously, was open to IVF, perhaps I could embrace the process as well.

I still felt ashamed that we needed help to do something that was supposed to be the most natural, basic, biological thing a heterosexual couple could do. And I still felt fearful that IVF was a last resort, that if we couldn't become pregnant this way, we might never become pregnant at all. But Bill pointed out that we already hadn't become pregnant any other way. If we did not take this risk, we would never know what IVF could make possible.

By the fourth week of meditation, I began to accept that I really didn't know what was "natural" and what was not. For Bill, the decision had been easy: IVF was the logical next step for us.

We called Dr. Colaum's office in mid-December and asked to be added to the rotation for the next available IVF cycle. We met with Tracey, Rachel, and Dr. Colaum in January and began the involved precycle regime. Bill and I returned to the office for a mandatory infectious-disease panel—$1,000 worth of blood tests that our insurance did not cover. We would be required to get this panel for each future cycle to confirm we did not have AIDS, HIV, syphilis, gonorrhea, chlamydia, or TB.

"Is this really necessary?" Bill asked, as we sat side by side in the lab, our veins popping from the rubber straps banding our biceps.

"It's the FDA's rule, not ours," Rachel said. After she'd finished filling the requisite tubes of blood, she handed Bill a plastic cup. "We always take a backup donation precycle," she said, "in case someone is unable to perform on the day." She motioned to the hallway. Bill trudged grudgingly toward the "man room," his shoulders hunched.

"Men can be babies sometimes," Rachel said. "Wait until he sees what you have to go through."

With these preprocedures completed, we would begin our actual IVF cycle in March.

But I continued to feel unsettled. I told him I just needed a little time to assimilate to the regimen that was coming. I prayed and meditated in the mornings, asking for courage and alignment with whatever we needed to do to have a family. I felt no different after the meditations, but by the Monday morning of our first Lupron injection, something had shifted. I woke feeling committed, like a warrioress going into battle.

If stim was like taking an intro-level class on fertility, IVF was a PhD program.

The first two weeks were easy. I went to the doctor's office for a monitoring ultrasound once a week. Each morning at home I injected five milligrams of Lupron into my abdomen and took a birth control pill and seventy-five milligrams of dexamethasone. On the fifth day of the cycle I stopped the birth control pill and my period started— right on cue. During week three, the medications increased. I continued the Lupron and dexamethasone in the morning. In the evenings I took Follistim, Repronex-Menopur, and an injection of estrogen on alternating days.

I guessed this was around the point in the cycle where people started having meltdowns or freaking out. A friend of mine told me she experienced paranoia and obsessive thoughts just from taking Clomid, and a friend of hers said IVF drugs sent her into a depression. Rachel had cautioned me about side effects ranging from sore breasts to bloating, and noted I might feel more easily overwhelmed than I typically would.

Aside from some general, low-grade anxiety over the process and a full feeling, as if my stomach had been inflated a few times with a bicycle pump, I felt normal. Tracey and Rachel seemed surprised.

"Do you think it's because I meditate?" I asked my friend Sandy over the phone. We'd met at a life-coach-training program the year I moved back from London and had become immediate friends. Sandy had been meditating for over twenty years and had often spoken of the benefits she experienced from her practice. When she moved to Santa Fe, I started to visit two or three times a year and we set up a monthly phone date.

"It might be the meditation," she said. "I think it's also the way you're approaching this process. You and Bill have chosen to be positive and let this bring you closer." I could envision Sandy on her back porch, drinking hot water with lemon, her cropped blond hair catching the light as the sun rose over the arroyos and canyons of the Sandia Mountains. I longed to be there for a day or two, to lay my body on the desert floor, to go hiking at night and see the thousands of stars in the black sky.

Sandy was one of the only people I told we were doing IVF. I no longer felt ashamed of our decision; I just didn't want people asking me if we were pregnant or when we would know. I found it challenging enough to be with the thoughts in my own head, the hopefulness tinged with fear, the useless attempts to not think about the outcome. We'd been general with our parents, too, sharing only that we were doing fertility treatments and we'd let them know when we had any news.

I tried not to think about catastrophic outcomes as I dutifully injected my abdomen each morning and night. As we neared retrieval (the procedure in which Dr. Colaum would go in and extract the eggs), my abdomen grew sore inside. The injections made constellations of angry red dots across my stomach, and in one or two places I had small purple bruises where the needle had punctured a capillary.

"Is there a way to avoid this?" I asked Tracey at one of my appointments.

"I'm afraid not," she said. "It just happens sometimes. It's nothing to worry about." The "injection site," as the instructions called my stomach, did not exactly hurt. But the skin felt itchy and stung when I rubbed it with the alcohol swabs.

Dr. Colaum measured the growth of my follicles and counted my eggs. I tried to count along with her but could still make out only fuzzy circles on the ultrasound screen. I would have guessed seven, but she consistently came up with nine. When the largest egg grew to her desired measurement, she would set the date for retrieval. We would transfer three days later, she told me, *if* we had embryos.

In the mornings, I read Zen axioms about being flexible with desires and supple as a reed, but as we neared the hoped-for retrieval and transfer dates, I felt like a violin whose strings were wound a few turns too tight.

When I was working, I focused on the work, but the drive back and forth to Evanston every other day gave me an abundance of unstructured time in which to fixate on our fertility process. My least favorite part of the drive was the long, utilitarian strip of Ashland Avenue that took up about twenty minutes of the commute. I logged the landmarks as I drove: car wash, a White Castle drive-through, and several blocks of sad, neglected-looking storefronts. Once I turned onto Ridge Road, though, in Evanston, the scene became more picturesque. The bare street opened onto a wide, tree-lined drive, and the long driveways and expansive lawns calmed my mind, so that by the time I reached the parking lot my spirits had lifted somewhat and I could breathe fully into my belly again.

On the drive back, I would feel calmer still, by a decimal point or two, having seen with my own eyes that the follicles were developing, that we had not hyperstimulated, that the eggs were growing "beautifully" (as Dr. Colaum liked to say), and that in about one week's time we would be ready for retrieval.

I didn't ask Bill to accompany me to the appointments. The frequent visits were disruptive enough to my routine, and we agreed it was better for him to work. In some way that I never named aloud, I felt that the monitoring was my responsibility: The eggs were growing in my body. I began to think of the appointments as part of my preparation for motherhood. When we had a baby, there would be errands and classes and check-ups at the pediatrician. IVF was like an early-start parenting program. I was taking care of our child before he/she was even conceived.

At night, as I lay in bed, I would imagine myself lying next to Bill heavily pregnant, feeling a tickle of excitement run up and down the front of my body. I knew what I was doing was a risk. The 33 percent statistic flashed in my head as a reminder. I would have been wise to keep my mind open to all possibilities, to stay in the moment, to be at peace with whatever was coming. But my heart already beat with these visions of pregnancy, and I started to find it hard to imagine that it could be possible *not* to be pregnant, after doing *all this*.

On my way home I stopped at Whole Foods to pick up groceries: bread, eggs, tea, spinach, and Ben and Jerry's frozen yogurt for Bill. I had told exactly one friend—Sandy in Santa Fe—that we were attempting pregnancy with IVF. I'd felt unburdened after I called her and longed for more connection as I sat in my car in the parking lot. Impulsively, I picked up the phone and dialed my parents' number.

"What a nice surprise," my mother said upon answering. I heard the score of some musical in the background. "Am I interrupting dinner?" I asked. It was five thirty in Chicago, and I sometimes forgot to factor in the hour time difference.

"Your father is out fighting for one of his causes tonight, so I'm going to get out of my work clothes, straight into pajamas, and eat a big bowl of cereal." She sounded thrilled.

"I wanted to share that Bill and I are doing IVF," I offered, bypassing any small talk. "We have two procedures—retrieval and transfer—sometime next week."

"How are you feeling?" she asked, continuing the conversation seamlessly, as if we'd just discussed fertility treatments the week before, instead of a single time many months earlier.

"A little anxious—about being pregnant but also about the retrieval procedure," I said. "I'll be out with general anesthetic while our doctor retrieves the eggs from the follicles."

I considered telling her about the eggs, how Dr. Colaum was pleased that I had so many. I began to, but stopped. If for some reason we couldn't complete the cycle, I worried I'd have her disappointment to contend with as well as my own.

"It's amazing what modern medicine can do," my mother said.

"I know. Thanks for letting me share," I said.

"It sounds like you're doing great, honey. We're praying for you. Keep us posted."

The following Wednesday, the first week of April, Dr. Colaum scrutinized the ultrasound screen and pronounced us ready for retrieval. I could make out the individual follicles on the monitor now and counted eleven or twelve viable eggs, ranging in size from nine to twenty centimeters.

"HCG tomorrow night," Dr. Colaum said to Tracey.

In an IVF cycle, HCG has to be injected at a precisely scheduled time, down to the minute, exactly thirty-six hours before the retrieval procedure. Unlike the other injected medications in the cycle, HCG is injected intramuscularly, which means in the buttocks, or in the "love handles," Rachel told us on the day of our first IVF consultation. "For you," she said, assessing my body, "I recommend the buttocks." Bill and I had henceforth referred to HCG as "the butt shot."

Our time for the butt shot was nine o'clock on Thursday night. I let Bill administer this one because the needle was longer and I couldn't work out how to twist myself around and inject the shot in either cheek. Bill said it would be fun—for him, at least, trying to make light of it—but I was jumpy all evening. A lot rode on this shot. I thought of the hours spent driving back and forth to Evanston, the month of injections, the lab tests, the $1,500 worth of extra procedures RMI included as part of its IVF package that insurance did not cover. If we screwed up, all of our efforts to this point would be wasted.

We ate dinner at home, turned off our phones, and watched a few sitcoms. At eight forty-five, we laid out the HCG vials and Bill began mixing the powder with a saline solution. I read the instructions out loud, checking both the manufacturer's instructions and the packet from RMI. I bounced my legs nervously while Bill prepared the syringe. At eight fifty-nine, I pulled down my jeans and turned my backside toward Bill. At nine o'clock exactly, Bill was still fiddling with the syringe and I started to panic. He'd found an air bubble and was flicking his finger on it, trying to get it to burst. I recalled horror films where people injected an air bubble into someone to murder them. I hadn't asked Tracey or Rachel about air bubbles. Could this injection kill me? The seconds ticked forward, and Bill squirted some air out of the top of the needle.

"Honey!" I yelled at Bill. "Don't lose any of it! It won't work if I don't take the whole dose"—as if he didn't know this as well as I did, as if he had an interest in anything other than success. Bill flicked the plastic tube again and the bubble burst. With a steady hand, he plunged the needle into my backside. I felt a small jolt of pain as the liquid entered the muscle. We counted to three and Bill removed the needle and massaged the area, as the packet instructed. He wiped the site with alcohol and I pulled up my pants and took over rubbing my behind. I wrote down the time on our chart. It was still exactly 9:00 PM.

When I called Dr. Colaum's office to confirm our HCG injection time the next morning, Tracey told us to arrive no later than 8:30 AM on Saturday for the retrieval. "Wear something comfortable and remember not to eat or drink anything after midnight tonight." The RMI packet also instructed me to remove any perfumes or nail polish. Later that day I got a message from an anesthesiologist with more instructions: not to swallow any water, even after brushing my teeth.

"They say that so you don't puke during the procedure," Bill said when I told him about the call.

When we arrived at RMI on Saturday, the office was already bustling. The overhead lights were on, and half a dozen staff members buzzed about the hallways. "Do you work every weekend?" I asked Rachel, who met us at the front door and gave us more forms to sign.

"We schedule all our patients' cycles in sync so that we work two weekends a month and have the other two off," she replied. I would not have wanted to work that many weekends; I was grateful for their dedication.

Rachel walked Bill and me past Dr. Colaum's and Rinehart's offices, past the lab where I'd had my blood drawn, and to the back of the clinic, where the procedures took place. I'd never been to this part of the office and was surprised by how big it was. A central space formed the nucleus for three patient waiting areas, a procedure room, where Dr. Colaum would perform the retrieval and transfer, and the fertilization lab, where embryologists, who'd taken on mythical qualities in my mind, introduced eggs and sperm to each other to create embryos.

Rachel escorted us to one of the waiting areas, a three-by-four-foot space partitioned off by curtains. Inside were a La-Z-Boy and a straight-backed chair, plus a shelf with a fanned-out row of magazines and a stack of surgical clothes: a cap, gown, and pair of socks for me. She handed Bill a cup for his "donation" and instructed me to change into the light blue ensemble. Bill slumped in the chair, holding his cup. "I'd almost forgotten about my part," he said with a weak smile.

"We need to get moving," Rachel said. "Dr. Colaum is almost ready." I donned the cotton gown, cauliflower-shaped paper cap, and terry cloth socks with rubber strips on the soles.

An anesthesiologist named Dr. Samuelson started an IV, which was attached to a pole with wheels. Rachel instructed me to wrap the light cotton blanket they'd provided around my waist and follow her to the procedure room. "The whole procedure only takes about twenty minutes," she said. The blanket trailed on the ground, and I had to focus not to trip. "But you'll be groggy for a while afterward."

Tracey was waiting in the room and helped me onto an operating table. Dr. Samuelson put an oxygen tube in my nose. "Just a precaution," she said. "I have your heart on a monitor, and I'll be right here with you the whole time." After the hysterosalpingogram, I'd been happy to hear that I wouldn't be awake for the retrieval. Now, however, I was scared. Last time I'd been put under anesthesia like this, I'd woken up with one less ovary.

Dr. Colaum entered the room with her usual good cheer and verve. Her long hair was tucked into a surgical cap; her dimpled hands looked poised and precise. "Are we ready to get those eggs?"

she asked, smiling. I smiled back at her and tried to focus on Tracey's face. Someone, I guessed it was Rachel, dimmed the lights and Dr. Samuelson told me to count backward from ten. Somewhere around seven, I was out.

"Time to wake up." I tried to open my eyes. Rachel's voice sounded gooey and slow.

"You did great, honey!" I could hear Bill, but I couldn't turn my head to see him. I blinked, trying to adjust my eyes to the light. I looked down. We were in the same patient area we'd been in earlier and I was wrapped in the blanket, reclined in the La-Z-Boy. "Dr. Colaum retrieved nine eggs!" he said. I struggled to open my eyes and focus on Bill.

"How long have I been out?" I asked.

"Um," Bill said, consulting the clock on the wall, "about twenty-five, thirty minutes."

"That's all?" I asked. I felt as if my arms and legs were being weighted down. I experimented to see if I could lift my hand. I raised it a couple of inches and then dropped it to the creased leather arm of the chair.

Tracey arrived with a bag of animal crackers and a 7UP. Rachel gave Bill strict instructions to call if I experienced heavy bleeding, high fever, or severe cramping. "Most likely you'll just feel tired and sleep a lot," Rachel said. "And one of us will call you tomorrow to let you know how many embryos we have. If everything looks good, we'll transfer in the next few days."

I contracted at the word "if" and tried to turn my mind to another subject.

"How did your donation go?" I asked Bill.

"Time of my life," he said, rolling his eyes and sticking out his tongue.

RMI policy required that I be delivered to the car in a wheelchair, which Lorelai from reception volunteered to push. "I'm praying for you guys," she told me as Bill brought the car to the front entrance. "Thank you," I said. "We'll take all the prayers we can get."

Of the nine eggs Dr. Colaum retrieved, five were fertilized successfully and were vital embryos the next day.

"Our guys like each other!" I said to Bill, holding my hand over the phone while Tracey gave me the details of the fertilization. I pulled the phone back to my ear, catching Tracey midsentence: " . . . Dr. Colaum scheduled your transfer for noon on Tuesday, so be here by eleven fifteen with a big bottle of water. You'll be awake for this one, and we need you to have a very full bladder by noon."

I felt giddy as we arrived at the office on Tuesday. Rachel took us directly to the same partitioned patient area we'd used for retrieval. Bill rifled through the magazines on the shelf, and I bounced a liter of Evian on my lap. We had five thriving embryos, one or more of which would be implanted in me in less than an hour.

Rachel introduced us to Carli, an embryologist from the lab. She pulled back the curtain and thrust a small square of paper at me. "Those are your embryos!" she said.

Bill and I stared at the image: three amazing circles captured by microscope, our potential future children—all five, six, or eight cells of them.

"Dr. Colaum wants to transfer all three of these embryos to maximize your chance of conception," Carli said. "Rachel has the paperwork for you to sign. Keep drinking your water. We'll be ready to go in twenty minutes."

We had already agreed to transfer three embryos if we had them. If we had additional embryos that looked healthy for freezing, we could store them with the lab to use in a future cycle. "These three were the strongest," Carli said, pointing out the optimal shape and formation of the cells.

I nodded without looking up. I was mesmerized by the images on the paper. I regarded this moment as a gift of IVF. How many people had the opportunity to see a visual image of their potential child at the moment of conception? I changed into a paper gown, hat, and socks similar to the ones I'd worn on Saturday. I felt hyperalert and appreciative that I would be awake for the procedure. I didn't care if it hurt—I wanted to see everything.

The clinic's policy was for the partners to wait outside in the patient areas. Still, I wished Bill could be in the procedure room, to be there as Dr. Colaum transferred the tiny potential lives to my body.

As in retrieval, the lights dimmed. To me, the room took on a reverent feel, like a sanctuary. Dr. Colaum arrived in her scrubs and asked how I was feeling. "Full of emotion," I said. She patted my upper arm. Tracey turned a flat computer screen toward me, and Dr. Colaum told me that I could watch as our embryos shot into my uterus.

From there, the procedure took on a well-practiced rhythm. Tracey positioned me at the edge of the exam table and put my feet in the stirrups. Carli stuck her head through a small window in the door that stood between the procedure room and the lab.

"Please state your full name slowly and clearly."

The doctors and nurses turned to me. "Sara Connell," I said. The process felt as if I were taking a wedding vow.

"Thank you," Carli said, and disappeared from the window.

"It's a double-check to ensure we transfer the correct one," Tracey explained. *How awful*, I thought. I'd never even imagined the possibility of a mix-up.

The activity in the room made me temporarily forget about the two liters of water sloshing around in my bladder, but now I felt the building pressure. The urgency to urinate increased, and I wondered if anyone had ever peed on the table. Tracey held up a plastic instrument that looked like a vacuum attachment, which was attached to the ultrasound machine. She squirted gel onto the roller and began to move it back and forth across my abdomen with firm pressure.

Now I *really* had to go.

"Good work!" Dr. Colaum said. She turned the screen farther in my direction. "The more full your bladder, the better I can see where I'm going." I stared at the screen, trying to make out the outline of my uterus. All I could see were fuzzy white pixels against black, like a photograph of outer space.

The window in the door opened again.

"Loading embryos," Carli called from the lab.

"Inserting speculum," Dr. Colaum announced, and deftly inserted the metal contraption and a small tube. "The tube goes through the cervix into the uterus," she explained. "I want to get them up high along the back wall."

I imagined the embryos like shooting stars being launched into the vast inner space of my uterus.

"Embryos ready," Carli said from the window.

"Ready?" Dr. Colaum asked me. I could just see the top of her gray hair peeking out from the surgical cap.

"Ready," I said. My throat was dry and my voice came out raspy.

I felt the light grip of Dr. Colaum's hand on my ankle. I lay back and tried to relax. *Come in, babies. Come in,* I repeated over and over in my mind.

"Transferring three embryos," Dr. Colaum said. I felt the cool line of the catheter tube inside me, and then, "Nice!" Rachel said from somewhere behind the table.

"Nailed it," Tracey said, pointing at the screen as if Dr. Colaum had just stuck a difficult landing in Olympian gymnastics.

"Doesn't get any better than that," Dr. Colaum said, attempting to show me on-screen where the embryos had landed.

I still wasn't sure I could see them, but I exclaimed, "Wow!" nonetheless.

"The rest," Dr. Colaum said, "is up to—"

"The Universe," I suggested, trying for something neutral. Dr. Colaum was a scientist, and I wasn't sure where her spiritual beliefs lay.

"—to whatever decides these things," Dr. Colaum said, gesturing upward and shrugging.

Carli closed the door to the lab window. Rachel and Dr. Colaum filed out of the room behind me. "See you outside in twenty minutes or so," Dr. Colaum said, squeezing my shoulder as she passed. Tracey stayed for another moment, removing the extra exam paper from the table, putting the metal instruments in a BIOHAZARD bin for cleaning, returning the ultrasound roller to a hook on the side of the machine. She tilted the bed even farther back so that my legs were up higher than my head. "Do you think you can hold it?" she asked.

The persistent *thump* in my bladder had escalated to a scream.

"Um-hmm," I said, willing my body to relax.

"See if you can rest," she said, and closed the door quietly behind her.

I heard Dr. Colaum's voice from outside the room and then Bill's laugh. One thought played over and over in my mind: *We might be pregnant. We might be pregnant.* I looked at the screen again and tried to quiet my mind. I stretched my hands across my belly the way I imagined I would if I was seven or eight or nine months pregnant. A lullaby came to mind and I started singing. I lay staring at the screen, feeling the pulse of my fingers and hands on my belly, humming and singing, welcoming this life the way I would want to be welcomed, in deep, soothing tones.

Under strict instructions not to exercise, lift anything heavier than fifteen pounds, drink alcohol, or have sex, I went about the next week in a state of wired anticipation. "Don't even think about trying to tell if you're pregnant," Rachel had told me, after I'd been allowed to go to the bathroom. "The hormones you've been taking can feel exactly like pregnancy symptoms. Your breasts will be sore, you will feel bloated, you could even come up positive on a pregnancy test because you took HCG—so don't take one." Home pregnancy tests were off the table at RMI. Rachel sounded like the seasoned parent of an adolescent, giving instructions on what not to do before she went out of town.

I filled my days with client sessions and preparing a talk, "The Feminine and Creativity," that I'd been asked to give for a local women's group. Many times a day, though, I'd stop in a hallway or when I was walking down the street to put my hands on my belly and squint my eyes, concentrating hard to discern any new sensation, any movement, as if there would be some way to feel cells dividing or the implantation that could be occurring at that very moment.

"Cut it out!" Bill yelled when he caught me standing in the doorway of our house, holding my hands on my belly, the Friday before our pregnancy test.

"My friend Michelle said she felt *the moment of implantation!*" I yelled back. "I haven't felt anything. I don't even feel the pregnancy symptoms from the IVF drugs that Rachel said I might feel."

"Those people are delusional about the timing," Bill said.

"What about my mom?" I said. "Is she delusional?"

My mother had long claimed to have known immediately when she was pregnant with me when she woke up and did not want a cup of coffee for the first time in her adult life.

"She was probably four weeks pregnant by the time she felt

pregnant. These people did not do IVF. People who are one week pregnant have no freaking idea," he said.

I tried to calm down, especially because I still had to make it through the weekend. RMI policy was to administer two pregnancy tests. Our first, which RMI would not tell us the results of, was on Friday. The "official" pregnancy test, as Rachel referred to it, would be on Monday. I tried to pretend the Friday test was just a fertility monitoring. I arrived at Dr. Colaum's office on my own at 8:55 AM and offered up my arm. I assisted the nurse, who was new to the staff, in labeling the vial with my name and birth date, ensuring my information appeared on my tube of blood. Before I left, Rachel explained that to confirm an advancing pregnancy, they would be looking for the level of the human growth hormone to double each day between tests.

I drove to Dr. Colaum's again early Monday morning. Bill and I both decided to work for the first part of the day. I met with clients in Evanston in the morning. At two thirty, I drove home and ate a late lunch, and then took my laptop upstairs to our bedroom to try and write. I stopped ten minutes later and alternated between reading and sending emails and folding the laundry that had piled up on top of the dryer. Bill was working in his office down the hall.

Three thirty slowly turned to three forty-five, and then it was four o'clock and four fifteen. I started to fear that Dr. Colaum's staff had left for the day, but I couldn't bring myself to call. Bill came into the room every ten minutes to check.

"Anything?" he asked.

"Not yet."

As the hour approached five o'clock, I figured we weren't going to hear from RMI. I scrolled through the numbers on my phone to find the after-hours number, when I saw an Evanston area code number come up on my cell phone.

"Sara?" Tracey's voice came singsongy through the phone. "Is Bill there with you?"

"I'm here," said Bill.

"We know we're calling a bit later than expected, but everybody wanted to be here."

"Everybody?" Bill mouthed to me. I shrugged. I was standing on my tiptoes, holding the phone up closer to Bill's and my faces.

"Hi, Sara!" I recognized that voice as Rachel's.

"We all wanted to be here to tell you . . . that . . . "

"Yes?" Bill said. I thought he might hyperventilate.

"You're pregnant!" The four or five voices on the phone announced this in unison. I dropped the phone and jumped onto Bill, straddling him with my legs, attacking him with kisses. He held on to the bedpost to steady himself, kissing me back and screaming, "Oh my god!"

We could hear cheering and applause through the phone. I released my grip on Bill and put the phone back to my ear.

"Dr. Colaum wants to see you for your first prenatal ultrasound one week from tomorrow," Tracey said, resuming a businesslike tone. I looked around for something to write with. "Whenever, anytime!" I said, drunk on the information we'd just received.

"We'll see you at nine o'clock AM next Tuesday," she said. "Remember to continue your medications. Dexamethasone in the morning and progesterone injections two times a day." Right. I'd forgotten about the shots.

We were pregnant! I spent the rest of the evening after the call from Dr. Colaum's trying to mentally tunnel down into my body to see if I could feel the growing life. Before we went to sleep, while Bill took a shower, I stood in front of the bathroom mirror, turning my body to the side, then to the front, the way I would hundreds of times during the pregnancy—shirt up, belly exposed, awestruck that there was life inside me.

The next morning Bill and I discussed how we wanted to share the news.

We didn't think we could wait until the three-month mark, regarded as the norm. We agreed to wait a little while, though, not to tell anyone yet.

"We can still celebrate—just us," he said. He booked a table at Japonais, a mutual favorite. The maître d' seated us at a table near the sculpted bonsai trees and dripping chandeliers made of branches. When the waiter asked what I wanted to drink, Bill said, "Just water for her. She's pregnant!"

"We just found out," I explained to the waiter. My face turned red, but I was thrilled. The pregnancy became more real each time we said it.

When I picked up my dry cleaning the following Monday afternoon, the couple who owned the cleaners greeted me with beaming smiles. "Congratulations, you. Your husband says you have baby!"

"I couldn't help myself," Bill said when I confronted him. "I want to be able to tell someone."

Despite our pressing desire to share, we made it to the first ultrasound appointment without telling our family. Dr. Colaum told us we'd have an ultrasound every week, so I drove to this appointment on my own.

"Look at that!" Dr. Colaum said, her voice full of pride as she turned the ultrasound flat-screen toward me. After seven months of looking at follicles and eggs, I saw the wand now focused on my uterus, where even I could make out a white blob, like a bright star, up along the back.

"That's the baby," Dr. Colaum said; then, giving Tracey a pointed look, "or babies."

I scanned Dr. Colaum's face for information.

"We won't know for sure until next week, but I think it might be twins."

Tracey printed a copy of the image on the screen for me to take home to show Bill.

I felt stunned as I left the exam room. Having one baby already seemed incredible. Even knowing the likelihood of twins was high for us, I could hardly comprehend we could be having two.

I stood staring at the photo in the waiting room, my hand on the front door to the office, unable to leave right away. "Psst!" Lorelai was beckoning me from the reception counter.

"It's twins," she said when I reached her desk. She looked to both sides to make sure no one was around, and then wrote some-thing on a yellow Post-it and slid the paper to me across the counter. In blue ballpoint pen she'd written two numbers:

194

633

"I heard Rachel talking," she said, again looking behind her. "Those were your HCG numbers from your blood test. There's two babies in there."

Bill and I stood peering down at the photograph as though if we looked hard enough, we'd be able to discern whether there were two individual forms.

"It doesn't really matter, right?" one of us would say. "Why do we care? We'll know in a week. We can just enjoy being pregnant."

We stuck the photo up in our kitchen, on the inner side of the refrigerator, where only we would see it. We'd leave it alone, and then one of us would pick it up again and we would laugh.

Bill dug out a magnifying glass from the garage to see if we could make out better details with an amplified image, but the white blob was indecipherable.

The night after the appointment, we made an event of calling our parents. Bill went to the store to buy ingredients for a beef stew made with eleven kinds of vegetables. We pulled names out of a bowl to decide the call order: My parents were last. I stirred the onions in oil while Bill shared the news with both sets of his parents. Bill's mother and stepmother cried. The mood was jubilant all around.

At nine o'clock eastern time, I dialed my parents in Virginia. My mother went to bed early; I hoped she would still be awake.

"Mom?" I said, motioning for Bill to turn down the heat on the stove so I could hear. "Are we calling too late? Do you have a minute?"

"We're here, honey. It's fine. I'll get Dad to pick up."

"Hi, Sara." My dad's voice was full of the evenness that made him a great moderator. My mother and I responded to things emotionally; there had been times when I was growing up when I hadn't known where my feelings ended and hers began. I imagined she could hear my excitement through the phone. I gripped the phone with my hand until my knuckles went white.

"Hi, Dad," I said, trying to control my pitch.

Bill came around the side of the chair where I was sitting and leaned his head near the phone. I looked at him and he nodded.

"We wanted to find out if you're ready to be grandparents."

"Oh, honey!" Mom's voice broke. I could hear her crying on the other end of the line. She breathed heavily and managed to speak. "You're pregnant?"

"We're pregnant, Mom!" I said, rejoicing in being able to say those words. "And," I said, pausing for dramatic effect, "Dr. Colaum thinks there's a good chance it's twins! We'll find out next week."

"It will be perfect whatever you have," my mother said.

"Get ready, Bill," my father said. "It gets really good from here."

"You're having twins," Dr. Colaum confirmed in the exam room the following Tuesday. Bill sat behind the table where I was lying naked from the waist down.

"You should see Bill's face!" Tracey said, trying unsuccessfully not to laugh. Dr. Colaum looked at Bill and, after several attempts to contort her face to maintain neutrality, broke into a laugh as well. I arched my back and tried to move my top half to be able to see him. The ultrasound wand was still inside me, and I didn't want to disturb the babies. His face was ashen, and he looked like he was in shock.

"I knew it was likely, but—" he stammered, "I just. Oh my god. To see it—them."

I looked back at the screen. Already we could see the amniotic sacs: two clear bursts of white life now, at least double the size they'd been the week before. My heartbeat accelerated, thumping hard in my chest. I raised my left hand to my abdomen.

"What's the due date?" Dr. Colaum asked Tracey.

"We already have a due date?" I asked, arching back to look at Bill.

Tracey pulled out a paper wheel and started turning it while she talked. "Your due date is based on forty weeks from the date of your last period," she explained. Tracey consulted her notes in our file. "So you guys are now technically four weeks pregnant, which makes you due on . . . January fourteenth."

"Aquarian babies," Bill said, "just like me." I had been squeezing his hand so tightly during the calculation that the skin had turned white. "Ow," he said. I let go. I felt as if light was being poured into my body. Twins. January 14.

Dr. Colaum told us she would monitor me weekly for the first nine to twelve weeks, at which point she would turn us over to our obstetrician.

Bill and I would need to find a new OB, having decided not to go back to Dr. Bizan and her overwhelmed practice, but we didn't discuss doctors on the way home. Instead, we called our parents.

"Just think of the cute little outfits and all of those little baby toes!" Bill's stepmother, Gail, said. Bill's dad sounded weepy. "We're thrilled, we're just thrilled." Gail told me later how he'd been pining for grandchildren and imagined carrying a granddaughter on his shoulders, walking into town and having the neighbors say, "There goes Butch and Buster."

"He thinks we'd call a girl Buster?" I laughed.

"It's just his fantasy," Gail said.

Bill's mother, Nancy, meanwhile, hoped we'd be having boys. "I loved having boys," she said.

His stepfather, Roger, had practiced as a child psychologist before creating his own consulting practice. "You're going to have your hands full," he said. "And the time of your lives." Through their voices, I could feel the arms of the grandparents stretching out to the babies, their desire to pull out the baby clothes they'd been saving and cuddle new infants almost as strong as our own.

When we called my parents, my mother wanted to know if I'd had any food cravings or aversions. "When I was pregnant with you," she said, "I could not bear the smell of fish. And I was obsessed with Hostess cupcakes—something I am sure horrifies you to hear, Ms. Holistic Medicine." But I relished receiving these unmentioned details about my own gestation, the intensely intimate time I shared with my mother, of which I had no memory. I wondered if I could transmit to the babies the excitement their larger family felt about their being here.

My mother and I started talking once and then several times a week. She told me about BabyCenter, a website that would send me a weekly update with illustrations depicting my children's development, comparing their size to pieces of fruit. We signed up, and on Mondays my mother would go to the grocery store and send a photograph of the comparison fruit in an email: a pea, an apricot, a lemon, and, later, a pear. Another day, my mother called to ask if Bill and I wanted my grandmother's rocking chair for the nursery. "It's polished dark oak, with a carved back and a cushion that she needlepointed herself. She left it in the will for you girls and your children."

I told her I would think about the rocking chair. I felt anxious projecting too far into the future. We were only five weeks pregnant.

At our six-week appointment, we saw the babies' heartbeats. Dr. Colaum had me hold still as she guided the monitor over the center of each baby. They now looked like two more delineated blob-circles. In the grainy picture of the screen, I could see what looked like the flickering image of an old black-and-white projector movie. "There it is!" Dr. Colaum said. She pressed a button on the ultrasound keyboard to freeze the image, and then the computer calculated the babies' heart rate. "Baby 1: 140. Baby 2: 141."

The ultrasound appointments were the highlight of my week. Dr. Colaum pronounced the babies "perfect!—in growth and appearance." Tracey and Rachel, like my mother, delighted in hearing about my pregnancy symptoms. The calls with our parents and visits with Dr. Colaum's staff were times when I could talk freely about the part of my life I was thinking about most. It seemed strange to feel so radically different and yet not be showing it on the outside. Any fatigue I felt (my primary symptom so far) would disappear the moment I had the opportunity to share.

"I was exactly the same in the first trimester!" my mother told. "Bone-aching, ridiculous tired—and I wasn't even working. Your father would come home from work, and I'd be slouched in the same chair I'd been sitting in when he left in the morning, a book half-open on my lap. I'd maybe read a page. It went away by twelve weeks or so."

I hadn't experienced any pronounced nausea, but I continued to feel as if I were on a barge, the ground beneath me moving and shifting at times. The breakfast of organic yogurt, dry cereal, and apples I'd eaten almost daily for the past five years now turned my stomach, as did fresh spinach and other raw vegetables.

I became spacey in the mornings. Bill thought my behavior was funny, as I was typically so disciplined and devoted to my routine. He cooked broccoli smothered in cheese and made vegetarian pizzas so I would eat some greens. He sent texts from the grocery store to inquire if I had any particular cravings.

At our eight-week appointment, Dr. Colaum approved me for exercise and, even better, travel. The twins had strong heartbeats and were growing in their own amniotic sacs, something physicians find very reassuring. Ever since I'd told my mother we were pregnant, I'd wanted to see her. I wanted to run to her and put her hands on my stomach, which had not yet begun to swell outwardly but held the growing lives of our babies.

I flew to Washington, D.C., the second week in June. "When you get back, we'll have your week-ten appointment," Dr. Colaum said, "and you can stop taking the injections." I marked the date on my calendar with a star. I'd been on shots steadily for over three months, and my backside was marked with purple and blue bruises. One night, the week before, the needle had gone in at an odd angle and hit a nerve. I had been up most of the night with pain radiating down my legs and back.

I brought my last batch of progesterone injections with me to my parents' house. My mother gasped in the kitchen when I pulled down my pants and she saw the punished skin. I'd also lost weight—something I didn't know could happen in a pregnancy but frequently can in the first trimester of a twins pregnancy. My jeans fell over my hips, and the back pockets sagged where my body had previously rounded them out.

"We're going out to eat right now," my father said. "We have to feed you and those babies." We went out to dinner, and in the mornings my dad bought bagels from the deli nearby, which we ate with cream cheese and soft butter.

At fourteen weeks, my stomach popped. Bill took a picture of me against the white of our kitchen door. I hadn't bought maternity clothes yet and was wearing a loose-fitting turquoise sundress. I pulled the material tight over my belly and stood sideways, facing our deck garden. I held up four fingers of my right hand, and Bill snapped the shot on his phone. We had reached the four-month mark.

Kaitlin and I had kept up our semimonthly call, every other Tuesday, since I'd moved back from England. She and her husband had been trying for over a year to get pregnant and had had two miscarriages, at six and eight weeks. The first week in August she told me they were pregnant again—just barely. I prayed for her baby daily. It terrified me to think about either of us experiencing such a loss, and I was grateful that Bill and I were well into the second trimester.

At the second-trimester mark, BabyCenter had sent an email that said: "Congratulations! Your risk of miscarriage has gone to less than 10 to 20 percent." We still had one final appointment left with Dr. Colaum when we met with our new OB.

Bill's business partner and his wife got us in to their OB-GYN practice with their doctor, Elsbeth Baker. Even though we'd done weekly ultrasounds with Dr. Colaum, Dr. Baker asked us to come in for an ultrasound. By week twelve, the twins had all of the important body parts and the doctors sent us home with photographs: crisp black-and-white images of little faces, hands, and feet.

At our final appointment at RMI, Baby A did a scissor kick right to camera and I was sure I saw *something* between his legs. Dr. Colaum saw it, too. She checked my face, presumably to gauge my response. "Was that—" I started to ask.

"Did you want to know the sex?" she asked. I nodded.

"What do you think?" she asked.

"I think I saw a penis."

"I think so, too," she said, angling the wand to see if Baby A wanted to reveal himself again. "That baby is a boy!"

To find out about Baby B, we'd have to wait until the twenty-week ultrasound. Bill said he'd wait for the technician to confirm the sex of both babies, as he did not trust my ultrasound reading and seemed offended about not having been there to witness it himself. Our appointment was scheduled for a Monday toward the end of August. We were five months pregnant now, and my belly amply filled out the stretch maternity tops I'd bought at Target and the Gap.

We'd dressed up for the appointment and planned to go out to lunch afterward. I wore a green wrap dress and liked being undeniably pregnant now, and the way my body rounded and curved. The twenty-week ultrasound appointment took place in a special suite several OB practices shared. The exam bed was covered in rich leather. The lighting was dim, like in a theater, and the walls were painted a soothing brown. Mounted on the walls were two fifty-two-inch plasma TVs. A dark-haired female technician wearing a lab coat entered the room. Without introduction, she invited me to the bed, switched on the ultrasound machine, poured gel onto a roller, and dimmed the overhead lights even more. "Enjoy the show," she said.

Bill and I watched as our babies were projected on the large screens. Having seen them weekly, I felt they were familiar now. I recognized the way they moved, the shape of their heads, the swimming motions they liked to do with their arms and hands.

"Ten fingers and ten toes," the technician said. "See?" She angled the roller to show us each baby's extremities.

She moved to the heads. "The brain looks good; skull bones are all forming nicely." She took us on a tour of the noses, lips, throats, and teeth. We saw the babies' kidneys and adrenal glands and even Baby A's bladder full of liquid. The technician zoomed in on the four beating chambers of the heart. Then she shifted to look at Baby B, who sat lower in my uterus. As the technician measured the femur bone, the baby stuck a thumb in its mouth.

"Is he?" I said

"Sucking his thumb," the technician affirmed.

"I used to suck my thumb!" I said, gobsmacked by the undeniably real infant gesture.

"I did, too!" Bill said.

"Hold steady if you can," the technician asked. The appointment took a long time. The technician had to do close to a hundred measurements for each baby.

Bill shifted in his chair. I started to feel lightheaded. My stomach grumbled. I wished I'd brought a snack.

"Do you want to know the sexes?" the technician asked. I stopped thinking about food.

Bill leaned forward in his chair. "Yes!" he said.

We held hands.

"Baby A is a . . . " She drew the words out slowly. I looked at Bill and then at the technician. "Boy!" she said. I nodded. I'd seen the confirmation already. "And Baby B . . . " she said, angling the roller so we could see with her. I waited for her to say "girl"; Bill believed we were having a girl as well.

"Another boy!" the technician said.

Bill dropped my hand. "Are you sure?" he said.

I looked at the screen and saw his little white member hanging between his legs. He put his thumb back in his mouth, and I melted into the table.

The revelation that we were having two boys took a few days to sink in. It seemed we now knew so much more about our twins. By the weekend, we were on baby websites, looking at names. On Friday, September 1, we went to Carnival, a cavernous Latin restaurant in the West Loop, to celebrate a friend's fortieth birthday. At dinner, she told me about a boy she'd dated in South Africa who came from a family of four boys. "Their mother was like you—creative and beautiful—and those boys adored her. I imagine that's the way your boys will be: lovely, fun, rambunctious, and adoring."

On September 4, I met with two clients in the morning. I invited my eleven o'clock client to meet upstairs in our living room, thinking the light was particularly beautiful that day. The sun filtered through the large dome window, bathing the sofa and chairs in light. Toward the end of the session, I felt a small cramp. Throughout the pregnancy, I'd had no cramping or pain. I'd felt flutters in my belly recently, though, and Dr. Baker had said these were the first movements of the twins that I could feel.

I walked my client to the door. Another cramp came, the kind that sometimes preceded an urgent need to go to the bathroom. I moved gingerly to the kitchen, taking my time and holding on to the railing of the short staircase that led up to the kitchen bathroom. I felt a slight rush of dizziness in my head, but it passed quickly. I switched on the light and pulled down my pants, getting ready to sit on the toilet. I felt another light cramp, and then I saw it: blood. A thick stand of it fell from between my legs. I braced myself between the two walls of the bathroom, praying that it was a trick of my eye. I looked down again and saw another streak running down the side of my right leg. More blood, coming faster now, falling into the basin of the toilet. A few drops splattered onto the blond boards of the hardwood floor. I bunched toilet paper between my legs and cupped my hand beneath me, trying desperately to think of anything I could do to stop it.

Chapter 6

I've heard people claim at dinner parties, or the occasional client intake session, that they are "good in a crisis." They mention this the way one might share about other useful skills, like being able to tie nautical knots or start a fire in the wilderness with a piece of wood and some flint. I have never aspired to have this skill.

I'm guessing, like intuition, the ability to be good in a crisis is something we all possess—perhaps a gift of Darwinian evolution. And I am sure we all benefit from this ability, yet I've also often heard it takes being in a crisis to know if one does indeed possess this skill.

When the blood continued to flow between my legs as I stood in the bathroom, a few drops now spilling onto the floorboards, I became hyperconscious of my body and my feet on the floor. My thoughts narrowed to a single message: *Get to the phone and call the doctor.*

Stuffing more toilet paper between my legs, I walked awkwardly across the kitchen to my cell phone, jeans still around my knees. My green maternity top stretched over my extended belly. I looked seven months pregnant because of the twins. I had to steady my hand on the kitchen island as I scrolled through my list of phone

numbers and called the OB's office. I kept my voice even as I provided details to the nurse.

"Are you bleeding through more than a pad an hour?"

"The bleeding just started."

"You're how far along?"

"Almost twenty-two weeks."

"Are you in any pain?"

If terror is pain, then yes. Physical pain, no.

The nurse sounded casual, unconcerned. I could picture the
bustling office, always overflowing with patients, running thirty to
forty minutes behind. At one point she asked me to hold the line
while she answered a question for a patient who was in the office. Her
demeanor both enraged me and gave me a shred of hope that perhaps
what was happening was not, in fact, dire.

The nurse finally gathered enough information to instruct me to
come to the office. Bill, who had been in a meeting downtown, said he
would meet me there. I called a taxi and walked out to the front steps
to wait. Taxis could take up to twenty minutes, and I wondered if I
should call an ambulance. I didn't have any pads in the house, so I'd
stuffed more toilet paper in my underwear. I brought nothing with me
from the house aside from my wallet and a sandwich (a last desperate
attempt at normalcy). The early September light blazed through the
trees and onto the sidewalk. I could not comprehend the bleeding.

Dr. Baker had told us to be prepared for the twins to come at
about eight months. According to our recalibrated due date, we were
entering our third trimester. Anything after twenty weeks was no
longer considered a miscarriage. I was terrified to think what was
happening. I put my hands to my stomach and tried to feel the babies
move. Everything inside my body felt normal. The cramping was
gone. Everything felt the same as it had the previous day. A woman
walked by, pushing her child in a stroller. I felt one of the babies

move, and I allowed myself to hope that everything would be okay. "Hang on, babies," I said to the twins. "Hang on."

In the taxi I started to pray. I texted Amanda and Kaitlin.

"Oh god," Kaitlin texted back. "All prayers with you."

Within minutes of arriving at the office, I was in the examining room. Dr. Baker slapped on a latex glove and examined me internally with her fingers. "Your cervix is dilated," she said. "Did anything happen? Have you been having any cramping? Did you have a hard bowel movement?"

"Could a bowel movement cause a problem?" I asked.

She said no. *Then why did you ask?* I thought, upset.

"I just checked you last week," she said. "Everything was fine."

Bill arrived and stood with his hand on my shoulder at the top of the exam table.

Dr. Baker looked worried and sent us to the hospital where she delivered, just a few blocks away.

"Go to the fourth floor," she said. "I'll meet you there in fifteen minutes."

The women's ward of the hospital was contained in the larger hospital building and had not been touched since the '70s, when it was built.

"You want us to walk?" I asked, confounded. Were we having an emergency or not? Bill took my hand and walked me out of the office and down the street. Dr. Baker's nurse had given me two pads, which I layered inside my thong. We tried not to imagine what might be happening. "Can you feel them?" Bill asked. I nodded and began to cry.

"Let's not panic yet," he said. "It might be okay." The hospital's entrance was grimy, like an old subway station, having been subjected to decades of pollution and smog from the El train and traffic nearby. I balked at the entrance, my body bristling like a cat sensing something malicious.

A nurse on the women's floor asked the same questions I'd now answered two times that day. She told me to change into a gown and admitted us to a large, ugly private room. I fought memories of being admitted to the hospital for my cyst. I felt the same taste of bewilderment I had experienced that day as people calmly asked questions and gave me forms to fill out as if I were applying for a car loan instead of bleeding through my jeans and onto the floor.

Dr. Baker arrived minutes later, wearing a lab coat and accompanied by a nurse with curly hair. Another doctor, an attending physician at the hospital who wore wire-rimmed glasses and had thick dark hair on his knuckles, joined her. They lifted my legs into stirrups, and Dr. Baker felt around inside me with her fingers. I winced as she pressed hard.

"She's dilated, probably three centimeters or so. I can feel the bag."

The other doctor checked to verify the dilation.

"You're in labor," she said. "Your cervix has dilated prematurely and the babies have begun to descend."

The labor I'd expected involved water breaking, not blood.

"It's too soon," she continued. "There's not a good chance they'll survive."

I twisted in the bed. I looked around for someone who could tell me this was a mistake. The doctors' faces were grim.

"Is there anything we can do?" I asked.

"There is one procedure we can try. It's called a cerclage." The attending physician with the hairy knuckles was speaking. "It involves trying to stitch up your cervix and push the babies back up into the uterus."

"It's a risk," Dr. Baker said. "We'd have to have a large needle right up close to the sac. If we burst the bag, the twins have to be delivered. There's a high risk of infection."

"If we don't do it?" I asked.

"You'll probably go into full labor and deliver them anyway."

"When would that happen?" Bill asked.

"Probably in the next forty-eight hours," Dr. Baker said. She looked down at her clipboard, avoiding our eyes. "An emergency cerclage like this one has about a 6 to 8 percent chance of success."

I noticed the clock on the wall, a generic circle with a white face and brown rim, reminiscent of the ones that were mounted on the walls of my junior high school. I watched the red second hand glide around the face.

"So, our only chance is the cerclage," Bill said. His teeth were clenched and his voice came out in a strained tone.

"I can give you a few moments," Dr. Baker said, moving toward the door.

Bill looked down at me on the bed. I couldn't imagine what the doctor thought we would need to discuss. I experienced the same tunneling sensation I'd felt in my kitchen.

"Order the cerclage," I said.

Dr. Eagen is the best in the hospital," Dr. Baker affirmed, as a surgical team prepared me for the procedure. We'd signed papers absolving the hospital of any responsibility if our twins did not survive. An anesthesiology team joined the growing party in the room. They told me that to protect the babies, I would not be able to have general anesthesia. Instead, they would administer a spinal tap to numb the area below my waist. I'd be strapped to a hospital table that they would maneuver to a steep incline, so that my legs would be up high in the air and my head would hang below.

"You'll have to lie very still," the older of the two anesthesiologists said. She spoke in a soothing voice and looked like an old hippie, with long hair that was just starting to gray.

"We'll use gravity to help us out," said a younger Asian anesthesiologist. He had a kind face, and I forced my mouth into a weak smile.

I turned my face away from the doctors. I could see my reflection in a glass cabinet opposite the bed. My hair was covered with a blue surgical bonnet, and I was still bleeding between my legs into a pad. A nurse started an IV in my arm. Someone else drew blood.

Sometime around 3:00 PM, Dr. Eagen's team assembled and two orderlies wheeled me into the operating room. The anesthesiology team rolled me onto my side and inserted the spinal tap. I was afraid to move. I was afraid of the rotating table. I was terrified that Dr. Eagen would not be able to save our babies.

Please let us be the 6 to 8 percent, I prayed silently as the table started to tilt.

Dr. Baker came into the room for the procedure. All I could see of her were her brown eyes, looking attentive and concerned through her scrubs and face mask. The head anesthesiologist inserted the needle into my spine. I closed my eyes but then opened them. Whatever was going to happen here, with my babies, I was going to be present for it. The younger anesthesiologist rolled me onto my back and secured me to the table with straps around my arms and across my abdomen and chest. I couldn't move my arms to my belly, so I said silently, over and over, *I am with you, babies. I am your mama. I have loved every minute with you. See if you can go back up inside. I love you so much.* I prayed that the highest good would unfold and then began to meditate. It was the only thing I could think to do.

The operating table started to move. The head anesthesiologist reminded me again to remain still. As my legs rose, I counted my breaths. I remembered a meditation I'd learned, the one about appreciating people and wishing them well. Silently, I thanked the two anesthesiologists for being kind, I thanked Dr. Baker for coming into the OR with me, I thanked Dr. Eagen for doing the training he'd done to allow him to perform this procedure. I wished good to the nurses and the lab technicians and the spinal tap that was numbing me, sort of, from the waist down.

Dr. Eagen centered a light between my legs, which were now high above me. I could see a large mirror on the ceiling. "It's there so the doctors can see what they're doing," Dr. Baker whispered, following my gaze. I remembered stories from Catholic school of upside-down crucifixions for people who had committed the most unconscionable crimes. I focused my attention inward, on the babies, on my breath.

I felt tugging and a light pulling sensation where Dr. Eagen worked. The energy in the room intensified. I thought the procedure might be working; the stitching had been going on a long time. Then I felt something gush and heard Dr. Eagen yell, "Shit!" I looked up into the mirror. Water and blood spilled onto the floor. I pulled at the straps at my arms. I wanted to push the babies back inside. I wanted to hold them there with my hands.

I put my attention back on the twins, the way I had each day since I'd learned we were pregnant. I'd always felt the warmth of their life, even imagined them giggling and talking to me. Now my belly was cold and I felt a void. The babies weren't inside me anymore. It felt as if they had fled, my womb had become an abandoned building in a state of emergency.

I heard a rush of sound near my ears and felt a hovering sensation around the sides of my head. I wasn't allowed to move and couldn't see anything except the ceiling mirror, a narrow strip of my body, and the tops of the doctors' heads. Dr. Eagen and his team were still active at the end of the table. I could feel fingers and metal instruments touching my thighs even through the gauze of numbness. The hovering continued for another few seconds, and then it was gone. Dr. Eagen pulled off the American-flag do-rag he'd been wearing and threw it onto the floor. He looked angry as he paced around the room. "Shit," he said again.

Dr. Baker approached the side of the bed, her palm outstretched like a marble statue of a saint. No one had to tell me what had happened. The sac had burst. The labor was irreversible now. I thanked Dr. Eagen and the anesthesiologists for trying. I started to thank the orderlies and the doctors for their attempt, but my words caught in my throat. I began to weep.

Dr. Baker began to cry as well. I wondered if she did so every time someone lost a baby. Now I understood the grooves around her eyes that seemed premature for age forty. She told me later that she cried because I was thanking people, because she'd never seen anyone do such a thing. The thanking didn't seem special to me, though. These people did their best to help us. Nothing I could say could change anything for the babies now. I felt as if their spirits were already gone.

Bill ran to the door as two orderlies rolled me into the room we'd been admitted to earlier. The strong men lifted me from the gurney to the bed in the middle of the room.

"What happened?" he asked.

"The cerclage didn't work," I said.

"So now what?" Bill said. "Now what!"

I stared at the wall clock, and then at the tubes and machines hooked up to the bed. I felt numb and strangely dispassionate. I would later learn about a form of trauma in which a person often does not feel the full force of the emotion during the event; the feelings emerge sometime later, like the pain of a sunburn that is not felt until the next day. I heaved once, drawing a craggy breath, but no tears came out. Dr. Baker arrived and told Bill I had been amazing in the operating room.

"The air was so still. I can't explain it."

I didn't bother mentioning that it was my meditation she had felt, a momentary balloon of some kind of grace hovering over the room.

"Your wife is one strong woman," Dr. Baker said.

"It doesn't matter," I said, more to myself than to the doctor. "It didn't save them."

Staring at Dr. Baker's face, I began to feel the first physical sensations of devastation. It was as if the outer perimeter of my heart were being singed by a tiny flame, the center still numb and exposed from the smash, like the pulpy core of a peach.

"We need to decide what to do now," Dr. Baker said. "The best thing, I think, is to attempt a D&C" (dilation and curettage). It dawned on me that this was the procedure used after miscarriages and in abortions, to remove the fetus. "You're pretty far along, but I think we can still accomplish this." I watched Bill's face crumple. His hand felt limp in mine.

"Your only other option is to deliver the babies," Dr. Baker said.

"You mean as in, going through contractions and pushing?" I asked. I couldn't imagine this scenario. Laboring for hours to deliver dead children. It sounded unendurable.

A therapist told me later that delivering stillborn babies can be a powerful healing experience and that she wished I'd been more informed at the hospital. But both then and later, I was grateful for the lack of explanation. The trauma of delivering sounded worse.

"I recommend the D&C," Dr. Baker said. Bill and I gave our consent.

"The earliest we can get you in is nine o'clock tonight." She left the room to consult with the surgical team. The wall clock read 5:00 PM. The four hours loomed like a chasm.

"I called your mother," Bill said.

"You what?" I asked. I wasn't sure Bill had ever placed a call individually to my mother. I would not have thought to call her. My mother was all the way in Alexandria, Virginia. I didn't want to worry her.

"She's on her way," Bill said. I felt confused. I knew we were reeling, but things must be really bad for my mother to jump on a plane. I started to whimper. My skin was damp with sweat, but I felt chilled. I pulled the cotton blanket on the bed up around my shoulders and neck.

My sister Ellen appeared at the door. Bill had paged her after he had called my mother. She was in the middle of her year as chief resident at Northwestern and had driven from Lake Shore to the South Side as soon as she'd received the page. When people saw us together, they commented that we looked like film negatives of each other: almost identical faces with wavy hair, mine black, hers blond. Her face was splotchy and swollen. She came to the side of the bed and grabbed my arms. She shook with tears. I pressed my face into her hair, which smelled faintly of almond from her shampoo.

She stayed and watched vigilantly as the doctor who was assigned to our case briefed us on the D&C. He was a middle-aged man with mousy brown hair and a thin, hungry face that reminded me of a greyhound's.

"You'll go under general anesthesia during the procedure and be in recovery for a half-hour or so. We'll aim to discharge you by 11:00 PM. You can go home and sleep in your own bed tonight."

He delivered the detail about our going home to sleep in our bed as if it were a special treat. As if it mattered where we slept tonight. Our children would still be gone.

I turned my face to the wall. The thin sheets scratched against my legs; the fluorescent lights hurt my eyes. The image of blood and water gushing from my splayed-open legs flashed over and over in my mind. I wished I could go under the anesthesia now.

By eight thirty, when a surgical team came to prep me for the OR, I was grateful we'd be leaving the hospital that night. The monotony of the room, the *blip* of the blood pressure machine, the Pepto-Bismol-pink walls—it had all grown unbearable.

Bill and I said little in the hours leading up to the procedure. When Dr. Eagen stopped in to check on us, he gave us the technical name for what had caused the premature labor: incompetent cervix. This single hospital in Chicago saw a case of IC about every nine days. I opened and closed my mouth soundlessly, like a fish. I had thought what had happened was some kind of freak occurrence. The statistic and its clinical name enraged me.

"It's biological," Dr. Eagen said, as if this would reassure us. "Nothing you could have done to bring it on or prevent it."

"And there's no test for this?" I asked, when I found my voice. I wanted to rip the IV out of my arm and start screaming. We'd had a hundred fucking tests since we became pregnant. We knew our babies didn't have Down syndrome, or cystic fibrosis, or nine hundred varieties of genetic mutations. We had satellites in space that could take the temperature on Mars, but we couldn't find a way to check the capabilities of the cervix in a way that would prevent how many deaths a month at hospitals across the country? Around the world?

"No."

I couldn't accept this reality or bear the looks of compassionate but passive acceptance of the doctors who delivered these facts. I clawed at the sheets on the bed with my fingernails. Dr. Eagen left Bill and me to wait out our time. When we were alone again, I kicked and pounded my feet.

When the orderly came to redress me in a surgical cap and gown, Bill stroked the side of my face.

"I'll see you when you come out. You're so strong and brave," he said, his voice breaking. I remembered Sam, the technician from my MRI several years before, saying I was strong, that I looked tough. I wanted to offer Bill some of that courage. I set my hands at my side and lifted my chin. I would be strong.

I woke in a haze of yellow light, aware of a dull thud of pain in my lower-right abdomen, down under my ovary. The thin-haired doctor was leaning over me, and I heard female voices in the room. "She's coming around," he called out. "Sara? Sara? Do you know what year it is?"

The question seemed ridiculous. I tried to open my eyes wider, to show my lucidity, but stopped; the pain was bad. Much worse as the room came into focus and I became fully conscious of my body. I was able to see the room was mostly dark, just a small desk lamp emitting the low light. Two nurses sat at a console with a computer and coffee mugs on coasters.

"Who is the current president?"

How long had I been out? These were questions I imagine were asked of people who had just come out of a coma. I tried to lift my head to look around me. It felt very late. Where was Bill?

"What year were you born?"

I answered their questions. The doctor looked relieved.

"We attempted the D&C but ended up deciding to deliver the twins via C-section," the doctor with the sallow face informed me.

I tried to focus on his face. The pain in my lower-right abdomen stabbed. I was finding it difficult to take a full breath of air.

"You're fine, though," he said. "You'll just have to stay in the hospital for a few days. We're going to stabilize your pain and then take you to a room upstairs."

A heavyset nurse appeared from the blackness. "How's the pain, on a scale of one to ten?" she asked.

I didn't understand why it was so dark in the room.

"Seven," I said, trying for equilibrium. "Maybe eight." She asked me to describe the pain. "Steady," I said, "and sharp, like the point of a blade."

She injected something into an IV tube connected to my arm that was still in place from the surgery.

The pain did not subside. The nurse tried another medication, and then her shift ended. The next nurse tried a stronger dose. The pain was thudding and constant. I was shaking and freezing cold. I would get warm and then start to sweat. I kept asking for more blankets. After the third medication attempt, I told the nurse the pain had reduced to a four. I wanted to see Bill. I assumed he knew about the C-section, that the doctors were keeping him posted about what was happening.

Bill was in a hypercaffeinated state upstairs in our assigned room. My mother had arrived around 10:00 PM, along with my brother-in-law. My sister had stayed through the surgery, leaving the room at intervals to see if she could find out any information from the doctors on the floor.

Bill nearly attacked the orderly who brought me into the room, demanding to know what had taken so long. "I thought I was going to lose you, too." My mother hung back for a moment and then rushed to me. "Momma," I said instinctively, reaching out my hands for her the way I must have when I was two. She pulled my head to her chest and put her arms around my back and waist.

My sister left to go home to salvage whatever sleep she could before she went on call at 8:00 AM. The night nurse tried a new medication, an opiate called Dilaudid that voided all the pain on contact. I wasn't at an eight or a three or even a one on the pain scale. The pain didn't exist. I was cogent and centered, but my body felt weightless. I sucked in a big, easy breath. The only other time I'd felt like this was during a meditation on a beach in Greece the summer after Bill and I got married. I had wished many times in the months and years that followed that emotional pain could be so easily medicated.

At around 5:00 AM, Bill went home to pick up some toiletries and clothes. My mother pushed a chair flush against the bed, so our bodies could be touching. I turned into her side, pressing my face into her sweater. I was barely conscious of the choking, sobbing noises that came from deep within me as she sat beside me.

The room was constructed in an L shape and faced east. The corridor outside the room was quiet, and I felt that if we stepped outside the room, the hospital would disappear and we'd find ourselves in some kind of infinite purgatorial wasteland.

A pink streak of light broke through the beveled metal blinds that covered the windows. I folded into the side of the bed and my mother and I cried together—for the babies, for the loss to all of us, a loss that felt fathomless, like the great yawning lochs in Scotland I'd seen when I lived in the UK, whose depths were still unknown.

The hospital room was a revolving door of nurses, doctors on rounds, interns. I was physically weak and had lost blood. Dr. Baker ordered a blood transfusion. I was terrified, gripped by archaic fears of diseased blood. I asked the nurse, and then my sister, to triple-check the blood type and its history. A symptom of posttraumatic stress disorder (PTSD), a diagnosis I would receive later, is hypervigilance. Another is flashbacks. When I closed my eyes, I saw the white lights of the operating room, Dr. Eagen's do-rag, Dr. Baker's worried face. I was afraid to sleep, fearing if I succumbed completely, I would hemorrhage and die.

My mother and Bill spent seventy-two hours camped out in the hospital room with me. Their presence gave me enough respite to take short naps, encouraged by antianxiety medication. I resisted the drugs until one of the doctors told me I needed the medication to recover.

"You need to be able to relax for your body to heal."

The day before I was discharged, a counselor named Danielle Perotti, from the perinatal loss department, stopped by our room. She told us that we would have a month to decide what to do with the twins' bodies and that the hospital would provide us with death certificates.

I didn't want to like Danielle. She wore a gray pantsuit with low heels and a silver cross that dangled on a chain at her neck. She was a mother, and, through our discussions, I sensed, a good one.

She talked to us like capable adults instead of victims. She brought us a large white shopping bag. "Inside the bag is a memento box for each of your twins," she said. "We made a card with each baby's footprint just after they were born." She extended the box toward us so we could see. The box was about a foot square, made of pulpy cardboard that showed the paper's fibers. It was tied with a dark green satin ribbon. I was surprised that the hospital provided such a service.

Danielle started to open the box when Dr. May, Dr. Baker's on-call associate, knocked on the door. Dr. May was a sturdy woman who'd grown up in China and was economical with her words.

"I need to tell you that in the next day or so your milk is going to come in. To get it to dry up, you can wear a tight sports bra and wrap Ace bandages over the top. The milk can be really hard for some women," she said. "I suggest you reach out for support if you need it." Dr. May gestured to Danielle in the chair.

I waited for further devastation, but the feeling did not come. I felt affirmed that my body would do this reproductively natural thing. I put my hands to my breasts and poked. They were hard like a preripe cantaloupe. I hadn't even noticed.

Something about the milk coming in felt hopeful; its existence was an offering to our babies and perhaps even, I allowed myself to think for the span of one breath, a practice run for a next time, when there would be a baby or babies to feed.

Dr. May had forgotten to shut our door when she left the room. We overheard her instructing the nurses on staff to take us out the back door of the hospital.

"I don't want them going out through the lobby, with all the new mothers and babies." Danielle rushed to close the door, but it was too late. "I'm so sorry you had to—" I shook my head, shame and anger stinging my face. Before we left, Danielle handed me a card and a hospital brochure. "You can come and see me anytime," she said. I gave her a lifeless hug.

Bill walked beside the wheelchair I was required to leave in and then pulled our car around the side entrance of the hospital while an orderly waited with me. The lake was the same gray as the sky. The wind was warm, but I shivered as I waited for the car. I held the white bag Danielle had given us, too drained to look through the contents. One of my teachers in England had said that when a death occurs, those who experience the death are forever changed. "Every death is a rebirth for those who remain."

I believed in the principle of rebirth. I believed anything could be healed and overcome. But I was afraid of what that rebirth might entail. I did not know what would await us when we got home and tried to resume our lives. And there, standing on the sidewalk already threatening to swallow me like quicksand, I felt the first conscious rip of grief.

I spent the greater part of the next three weeks roiling on the floor. However I lay, I could not get comfortable. I would find comfort only for several seconds or a minute in a new position, before the nausea found me again and started its exhausting churn.

My mother flew back to Virginia to regroup with my father. The day she left, Bill's father and stepmother drove in from Cincinnati and asked what they could do to help. Gail outfitted our house with new sheets and towels and comforting foods they knew we liked. Bill's mother and stepfather called from Nebraska, where they had recently moved from Manhattan. They, too, wanted to help. People sent cards and flowers that stacked up on the countertops in the kitchen and overflowed, unopened, onto our dining room table and TV console. I told Bill I didn't want to see anyone and spent my time on our bedroom floor. Danielle left several messages asking us to call the hospital, where the babies' bodies were being kept, to tell them what we wanted to do. The brochure she had given us listed our options as disposal, burial, or cremation, but I didn't call her back. Bill told me he could not stand to hear the sounds I was making, and that he was going to his office downtown. I told him to go; I preferred to be alone.

The day we came home, I moved the picture of Quin Yin, which had remained beside my bed throughout the pregnancy, to the shelf in our Chinese cabinet across from our bed so I could see it easily from my new post on the floor. For ten days I wept beneath the image and beseeched the Great Mother to offer me some comfort and support. I continued to meditate daily but felt no connection, no solace or relief. When I closed my eyes at night, violent images flashed through my mind: rivers of blood and dead babies. I'd twist in bed as great paintbrush strokes of fear rushed up and down my body, until I finally took the antianxiety drug Dr. Baker had prescribed. Only then did I succumb to sleep.

On the eleventh day, the house was quiet. Bill's parents had left and Bill was at work. I kneeled before the picture of Quin Yin. "I'm not asking you to bring our babies back," I cried. "But I thought you were real. I trusted you. I need help. I am in agony."

The house remained quiet. I heard several birds squawking outside the window. I felt too tired to cry. My heart began to flutter in my chest as if it had broken out of my ribcage and had been pushed up high against the skin.

My rational self reminded me that people had suffered worse losses. I understood this intellectually, but I could not get off the floor. I felt as if I were being burned slowly with an invisible fire. "Please," I said to the air, "help me."

The light in the room expanded, and I felt a breath of air brush my face. I turned onto my stomach and pushed myself up into a squat, then rolled onto my knees so I was sitting with my legs folded under me. The Chinese cabinet started to wave like a mirage in the desert. I had the ridiculous idea that the Great Mother was standing in the room.

Two things.

I heard the words not as an audible sound, but in my mind, the way I'd heard the voice say, *Open your heart to your family*, in my meditation several years before.

First: *Some babies die. Dog babies, dolphin babies, human babies. This is not personal.*

I held still. My heart continued to flutter. I pressed my hand against it, asking that it be still so I could hear.

Second: You have been initiated.

The light in the ceiling lamp swelled and then dimmed. The wavy energy I'd felt was gone. The afternoon sun spilled onto the carpet. It was 3:15 PM.

I did not write the experience off as a figment of my imagination. Raised bumps covered my arms; the hair on the back of my neck stood on end. I accepted the possibility of the visitation as real, at least as real as the voices in meditation, perhaps only because I had not heard some pat answer, the words I wanted to hear: *Your babies are coming. You will have children.*

.A spiritual teacher my father had introduced me to said in a lecture once, "Paradox is at the heart of spiritual truth." I spent several hours contemplating the paradoxical message. *Some babies die:* not personal. *You've been initiated:* deeply personal. The meaning was trying to make itself clear in my mind. With the twins' death, I had not been rejected from being a mother; I had been initiated into motherhood.

I still felt upset and alone and afraid. But I took the first full breath I'd taken since I'd come home from the hospital. That night, I joined Bill at our dining room table for dinner. The next morning, I took a shower. Over breakfast, Bill and I made some decisions about what we would do next.

Bill supported me in taking a three-month sabbatical from my coaching practice. I would accept an offer to teach the graduating class of the counseling program where I'd done my training, which would take place one night a week for three hours. With work accounted for, I took out the bag Danielle had given us at the hospital, the one with the twins' boxes. The corners were bent a bit, but the boxes had traveled well. I set them side by side on the table.

"I don't want to be having this conversation," Bill said, his eyes squinted and tense. "And I don't want to have a funeral."

"I don't want to just leave the bodies with the hospital," I said, starting to cry.

My meeting with the funeral director who handled cremations was my first venture out of the house. Part of the reason I stayed inside so long was that I felt demoralized by most things people had to say about the twins and what had happened. I bristled at any allusion to this being "God's plan" or notion that this was an experience that would provide life lessons and growth. Nor could I embrace the opposite and also popular offering that this never should have happened, that it was a tragedy that went against nature.

I believed the Great Mother's message—that sometimes babies die. As much as I wanted to, I didn't feel we were entitled to children, or that we deserved them because we were nice people or because we'd make good parents. I didn't believe it should or shouldn't have happened. My favorite card was from a friend, a screenwriter in Los Angeles. In telegram style on a thick white piece of Crane stationary, he wrote: "Just heard what happened. Completely sucks. I love you."

On my way to the funeral parlor, my phone rang. I answered, thinking it could be the director I'd spoken with the day before. A female voice with a rolling Southern accent announced that she was calling from my insurance company. She said she'd left several messages, as they needed to register me for labor and delivery at the hospital.

I felt unnerved being out of the house. The sunlight hurt my eyes and was bringing on a headache. My thoughts were scattered and disjointed. Bill found the idea of the funeral home unbearable, so I had volunteered to go on my own. As excruciating as it felt to schedule the meeting, I felt as if I were taking some small action as a mother. I was taking care of our babies in some way. I started the drive feeling, if not good, strong and more energized. The insurance call came as a slap.

I informed the woman that we were no longer pregnant, that the twins had died. The woman paused for a moment and then said. "Oh, well. God knows what he is doing. It obviously wasn't meant to be." She said this casually, as if I were on the phone with J.Crew and she was informing me that a sweater I wanted was sold out.

"I'll just go ahead and take you off the list," she said.

"You do that!" I said, throwing the phone to the floor of the car. If it wouldn't have hurt me or anyone else, I would have driven my car into a tree.

I found other people's attempts to reconcile what had happened challenging, too. A few people in the holistic community who believed we are 100 percent responsible for anything that happens in life suggested that perhaps Bill's and my marriage wasn't strong and that was why the babies hadn't stayed, or that the twins' death was a good thing in the sense that now I would be able to really help people because I'd suffered a loss. I fantasized about smashing plates.

On a Friday in early October, Bill and I drove to Joliet, which Bill dubbed "the anus of Illinois," for the twins' cremation. We'd met previously with the funeral home to pick out two small urns, one with dolphins and the other with flying seagulls. We'd been told that we could bring any special items, such as toys or clothing, to be cremated with the twins. I'd gathered some flowers from our garden, some incense I'd bought in Glastonbury, and one little outfit for each baby that someone had given us as an early shower gift. I bundled them all in my favorite pashmina, made out of soft teal wool.

Bill drove eighty miles per hour down the highway. His face looked wan. I felt sick, too, driving to this industrial site, holding in my hands items that would be burned with our babies' bodies. But I felt compelled to attend the cremation. I wanted our babies to know we were there for them at every moment.

The road leading to the cremation site looked postapocalyptic. Massive construction on something had begun and then been abandoned. The choppy drive took us through loose rock and asphalt piles, uninhabited construction trucks and cement mixers. I checked the directions multiple times to ensure we were on the correct street. We pulled up at a building—*the* building—a one-story cinder-block box about twenty-five by twenty feet. The worst part was the sound—a great roaring churn that echoed far out into the woods behind the site.

"It's just a giant incinerator," Bill hissed, as I opened the door and double-checked that the twins' things were contained in the wrap.

Bill scraped his feet in the gravel at the side of the car, looking like a spooked horse. "I'll go in and check it out," I said. The whirring noise was louder inside, and I had to shout when giving my name to a short woman sitting at the front desk. She wore what I would call a church dress, red with a pattern of white flowers and a lace collar; her gold name badge read DOREEN.

Doreen confirmed that the twins' bodies had arrived from the hospital and walked me through to the family viewing room. Someone had tried to make it lovely, but the room looked like a blown-up dollhouse with inexpensive, chintzy furniture and doilies against pale yellow walls. Cut into one wall was a window that had a view into the incinerator room. Bill could not come in here.

"I think I'll wait outside with my husband, if that's okay," I said. I held out the bundle that was still in my arms. "I brought some things for the boys," I said. My voice came out cracked and hoarse. Doreen assured me whatever we wanted to do was fine. She said the cremation would begin in fifteen minutes and take about an hour.

"It takes less time for babies," she said, giving me a sympathetic look.

I handed her the keepsakes we'd brought, and she walked me to a tray in the wall between her office and the incinerator room. I placed the items inside. The tray was made of shiny steel and felt cold to my hand. Doreen assured me these things would be cremated with the twins. I double-checked that I'd given her everything we'd brought, and then I ran out of the building to the car.

Bill had spotted a park on the other side of the construction. "Let's go there," he said. "I think we'll be able to see the place but not hear it."

The park was a state-run forest preserve. Ours was the only car in the lot, and from what we could see, we had the park to ourselves. We'd dressed up for the occasion: Bill in a white button-down shirt and suit pants, I in a blue dress, a shade darker than the wrap I'd brought for the babies. We looked for an easy trail on the map, one we could manage in our attire, and hiked for a few minutes into the woods. We walked in until we could see the small cement building through the trees. At nine forty-five, the time the cremation was set to begin, we grabbed on to each other and I said a prayer for our boys. Bill kept track of the hour on his watch. Our prayer took only a few minutes, and then we stood in the circle of trees, uncertain of what to do. Bill suggested we list the reasons we were grateful for the twins: "that we got to experience over five months of pregnancy"; "that they allowed us to be parents for the first time"; "that they proved our bodies could do this, that our eggs and sperm liked each other"; "that we *could* get pregnant and have children."

We listed things until we were sobbing, holding on to each other in a viselike embrace. As I clung to Bill's chest, I felt wrenching sadness and also a sensation of release. I felt that we might be leaving a chunk of the sadness in the woods that day, and that the woods were happy to take it. When the hour was over, we walked to the car. Bill had sweated through his shirt. His sleeves were smeared with mascara and salt from my tears.

"I'm sorry I couldn't go in there," Bill said, gesturing over the trees toward the crematorium.

"It was just their bodies in there, anyway," I said. "Their spirits had already left." Bill said he wasn't sure what he believed about that.

"You think it's okay, though, with them, that we didn't wait in the building?" Bill said. He put the key in the ignition to start the car.

"It think the park was much better, actually," I said.

Bill looked concerned as he pulled onto the highway.

We decided we'd go to lunch, even though it was early, somewhere new that didn't remind us of anything. Lunch out would be better than the emptiness of our house. Our home had never felt so before, but on some days now it seemed cavernous. Bill drove more slowly than he had on the way out that morning. We listened to classical music on the radio and held hands over the gearshift. I felt close to him, and tired in a good way.

When we arrived at the restaurant, Bill called me to the back of the car. He had been crossing to meet me on the passenger side, when something had stopped him. I ran around the side and looked where his fingers were pointing. In the beige rim of the roof was a large Y-shaped tree branch.

"It wasn't there this morning," Bill said. "I'm sure of it. I got gas and had the car washed before we left."

I had not seen the branch on the car at the crematorium, either.

"Do you think?" Bill trailed off, unable perhaps to give voice to what he was thinking. I kept quiet. I typically would have been the one to suggest some kind of metaphysical possibility.

"What do you think?" I asked.

"I think the boys put it there," Bill said. He stood straight, his chest slightly puffed out, as if to defy anyone who would challenge him. "I think they put it there to say they were with us and it was okay that we witnessed their cremation in the woods."

We took the branch into the restaurant with us, and later, when we went home, I held it in my lap for a long time, feeling the smooth bark and small woody knots. We placed the branch in the solarium alcove on a small table where we'd place the twins' urns when I picked them up the next week: facing west, the place of our ancestors, overlooking the garden.

After the twins were cremated, a single mission moved me out of bed each day: *Get well so we can have a family.* Condolence cards liked to say, "Time heals all wounds" but I had experienced, with previous traumas, that some rigorous inner work was also necessary. At my follow-up appointment, Dr. Baker told me I was showing signs of PTSD.

I sought out a therapist named Eleanor, a specialist in EMDR (Eye Movement Desensitization and Reprocessing), a therapy being used with Iraq War veterans and 9/11 firefighters, as well as lay trauma survivors. Eleanor told me we would have to start with any unhealed trauma from my past that was reminiscent of the twins' death.

"Have you experienced any previous sexual or reproductive trauma?" she asked.

"Yes, Eleanor, I have."

I left feeling angry. I decided to walk the long way to my car, through Millennium Park, where I could see the lake. The water was gray-blue, like the sky, and seagulls were chasing and calling to each other.

Eleanor's office was not the first place I had heard that traumas were connected, and I felt angry at the potential relationship. If the childhood traumas somehow led to my reproductive issues, I felt kicked while down—punished for having been hurt.

I walked all the way to the lake. At the place in the path where the water came up to a cement embankment with a swimming beach, I stopped and picked up two gray stones from the grass and threw them, one at a time, into the water. There was a headwind, and the stones did not fly far. They plopped almost in tandem into the waves and sank to the bottom. When I thought about the traumas' being linked together in a thematic chain, I felt broken. But if this work helped me heal, and helped Bill and me have a child, I would do what Eleanor recommended.

Grieving as a couple presented challenges. If Bill was having a good day, he would scowl if he found me crying at the bathroom sink. If I experienced him as angry, I'd feel hurt and want to retract. We committed and recommitted to staying open and present with each other, but doing so was not easy.

One day he came home from a meeting with a new client feeling lighter, happy to have felt "normal" that day, he said. I had not felt well; a wave of breathless pain had hit somewhere around four o'clock that afternoon, and I'd lain in a heap in the bathroom with our dog for several hours. Bill saw my splotchy skin and my red-rimmed eyes, and did an about-face toward the door. "I feel like you want to leave and never come back," I yelled at him.

"I *do* want to leave and never come back," Bill said, standing in the open frame of the door, a Halloween sky of translucent clouds and the sliver of the moon behind him.

The moment felt charged, the way the air does before a storm. We locked eyes, mirrors of pain and sadness. After a moment, Bill closed the door and came inside the house. We ate dinner together and afterward held hands. I went to the bathroom to wash my face.

"It gives me great faith that you two can be so honest," Eleanor said when I told her about the interaction.

I'd feel as if I was getting better, and then I'd wake up feeling flattened. As I continued EMDR, I felt a regular urge to scream. I feared if I gave voice to the sound I felt inside my body, the neighbors would be terrified and call the police, so I got into my car and drove to the expressway, onto I-94 heading north. I went back and forth between North Avenue and Lawrence, waiting until I was staggered between semitrucks and smaller sedans in which the drivers wouldn't be at eye level. I picked my moment and began to shriek. My throat was scratched raw in seconds. My chest protested the intensity of the sound. My hands shook on the wheel. I tried to keep my eyes clear of tears so I would not hit anyone on the road. The car became a new vehicle for grief.

As soon as Dr. Baker cleared me for exercise, I went to yoga. My mantra as I prostrated myself on my mat was full healing, to get well so I could try and be a mother again.

"We must really want this," Bill remarked to me after yet another friend tentatively asked us if we thought we would continue to try to get pregnant.

Instead of lessening our desire, the loss had intensified it, and continued to; the depth of the pain acted as some kind of bellows that increased the fire of our longing.

I sought out a new yoga studio, where I didn't know anyone who would ask me about the pregnancy. I found a teacher I liked. One day I arrived to find the class had been changed to a prenatal workshop. Several chatty women in various stages of pregnancy greeted each other and began setting up props by their mats.

I looked around at the lululemon-clad mommies-to-be, in their cheerful blue and cranberry tops stretched wide over baby bumps, and fully believed that all of these women had effortlessly conceived and would have these children. *Everyone* else had children when-ever they wanted, *easily*. Even though one in six U.S. births is helped by some kind of fertility treatment, and somewhere around 136,000 adoptions take place every year in the United States, I felt I was the only one who had struggled, who would not carry a baby to term, who wouldn't get the joy of raising a child. The hurt inside me felt so great I thought I might implode.

"You're welcome to stay." I turned to find the instructor, a wide-hipped woman with hazel eyes, pointing to an available place on the floor. "I can adapt the class for a mixed group." I could imagine no scenario in which I would choose to stay for a prenatal yoga class. But the day had turned blustery and overcast, and I felt too tired to walk to the car. "Fine," I said, huffing toward my mat. "I'll stay."

I'd taken to running away from the phone when it rang.

"It's someone else calling to tell me they're pregnant," I'd say to Bill if he brought the phone to me, pushing it away from my body with my hands.

"Not everyone is pregnant right now," Bill said.

It felt like they were. In the same week, Kaitlin, Amanda, and my childhood friend Heather had all called to inform me they'd entered their second trimester. I felt simultaneously happy and emotionally impaled. A part of me wished that I could hide until I felt better or we had a baby of our own.

It seemed that anytime I arrived at the gym, mothers and pregnant women were working out en masse. I would pick the line in the grocery store where a woman with a baby or small children were practicing words.

"Are you jealous or envious?" Eleanor asked me in a session. "Jealousy is not wanting them to have what they have. Envy is wanting it, too."

"Both," I said, hating myself for the ugliness of it. "Jealous of strangers, envious of friends," I confessed.

In October, I flew to D.C. to my parents' house for the wedding of a friend of the family. My mother had retired in September, and we spent Friday having lunch and shopping in Georgetown. It had been only a few weeks since her retirement, but she'd changed. She seemed more vibrant. She arrived at the airport to pick me up wearing a green sweater and dark jeans that flattered her shape.

"I've been going to the gym five days a week," she said. "Dad and I are taking a cooking class at the Smithsonian." Preretirement, she had worked sixty to seventy hours a week, ingesting Diet Coke and bags of pretzels at her desk, wearing navy blue or black suits or boxy Jones of New York separates.

"I'm calling her my trophy wife," my dad said. In a gesture I'd never seen before, he twirled my mother around the living room, holding one of her arms in the air and putting his other on the small of her back. My parents had always been affectionate, but my father had never seemed interested in appearances. His interests were his spiritual pursuits and sports, basketball and tennis.

"Retirement is working for you guys," I said, laughing.

"I don't know why I'm able to get healthy now. I've made plenty of attempts in the past," my mother said.

I felt joy seeing her be able to devote time to herself. It was something my sisters and I had always wanted for her.

"You look great, Mom," I said.

The night of the wedding, I felt broken again from a day spent seeing people's babies and explaining to extended family friends that no, I was not pregnant anymore.

By January, with the turn of the New Year, I felt physically stronger and was enthusiastic to make it to May, when we could do IVF again. I had begun to believe we could have a baby again, and I would act accordingly. The success rates for pregnancies with a cerclage were still 60 and 80 percent. Gambling had never appealed to me, and it occurred to me that if I carried the baby, we would be doing exactly that with our child's life. But even still, Bill and I were on board to try again.

On January 14, I took a shower before bed and turned up the water extra hot, languishing in the heat and steam. I bent to fill a washcloth with a shower gel and noticed my nipples were erect, and that despite the heat they were sore. A stream of white jettisoned out from my right breast. I put my hands to the nipple, concerned I had some kind of infection. The liquid was creamy and opaque. I raised my hand to just under my eye, where I could examine the liquid in the light. I stared for a moment, trying to remain objective. It was breast milk.

I ran into the bedroom, trying to keep enough of it in my hands to show Bill. Dripping water onto the carpet, I extended my palm. "Do you see this! Look!"

Another thought came, so I went to the folder we'd kept of the twins' ultrasound photos and doctors' notes. A paper from our first appointment with Dr. Baker confirmed it: January 14 was the twins' original due date.

I told Dr. Baker about the incident at my follow-up appointment the next week, fascinated to hear what she would make of the amazing mind-body connection.

"There are so many things we cannot medically explain," she said, and changed the subject.

Her examination confirmed that my uterus had healed completely and we were clear to begin IVF again in the spring. "Just one embryo at a time though, Sara," she said. Bill and I had come to the same conclusion, based on our own research. I'd also discovered that the term "incompetent cervix" did not apply in the case of multiples.

"So, it was more of an incompetent diagnosis," I joked when I told Eleanor what I'd discovered.

"It's a punishing name," she said. "I support you in relinquishing it."

The team at RMI welcomed us like family when we went for our next appointment.

"We want this for you now more than ever!" Tracey said, engulfing me in a hug. Dr. Colaum mapped out a new plan based on transferring one embryo. She added baby aspirin to offset the chance of blood clots (which can cause miscarriage) and Viagra to plump the uterine lining.

"Women can take Viagra?" I asked, feeling afraid of what effects the infamous medication might have on my body.

"You'll be fine," Dr. Colaum said. "You'll insert three to four suppositories a day to increase the likelihood of implantation. If we're going one embryo at a time, we're going to use every possible resource."

I warmed under Dr. Colaum's enthusiasm. My body felt receptive and strong. This time, when UPS delivered the medications from Braun, I ran to the truck to sign and carried the box inside myself.

The day of our pregnancy test, Tracey said she would call us by 3:00 PM. I waited next to my phone like a loaded spring.

"I'm so sorry, Sara," she said when she called. "You're not pregnant this time."

"It's okay," I said, feeling a need to reassure her.

We took the requisite two months off between cycles and did our next cycle in June.

The day of the pregnancy test, Rachel called. Bill had worked from home that afternoon, and we both felt hopeful.

The phone rang at 2:00 PM. When I saw the RMI number come up on my phone, I didn't have a positive feeling.

"It doesn't look good, Sar," Rachel said. "Your HCG level is a three."

Bill and I spent the weekend trying to talk ourselves through the disappointment.

"I understand statistically it's a 33 percent chance. But I still think we will be pregnant every time," he said.

Statistics meant little to my emotions. After a negative pregnancy test, fears swarmed like locusts. *What if we never get pregnant again? What if something else is wrong with my body?* The "no" ripped the scab off the wound, exposing grief that was still close to the surface. It erupted like a rash.

"I saw a woman slap her child in the checkout line, and I actually thought about taking her baby," Bill said when he returned from the grocery store one evening. "I stood there thinking, *You don't deserve children. If you don't treat that baby with love, I'll take it.*"

I brought my hands to his forehead and rubbed his temples.

"I'm losing it," he said, leaning back into me.

A week later, we continued to feel low.

We were open to the idea of adoption and had discussed the option many times. But once we'd confirmed we had all the necessary parts to have children ourselves—good eggs and sperm, a healthy uterus—we felt called to continue, at least for now. On Tuesday after I got my period, we called Dr. Colaum's and signed on for an August cycle.

At midnight on Friday, August 8, our house phone rang. We didn't answer, assuming it was a wrong number. A few seconds later, Bill's cell phone lit up next to the bed. Dread spread across my stomach like a brushfire. The landline rang again. Bill roused himself, his hair tousled and his face creased with sleep. *Don't make assumptions,* I said to myself, trying to give whatever was on the line the benefit of the doubt.

"My mother's dead," Bill said, after a pained few seconds. His mouth had gone dry, and the saliva on his lips turned the skin white. He ran to the guest bathroom and threw up. He'd told his stepfather we'd leave for Omaha in the morning. I stood next to the bed, stunned and cold. Bill walked back and forth to the sink in our bathroom, drinking glass after glass of water. His skin began to look blue, and I wrapped the duvet around his body. For the next few hours, I held him in the bed, stroking his head until he fell into a fitful and exhausted sleep.

My mother drove through the night from Virginia to Nebraska to attend the memorial.

"I know you have so many people to attend to," she said, surveying the crowd from the back of the chapel. "I'm just here to honor Nancy, to support Bill."

"It is *beyond* beyond that you came," Bill told her when he spotted her in the doorway.

"I'm here for you," she said. "I'm so sorry."

She stayed in town, nearby with my grandmother, as we helped sort through Nancy's things. When she stopped by the house before she drove back to Virginia, Bill asked if, moving forward, he could call her Mom.

At the end of the month, a tornado came through Chicago, throwing out power lines and flooding the basements on our street. A month later, a pipe broke in my office and sent two feet of water spraying through the walls, requiring that the entire floor and moldings be pulled out and redone.

I'd stopped taking the antianxiety medication in preparation for IVF and had begun having nightmares again. I would get out of bed multiple times a night to check that the front door was locked, that the floors were still dry, that the burners on the stove had not switched themselves on and started a gas fire. Bill said he felt cursed.

Sometimes, though, after my nightly rounds, I would sit in the solarium alcove and talk to the twins in their blue metal urns. Kaitlin had sent me an article about a sect of Judaism that believes the babies who "do not stay" become intercessors and guides for the children who are to come. I found the same lore in Mexican traditions describing how "the babies that pass through" are given a place of reverence in the family.

We'd installed a water feature next to the twins' urns, and the constant gurgle was soothing. I looked out through the sliding glass doors up at the moon, a slash of light in a cloudless night. The Great Mother was there somewhere, I thought—existing, at least, as part of the collective consciousness, as Jung would say. I ran my fingers over the Y-branch that we'd found on the car after the twins' cremation. The sight of that branch and the way it had come to us motivated me to continue.

Our fourth round of IVF started under a new moon, which was said to be auspicious for new projects. I'd stopped trying to feel for an intuitive knowing about the outcome of the cycle, surrendering myself to the idea that I was not in control. All I could do was take the medication and bring my body to the procedure.

Dr. Colaum transferred one blast. I watched the screen as the blast shot into my womb. My eyes had become more practiced over the past three cycles. This time, I saw the embryo land, a white meteor falling from space.

"It doesn't get any better than that," Dr. Colaum said with a confident smile.

Nine days later, Tracey and Rachel called together. "You're pregnant, Sara! Your HCG levels look good."

We called all the grandparents in a round; they rejoiced and expressed having felt parched for good news. My mother and I signed up for BabyCenter again. I did my best to join the excitement, but felt wary and afraid. I told myself I was having a new experience, that I could trust this baby to grow. The bubble of impenetrability was gone, though, and I clenched with every twinge in my abdomen, squeezed my eyes shut each time I went to the bathroom, terrified to see blood. I worried that the stress and anxiety I was feeling would hurt the baby; pregnancy books and the Internet stressed the importance of being relaxed and joyful in order to have a successful pregnancy.

Kaitlin reminded me what her doctor had told her when she became pregnant after having three miscarriages: "Women have babies in the middle of war-torn countries; women have babies from rape. I'm not saying stress is wonderful or that it wouldn't be good to relax, but you are not going to kill your baby from being anxious. Anyone who says so is misguided." Kaitlin was eleven weeks pregnant again. Six months later, her son, Eli, was born a healthy eight pounds, three ounces, at forty-one weeks.

On a Wednesday night six weeks into the pregnancy, I started to bleed. It was nine thirty. Bill was at the sink in the bathroom, brushing his teeth. I stood over the toilet; the halogen lights in our bathroom glowed happily, the white spa towels were stacked high, the rows of my essential oils stood straight. No sign that anything was amiss.

"I'm bleeding!" I called to Bill.

"No," Bill said, opening the door that separated the toilet from the greater bathroom. He looked at the toilet paper in my hand, thick drops of red and brown blood. "No. It's just spotting. All the websites say you can spot. Remember your friend who had almost a full period and her baby was fine?"

"I think it's too much blood for spotting," I said.

"It's not," Bill said, the way a child might when not getting the toy he wanted.

I placed a thick pad in a clean pair of underwear and shoved the stained pair into a plastic bag.

"I guess we can wait a little while to call," I said. Dr. Colaum's staff had left hours ago. The RMI literature said to call the emergency number only if I was bleeding through a pad an hour. I kept a watch on the bleeding.

I walked in circles around the bathroom. Maybe it was just spotting. Maybe the pregnancy would continue. The cramps intensified, and I felt the warmth of more blood. I could not imagine that this was good. My forehead felt prickly and hot.

"I don't feel good," I said to Bill.

His eyes were glassy and he looked crazed. "Don't you say it," he hissed, his words menacing and sharp. *"We are not having . . ."* He refused to say the word. His voice was raised and hot with anger. "My *mother* wouldn't let this happen."

Grief enfolded Bill like a cape. I wasn't sure he could even see me anymore.

I felt like I was cracking, like a stone statue turning into dust. Bill turned away from me, jumped in bed, and pulled the covers over his face. I felt fully abandoned. I slept, or rather lay awake, in the hallway between our bedroom and the bathroom, arms and legs curled into a circle, the way our Labrador slept when he was sick.

Dr. Colaum performed an ultrasound the next morning. Bill had apologized on the drive to Evanston and now seemed himself, his face poised like that of an army general about to hear news of a battle. I felt empty and bereft.

"It doesn't look good," Dr. Colaum said. The blood had washed the embryo and growing placenta away like rain. "I'm guessing it was something with the embryo," she said. "Sometimes it's as if nature knows there's a problem; the embryos self-select out."

In equal part with the sadness I felt, I also felt relief. Relief that the miscarriage had happened this early, that there was no physical trauma. I felt relief that I did not need to spend every minute of every day and night gripped by anxiety and fear. Going into this pregnancy, I'd been so worried about my body and its ability to carry the baby, but now, as I felt the cascades of relief course through me, I wondered for the first time about my mental ability to carry a child in the future.

I doubled up on therapy sessions and EMDR. I met with a woman named Sheila Swenson for hypnosis. I increased my meditation time and upped my yoga practice to two or three times a week. I knew myself to be a courageous and capable person. I was determined to overcome the plaguing terror and doubts I felt about pregnancy.

Bill and I took on more work to generate the money we would need for a next round of IVF. We'd used up the allotted three cycles covered by insurance and would need to pay the entire $20,000 ourselves. "Do you offer frequent-flyer discounts?" I joked to Lisa Rinehart when I saw her at the end of our next consultation. If we paid in cash, RMI would knock 5 percent off the cost.

A friend of Bill's from college contacted him through email and shared that he and his wife had stopped trying after three cycles. They had decided not to have children. Other people told us stories about couples that stopped trying and then became pregnant. I did not believe we would become pregnant unaided. I was afraid of pregnancy and did not love doing IVF, but I wanted to have children and believed this was our way.

We did our fifth cycle of IVF at the beginning of 2009. For the first time, a small part of me actually hoped that we were not pregnant. As hard as I tried not to, I kept seeing blood, Bill screaming at me while I miscarried. When the pregnancy test was negative, I felt both crushed and relieved.

Bill and I agreed we needed a break. Financially, we would need time to fill up our reserves again. Emotionally, we felt brittle and spent. We decided we would take eight months off from doing any fertility treatments. We would take a vacation. Friends told us about a new place in Mexico that looked nurturing and serene. We would go away, cleanse our palates, reconnect with each other as a couple.

We agreed to check in with each other once a month. In between, we would spend time on our own considering all options, listening for what we felt guided to do: more IVF, surrogacy, adoption. Outside of the check-ins, we would not talk about babies or fertility.

We shared our intentions with our parents. "We're taking a break," we said. "We will let you know when we have something to share."

"This sounds really healthy," my mother said. "You can take some trips and focus on your coaching practice. Frankly, I could use a life coach. One of these days I am going to come to one of your workshops and see what it is, exactly, that you do."

Every January, I facilitated a vision workshop in Chicago where participants explored a vision for their year, using coaching exercises and techniques. Unbeknownst to me, my mother called Bill to find out the details and arranged to attend that year's event. The workshop had grown in number in the four years I'd offered it, and when she arrived there was a line out the door of the venue in Lincoln Park that was sponsoring the event.

I was shocked when I saw her, standing in a new gray peacoat, snowflakes sticking to her eyelashes and the tops of her hair.

"I'm here as a participant," she said. "I think I need what you're teaching today."

I tried not to think about her reaction to the activities of the day. To my knowledge she had never tried life coaching and had always seemed skeptical of counseling and therapy work. Facilitating demanded all of my attention. Nearly eighty people showed up, and I had to adapt some of the exercises to accommodate the large group. I didn't think about my mother's reactions again until we'd finished and I'd helped the volunteers restore the room. Then I saw her, standing patiently by the door, as a few last people surrounded me with questions.

She spent the ride back to my house telling me about the small group exercise and how interesting the people in her group were. "We visioned that one of the men's screenplays won an Oscar," my mother said. "And that this other guy, Kurt, who does standup, emceed a roast for Bill Gates."

My mother had also told my sister and brother-in-law about her surprise visit. They were in our kitchen with Bill when we came in from the garage. Bill had spent the afternoon cooking a stew. We entered the house to a crackling fire and rich smells of black pepper and red wine coming from the stove.

"How was it?" Bill asked.

"Fantastic," my mother said. "But Sara is going to have to explain the vision board I made. I don't understand over half the things on it. Will you come upstairs with me?"

I carried my mother's suitcase to the guest room and she laid the vision board on the bed. The lower half of the board was full of images of fresh vegetables and healthy food, a bike and active people running. In the top left corner, there was a young woman with a baby.

"That's you and your baby," my mother said. My eyes filled. "Is it okay to include visions for other people?"

"No rules," I said, my throat tight. In one corner was a red magazine page with the words "women after menopause have a choice." In the center she'd pasted a large baby ostrich with its beak wide open, eyes bulging with joy. "I don't know what to make of this image," she said. "I chose it because I want to find or do whatever makes me feel like that ostrich," she said. She ran her hands lovingly over the glossy photo.

"I really don't understand the menopause part," she said. "I think I meant retirement, that people after retirement have a choice. I'll cover it over when I get home."

Over hot plates of stew, my mother told Bill and my sister and brother-in-law about the big crowd and the part at the end where they imagined scenarios in which their visions had already happened. "Sara is a great teacher," she said. "Everyone loved it."

Over the next few months, my mother called with coaching questions. "What I want is to find my calling," she said. "I have my vision board up on the wall in my room where I see it every day, but I still don't have a clue."

I recommended some books and asked if she was open to meditation. "It's the only practice I recommend for everyone," I said. She found a rock in the woods near her house and began meditating on it daily after her morning walk with her friends. "I hope no one sees me," she said. "They'll think I'm the crazy woman in the woods."

"Dad meditates," I said.

"Only in the house," she answered.

Sometime in April she called me, agitated. "I've got nothing," she said. "I'm meditating every day. All the coaching books say to think of the time you were happiest in life, the thing that brings you more joy than anything else in the world." Frustration echoed in her words.

"The only answer I have is being pregnant with you girls. It's the same thing when I meditate. I see images of being pregnant. I'm fifty-nine years old. I've been through menopause. I'm trying to see it symbolically—pregnant with a vision, birthing an idea—but honestly, I don't see it." She hung up the phone muttering something about looking into microloans for mothers in Africa.

Bill and I did our "check-ins" at the beginning of each month. In May we sat outside under our new green patio umbrella that Bill had found on sale. We'd spent the previous weekend clearing pots for a new crop of tomatoes and packing the herb boxes with fresh, dark soil. The wind that felt omnipresent in Chicago in the winter months was lessening but still cool. I was counting the days until our vacation to Mexico. We were leaving in a week. I moved out from under the umbrella's shade to sit directly in the sun.

Our conversation was the same as it had been in February and March: Bill wanted to do more IVF. I wanted to say "great!" and share his enthusiasm, but more IVF was not the answer that came to me when I sat in my quiet times and took walks in the forest preserves north of the city. Often before starting on a trail, I'd ask for guidance about having a family. I never heard a clear answer, the way I'd heard from the Divine Mother in my bedroom, but I would regularly find a Y-shaped branch, often in the middle of the trail, so obvious it was impossible for me to ignore. I brought these branches home and was starting to form a little forest on the twins' table in the solarium. The branches did not give me a specific answer, but my heart did. The answer that rose up again and again was surrogacy.

"We have good eggs and sperm. They like each other and make great embryos," I said to Bill. In April I'd attended a meeting of an organization called Resolve that ran support groups for people going through fertility struggles. The group was self-run by members, and I'd been surprised by the accounts of women years further into a journey than we were, people with different challenges than ours: older or defective eggs, partners with low sperm count, deficient embryos. I hadn't realized how much we had going for us.

"We have great biological components," I said. "The part we need help with is the carrying of the baby."

"I don't want a stranger carrying our baby," Bill said. "I want to share the experience with you. I want to rub the belly and talk to the baby the way we did with the twins. What happened wouldn't have with one baby."

I didn't know how to explain that I didn't trust the process or the doctors or my body anymore. Dr. Baker imagined I would be put on bed rest for the second and third trimesters. I could be hospital-ized for a large majority of the pregnancy. And that was if my cervix stayed closed. I'd looked up success rates for pregnancies with a cer-clage again: still 60 to 80 percent.

"Every pregnancy is a risk," people told me.

But things changed for me when I knew the odds going in. Sixty percent was not high enough for me; neither was eighty.

Bill and I were at an impasse, but we agreed to stick with our agreement. We'd continue considering options and check in again after our vacation in May.

Every day, after my quiet time, I prayed.

"If it is only fear that is keeping me from carrying our baby, please take it," I said to the Universe, the Great Mother, whomever or whatever might be listening and available for help. "Please give me the clarity and courage to do whatever is for me to do."

I thought about surrogacy during our time in Mexico. Once, a few months after the twins died, a woman from my meditation class had said, "I wish I could carry your baby for you." She was a beautiful young mother of three children. I daydreamed about calling her up.

When we returned home, happier and relaxed, rejuvenated by the lapping waves of the Caribbean Sea, Bill said he felt differently and was open to the idea of surrogacy.

"I don't think I've been hearing you," he said. "I wanted you to want to carry our baby. I wanted you to say you're ready to go again. I hear now that you're concerned. I hear that you aren't sure that you're able."

I told Bill I wanted to feel confident in carrying a baby, too. "We won't do anything until the fall, anyway," I said. "Either of us could feel differently. All options are still on the table."

I came home the following week from a meeting to find Bill storming around his office. "Do you know what it would cost us to have a surrogate?" he asked. He whacked a pile of papers down on the desk. "Well, I do. I did a little research after my conference call ended with our not getting a new client. A whole IVF cycle *plus* $30,000 to $50,000. That doesn't include legal fees and extra medical expenses for the surrogate," Bill said. "We are getting tapped out."

"We could see if any of our parents want to contribute," I said. "You mentioned Roger—"

"We're not asking our fucking parents for money," Bill said. "I just turned forty years old, for Christ's sake. I have my own business. You have a business. We have to figure this out."

"Maybe we can adopt, then," I said, feeling responsible and panicked. I'd been bringing in only $30,000 to $50,000 a year since we'd moved to Chicago from London.

"Adoption's expensive, too," he said. "And it can take years. I don't want to be in my seventies when our children graduate from college."

"It will be expensive to do more IVF," I said.

"I don't know how we're going to do more of that, either," Bill said.

Bill was able to move past what he called his "financial freak-out," and by Memorial Day we were imagining hilarious surrogacy scenarios where some friend or one of my sisters would say she wanted to carry the baby and we'd do insemination at home using a turkey baster. "I still don't like the idea of a stranger surrogate," Bill said. "I just wish it could be someone we know."

Even if one of our siblings had wanted to volunteer, none of them would have been accepted candidates. Bill had one brother. My

sisters were both younger and hadn't had children yet. Doctors typically required a woman to have had previous successful pregnancies
to be a surrogate.

My mother called to ask if we were free the third weekend in
June. "Your father found a mediation conference in Chicago. We'd
love to stay with you."

"Wonderful," I said. "While Dad's at the conference, we can go
for a long walk by the lake."

"Maybe I'll have better luck finding my passion in Chicago," my
mother said despondently. "I'm not having any success at my rock."

"I hear you, Mom," I said.

I picked up my parents at the airport, joyful to see them. Their
flight arrived on time, and the sky was a cloudless blue when they
landed. "Look at this five-star treatment," my dad said, as I jumped
from the car and hauled their bags into the trunk.

"Did you get my letter?" my mother asked when we arrived at
our house and planted ourselves in the kitchen. Bill was on a conference call in his office. My mother seemed jumpy. She walked around
the kitchen, touching the leaves on a plant, inspecting the new cof-
feemaker on the counter.

"I didn't check the mail yesterday," I said. "Bill probably brought
it in." I walked over to the bookshelf where we kept the mail and
sifted through a short pile of bank statements, catalogs, and coupon
books. Toward the bottom of the stack, I pulled out a small white
envelope with my mother's familiar, slanted handwriting. "This one?"
I asked, as if she sent me letters every day. My father sent thank-you
cards, and Bill's stepfather sent us weekly packets full of "articles of
interest," but I could not recall the last time my mother had sent a
letter through the mail.

"That's it. You haven't read it?" she asked.

I shook my head. "Shall I open it now?"

"Um, probably later," she said. She extended her hand to reach for it and then pulled back, letting her hand drop to the counter.

"Let's go out for our walk," she suggested.

My father said he'd stay at the house to keep Bill company once he finished working.

We headed east. "This will take us all the way to the lake if you're up for a longer walk," I said.

"Maybe I should have brought the letter," she said. I slowed my stride to try to get a look at my mother's face. Her hair was cropped short in its usual style. Her arms and legs were brown and lean from long bike rides she'd begun doing around D.C. She kept stopping and starting, looking in front and then to the sides of the street, as if to ensure we weren't being watched.

"What is going on, Mom?" I said. "Have you had an inspiration?"

"I don't know whether to tell you or have you read it first."

We'd walked only five blocks. I started to suggest that we walk to the lake and then circle back for the letter, but the full walk would take over an hour and my mother was acting like a firework with a lit fuse.

We turned around and doubled back to my street. On the way, I tried to guess what she'd thought of for her vision.

"Microloans in Africa?" I asked, remembering our call a few months earlier.

"Nope."

"Starting an online random-acts-of-kindness group?"

My mother shook her head. "Read the letter," she said.

My heart pounded as I walked with the letter to my bedroom. I didn't know why I was choosing to read it upstairs, instead of in my office or out on the deck. I could hear Bill talking on the phone as I shut the bedroom door. I sat in front of the picture of Quin Yin, where I'd spent all those months grieving on the floor. I couldn't make sense of my nervousness; this was my mother's vision, not mine.

I peeled back the flap of the envelope with care and unfolded the three sheets of unlined paper. I read, and when I had finished, my heart thumped like a fist in my chest. I walked into Bill's office and handed the letter to him. "I'll stay here while you read it," I said. I didn't take a breath while he read. His eyes grew wide as he turned the pages.

"Is this even possible?" Bill asked.

"Do you want to find out?" I asked. Bill nodded.

We found my mother sitting on the deck, under the green umbrella. "Pretty crazy, right?" she said.

I replayed phrases from the letter in my head: *Postmenopausal women have given birth . . . I'm pretty good at this . . . reason I've been able to get into great shape, have such great health . . . The happiest moments of my life were being pregnant and having you three girls.*

I began to cry. Bill squeezed my hand.

"That you would even consider this," I said. "That you would even think to."

"It's my ostrich," my mother said.

"And you seriously would do this?" Bill said. "I mean, if it's possible."

"I would," my mother said. Her face was serene. I thought of a female preacher I'd seen, who had introduced herself as a "woman of power."

My mother looked the way that woman had that day. She was offering to be our surrogate.

Chapter 7

In light of what my mother had just offered, we decided to spend the evening at home. My father had been notably absent during the revealing of my mother's proposition, and now I set out to find him.

"I can't wait to hear what he thinks of this," Bill said.

I assumed he was in the guest room. I folded the pages of the letter back into the envelope, tucked it into my bra strap, and ran up the stairs.

I found my dad in Bill's office, reading one of Thich Nhat Hanh's meditation books.

"That apple didn't fall far," Bill said when we returned to the kitchen and my father set the meditation book on the counter. I smiled at my dad. Our shared interest in spirituality reunited us. More than an olive branch, it had become a lifeline. That day after the phone call in which I'd disclosed the traumas of my youth, he had confessed that he had experienced emotional trauma as a child and had grown up feeling marginalized in his family, too. Since then, he'd sent me articles and books he thought I would like, and had introduced me to Buddhist teachings. Through our discussions, I saw that we were both on a path of healing. I had always admired my father; now I felt closeness and love.

We all looked around at each other; everyone seemed uncertain how to begin. Suddenly, we were all busy helping to prepare dinner, having decided somehow that *the conversation* would wait until we were seated at the table.

My mother helped Bill wash vegetables and season a pork tenderloin for dinner. My father let our dog out into the front yard. I lit votive candles in a row and laid out white linen napkins. My heart continued to hammer. Was this a real possibility? And if it was, would we, as a family, be able to do it? Our bond still felt nascent. We were talking about an intimacy here that surpassed anything I'd ever heard of.

My parents helped Bill carry the food to the table. Outside, the sun had dropped and filled the sky with an unusual orange light. My eye moved to the Chinese table where we kept the twins' urns and our collection of Y-shaped branches. I traced my fingers around the shape of the letter under my shirt. If we had a child this way, it would blow my mind.

At eight o'clock, we sat down. The candle flames made dancing shadows on the walls. Crickets chirped through the open windows. Below the hum, I could hear the low tick of the grandfather clock Bill's mother had given us several years ago. The paper of the envelope scratched against the surface of my skin. I glanced at my mother, waiting for her to speak, but my father spoke first. He set his knife and fork across his plate and smoothed his napkin in his lap.

"This is all Lissa's fault."

Lissa was a close friend of my mother's, also recently retired, and also a core member of the daily walking militia my mother and her friends had started to help each other lose weight. To keep themselves entertained, they shared book recommendations, recipes, the comings and goings of their children, and interesting stories they'd seen in the news.

My mother interjected to tell us how, three weeks ago, Lissa had told the group about a story she'd seen online about a postmenopausal woman who got pregnant and carried a baby to term.

"Do you think we should be concerned?" The members of the group had laughed, poking each other's arms. "Maybe we need to start using birth control!"

After the walk, my mother went online to find out more about the story. "I found stories about women in their fifties doing IVF to become pregnant," she said. "It didn't seem these women were getting pregnant by accident, though, so I was able to report back to the group the next day that we probably didn't need to be concerned about birth control."

My mother laughed and took a bite of her pork. "This is really good, Bill," she said. Bill and I had set our forks on our plates, not even pretending to eat.

"So?" I said.

"Well, I wasn't thinking any more about it. But then later that week I was doing a meditation in my room. I lay back in the window seat and looked up at my vision board. Your father came in from playing tennis, and I heard him go into the bathroom to take a shower. I could hear the water running as I looked up at the ostrich and the healthy food and the sign WOMEN AFTER MENOPAUSE HAVE A CHOICE. Then, all of a sudden, it was like the images began to move—just the tiniest bit, barely perceptibly. The skin on my arms and neck raised; I think my body knew before I did. I stared at the board and I started to weep."

I urged myself to remain calm. I considered that Bill and I might have taken more time to talk more just the two of us, before dinner. Just because postmenopausal surrogacy had been done, it was obviously rare, and we had no idea of the risks involved. I looked at Bill, trying to get a read on his thoughts.

My mother watched our faces and halted. "I may have gotten a little carried away," she said. Her hands fell to her lap, and she looked hesitant.

"There are so many options. I understand if you don't want to pursue this."

Bill interrupted before my mother could go further. "What you are offering is the most selfless, the most incredible . . . I really don't have words." His voice broke and he blinked to clear his eyes. I reached under the table and squeezed his hand. I ran around from my seat and wrapped my arms around my mother over the back of her chair.

"Mom! As far as I'm concerned, if we can find a doctor who will do this—if there is a way for you to safely be our surrogate—I would do it today."

I felt self-conscious, draped over her shoulders. Aside from the period just after the twins died, our only physical contact had been a hug hello or goodbye. The closeness felt strange and good. My mother's arm, with its pattern of freckles in a cluster near her wrist, looked so like my own.

My father was watching my mother. I thought I detected pride in his gaze. Then he turned to Bill and me. "I have feelings about this, and concerns, to be sure," he said. "But your mother has supported me in my pursuits throughout our marriage. I've come to believe, without doubt, that this 'vision'—to use your word, Sara—comes from your mother's soul. I would never stand in the way of her or of this. If you can find a doctor willing to do this, I support you."

"I'll call Dr. Colaum in the morning," I said, struggling to believe this conversation was happening. Out of nowhere, we had a new option where there had been none.

We began to talk about potential scenarios and timing, but stopped ourselves. Even in the exhilaration of possibility, I felt too guarded to think too far into the future. My father yawned and announced he was going to bed. Bill left next, retreating upstairs to his computer. "I need to unwind," he said. My mother and I had pulled our chairs closer so that our knees were almost touching. I pulled the letter out and set it on the table, smoothing its pages with my fingers. My mother held one side while I held the other, re-reading the remarkable words. The small candles had burned down to liquid in the tin holders.

"We should probably go to bed, too," I said, not wanting to leave the moment, the candles, my mother's hands.

Bill was already asleep by the time I crawled into bed. I pressed my cold feet against his legs. His body was always warm. Lying there, I remembered a talk I'd seen by an artist in Chicago. I'd forgotten her name but remembered with clarity her saying that she had come to a point in her process where she almost exclusively followed her wildest-sounding ideas. "I believe the crazy ideas are my truest inspiration," she'd said. "They are the ones that have become my greatest successes."

Bill rolled over and laid his arm over my chest. I lay awake for some time, eyes open, praying that this new idea was an inspired crazy idea, rather than just a crazy one.

We had our first appointment with Dr. Colaum on a Wednesday in mid-August. My mother had flown into town for the meeting, and the three of us barely spoke on the forty-minute drive to Evanston.

I felt like a charged particle, bursting with potential energy. I'd reminded myself repeatedly in the past six weeks not to think beyond the appointment: We were meeting with Dr. Colaum for an exploratory discussion only; nothing would be decided today; there were other options should this idea turn out to not be valid. I told myself these things, but the truth was, I was already invested in this idea. I felt in my soul that my mother had come upon something great and now the medical viability of this vision was about to be determined.

As Bill turned the car into the COS building parking lot, adrenaline shot through my body.

"I hope we don't show up to find men in white coats waiting for us at the office," my mother joked. But in fact she was naming the fear we'd voiced more than once since we'd decided we'd go through with the consultation.

Wanting to give Dr. Colaum time to respond, I'd presented our idea in a letter—a letter that took me seven rough drafts and sixteen pieces of stationery to write. I'd sent the letter two weeks before the appointment. All we knew walking into the office was that Dr. Colaum had received it and agreed to the meeting.

While I'd been composing the letter, my mother had gone back to Alexandria, where she'd heard from a friend about a women's conference in Albuquerque. The conference was taking place also in August, so we booked two places and made our appointment with Dr. Colaum for the Wednesday before the conference began. We'd meet with Dr. Colaum that morning and fly together to New Mexico the following day. "If she wants to do any follow-up testing, I can come back through Chicago on the return trip," my mother had said on the phone once we had an appointment. The thought that we could be taking next steps was thrilling.

Dr. Colaum met us in her office; it was the same as it had been each time we'd prepared to start an IVF cycle: I allowed myself to hope. Dr. Colaum invited a spirit of optimism metered with a heavy dose of science. She continually looked for options and focused on positive actions. Today, though, I could not bring myself to meet her eyes when we entered the consultation room. I focused on her hair, pulled up in her usual bun on the top of her head.

Rachel dragged an extra chair across the room and positioned it in front of Dr. Colaum's desk. The room contained the now familiar Frank Lloyd Wright artwork and framed photographs of Dr. Colaum's many grandchildren. But the desk itself looked bigger, even though there were now three of us sitting across from Dr. Colaum, whereas before it had always been just Bill and I. I thought of the axiom about there being strength in numbers.

Dr. Colaum regarded us each individually. Rachel took a seat in a chair on Dr. Colaum's side of the desk, pen poised over our folder, like a court stenographer ready to take notes. I looked at our folder; once flat and pristine, it was now frayed at the corners and over four inches thick, containing ultrasound photos and notes from the past five years of fertility processes. My throat felt dry; I wished I'd brought a glass of water in from the waiting room.

"I read your letter," Dr. Colaum began. I tried to gauge her point of view but was unable to detect anything from her body language. Her face was inscrutable.

"I've done some research," she went on. "As you already know, there have been some cases of successful pregnancies in postmenopausal women, including surrogacy pregnancies through IVF." She seemed to be speaking unusually slowly, elongating her words and pausing between phrases. I sensed hesitation, but it could have been my imagination.

"Such pregnancies are possible," she said, rephrasing what she'd already said. Finally, she pulled her reading glasses off her nose and let them dangle from the chain between across her chest. "Why don't you ask me what you want to know?"

Bill spoke first, his question already poised like slingshot. "When is such a pregnancy possible?"

"A pregnancy is possible any time a woman still has a functioning uterus. A pregnancy such as the one you are proposing is feasible if a woman has a healthy uterus, is in excellent overall physical health, has normal to low normal blood pressure, and has had previous successful pregnancies." I felt encouraged and sat straighter in my chair. I looked at my mother, whose eyes had widened, and nodded.

"From the information you've shared with me," Dr. Colaum said, now turning to my mother, "Kris, you fit this profile."

What followed took on the form of an interview. Dr. Colaum asked my mother questions about vaginal births, tearing afterward, menstrual cycles before menopause, and symptoms during. My mother hesitated a few times, looking at Bill and me for cues about how descriptive to be. At one point Bill asked me in a whisper if he should step out of the room, but this was only the first of the awkward moments to come. They came to be amusing.

"Stay," my mother said. "This is something you may have to get used to . . . "

" . . . if you go down this path," Dr. Colaum said, finishing my mother's sentence.

"Do you think we can pursue this?" I asked, calling the question. I could bear the anticipation no longer; I wanted to know. Bill and my mother leaned forward in their chairs. The room was charged with our hope.

"If we were to pursue this," Dr. Colaum said, emphasizing the word "if" yet again, and addressing my mother, "Kris, you will need to have a battery of physical tests and get the approval from an OB who will take you on as a patient. You'll need to have legal documents drawn up and signed, and you'll all need to have a psychological evaluation, which Illinois law requires of all parties engaging in surrogacy."

"But we *can* pursue this?" I asked, reframing my question. "A surrogacy pregnancy with my mother is a real option?" I sat on my hands to keep them still.

Dr. Colaum didn't answer right away.

After a moment she said, "Providing your mother meets the medical baseline criteria, then yes," Dr. Colaum said, "it is possible."

I held my eyes open, not wanting to breathe or blink.

I realized in that moment that I felt suspended in time, that I wanted more than anything in the world for Dr. Colaum's answer to be an unqualified yes.

I would have loved to have had a pregnancy with just Bill and me. But the new place, a surrogacy with my mother, called to me as a song in my heart. "The body never lies," my holistic medicine teachers in London had said over and again.

When had our relationship changed? And how? Friends would later ask me about this, having heard me talk about how distant I'd felt my relationship with my mother to be. I cited what the therapist in London had charged me with: offering unconditional acceptance to my family and working to change myself. At the time her words had seemed cryptic, but I could see fruits from the seeds that she planted.

I wasn't the only one to change, though. Mental-health professionals like to say that when one person changes, the entire unit can change. In our case, I think my mother and I both changed. And I had begun to think that it was perhaps our desire to find and follow our individual calling that moved us out of the way so that the love that had always been there could flow through—the love now a force bringing us together for an experience unlike anything either of us could have imagined.

"What other questions do you have?" Dr. Colaum said. The memory of London and therapy had spun me into another place. I sat on my hands again to ground myself.

"What are the risks to my mother?" I asked, fully back in the room. This was the question Bill and I had committed to ask at the appointment, should the conversation progress this far.

"If you prove to be in strong overall physical and reproductive health," Dr. Colaum said, addressing my mother again, "there are only slightly elevated risks compared with those in a normal pregnancy. Elevated blood pressure can occur," Dr. Colaum said. I waited for her to continue, to say something horrible, something life threatening or compromising that would constitute too great a risk. Dr. Colaum looked at my mother for another moment, as if she were trying to assess her emotional makeup. Dr. Colaum's glasses rose and fell against the silk of her dress with her breath.

"Fatigue," she said, finally.

We waited. I held my breath again. I waited for "fatigue and mortality," "fatigue and possible stroke."

"Fatigue?" my mother said. "You mean I'd be tired!"

"Really tired," Dr. Colaum said.

My mother leaned far back in her chair and began to laugh. "Tired!"

"*If* your blood pressure was stable and *if* there were no other issues that can come up with any pregnancy, then, yes, I think fatigue would be the main symptom caused by age," Dr. Colaum said. "Be clear these are big ifs," she said.

My mother continued to laugh.

"I was tired when I had no help and two children under five to run after every day. I'm retired now—I don't have to do anything. If fatigue is the big factor, I think can handle it."

Dr. Colaum studied my mother in a way that suggested she approved.

"We'll know more after your tests," Dr. Colaum said.

Rachel touched Dr. Colaum's shoulder and whispered that her next appointment was in five minutes.

"Other questions?" Dr. Colaum asked. I hadn't imagined the appointment would take us so far, and yet I couldn't think of any other questions to ask.

Bill cleared his throat. "I have one—something I feel it's important to ask." Dr. Colaum nodded.

"What is the difference between a thirtysomething uterus and a . . . " Bill halted, his face reddening for a moment as he searched for the right word.

"An old one," my mother offered. "It's okay," she said to Bill, placing her hand on his arm. "I *am* old; it's a good question."

"The medical term we use is 'advanced maternal age,'" Dr. Colaum said, "advanced maternal age being anyone over the age of thirty-five."

Bill poked my ribs through the chair. According to that definition, I was only one year away from joining this group.

"There's no difference," she said, answering Bill's question.

My mother's mouth parted. I pulled back my head, uncertain if I'd heard her correctly.

"The age of the eggs in the ovaries is the primary factor of age in fertility," Dr. Colaum said. "In a certain capacity," she said, a small smile breaking over her face, as if she were having the opportunity to share something little known and rare, "the uterus doesn't age."

Rachel said, "Okay, then," signaling that we needed to stop.

"Tracey can give you a list of our recommended OBs who can do the baseline tests," Dr. Colaum said. If you're willing to come to Evanston, I recommend Dr. Allen at Evanston Hospital. His office is just three blocks from here."

As we gathered our things to leave, Dr. Colaum stood up to see us out. "If you are approved for the surrogacy," she said, "we would be honored to be your fertility team." She gestured my mother to her desk and showed her a photograph of her sixteenth grandchild in a gold frame. As Bill and I exited the door, I heard her say to my mother, "You are an extraordinary woman."

We were jubilant on the way home. Bill was the most reserved, saying that we still had to go through the screening tests, which would be extensive. But he smiled and held my hand across the front seat. "I wish you could have seen Sara's face when Dr. Colaum said the idea was possible," Bill said, looking at my mother through the rearview mirror. "I thought she was going to faint." I nodded and laughed. I was still taking fast, shallow breaths.

My mother and I continued to celebrate cautiously in Albuquerque. The conference opened with a twenty-minute silent meditation and a concert of several female artists. We sat on folding chairs in a large hotel ballroom filled with three hundred other women. I remembered meeting a mother and daughter once at an aromatherapy workshop I'd attended in England. They both had pale, creamy skin, blue eyes, and blond hair. All weekend I had watched them, probably conspicuously, as they sat, the sides of their arms touching at a worktable, holding smelling strips under each other's noses, testing each other's blends on their wrists. I envied their shared interests and tangible closeness. I tried to imagine my own mother and me attending such a workshop, but could not.

And now my shoulder touched hers in the ballroom, where speakers were presenting on and we were discussing creativity and personal empowerment and the sacred feminine. When one of the presenters talked about the importance of finding a calling or purpose, my mother poked my arm. "They should take your vision workshop." We imagined presenting the workshop there.

"Hopefully, I'll be home with a baby!" I said, and she squeezed my hand in my lap.

In between speakers, we spent our time talking about "the vision." We explored the hotel gardens, filled with rows of leafy plants, the air thick with the smell of cedar from the mountains nearby. We couldn't rehash the meeting with Dr. Colaum enough.

We ate dinner one night in the Old Town district of the city. On the porch of a hacienda-style restaurant, we ate red and green chilies and dipped warm sopapillas into honey while we talked about the female reproductive system and menstrual cycle and how mystical the female body seemed.

In the mornings, while walking down a stretch of industrial road to conference site, we broke into a skip, chanting, "No difference! No difference!" to the outstretched desert sky. Dr. Colaum's revelation about the uterus had become our mantra.

We made an appointment with Dr. Allen for the week after the conference. As the day approached, my mother and I seemed to take turns being nervous. Riding up to Dr. Allen's office, we were both antsy. Bill was in D.C. for the day, meeting with a television network about a new show he was going to executive produce. I drove my mother to Evanston, relieved for the moment that we had only our emotions to manage. My mother held her purse in her lap; a banana and a bottle of water peeked out of the top. "To show Dr. Allen I'm healthy," she said.

"I also brought a pad of paper and a pen to take notes." She was like a student on the first day of class. Her fingers kept clutching and unclutching the black leather straps of her bag.

"Now I know how you feel," she said after we'd driven another mile in silence. "I'm suddenly self-conscious about what my body will be able to do."

"I hear you," I said, trying my best to separate the memories of my previous fertility appointments from this one.

Dr. Colaum made it clear she would work with us if we had an OB's approval. I had the noxious thought that Dr. Colaum had only said yes to appease us.

Dr. Allen didn't have a five-year relationship with us. He didn't know anything about my history. Our meeting that morning would be the first he'd hear of our proposal.

My mother began listing points to share with Dr. Allen:

- normal physical two years before
- no abnormal Pap smears or mammograms
- exercise five to six times a week

A smile pulled at my lips. I might be scared of Dr. Allen's response, but I was not worried about my mother's physical abilities. Her ribcage held a healthy heart and her body was built of long, lean muscle. My hands were clenched on the steering wheel and I focused on relaxing my grip. I reminded myself that the women in our family had unusually low blood pressure. The highest either my mother's or mine had ever been was 100/70, even when stressed.

The traffic slowed for several minutes near Lawrence Avenue, but opened up again north of Devon. We arrived at the hospital, parked in the garage across the street, and took the elevator up to Dr. Allen's office. There we sat waiting, nervously waiting to get the go-ahead for the next step of our journey.

Dr. Allen came to the waiting room to greet us himself. He was ex-military and looked it with his closely cropped hair and towering height. At sixty-one, he still possessed the trim, muscular build of an active duty officer. On the way to his office he shared that he started his career in the army before his enjoyable twenty-five-year career in obstetrics. I imagined he inspired great confidence in a delivery room.

He guided us into a small consultation room with a single metal desk and three chairs. He invited us to sit and finished his introduction by saying that his team worked with a lot of high-risk cases. I sucked in a breath. Dr. Allen seemed forthright and skilled. I believed he would listen and give us an honest opinion.

Dr. Allen asked me to begin and to detail my pregnancy history and why we had come to see him. He showed emotion, twice, at the stillbirth of the twins and at my mother's offer to be our surrogate, moving his head back in the chair slightly and letting out a small wow.

He interviewed my mother next about her health, medical history, and previous pregnancies. He jotted down her answers on a small notepad he had pulled from his lab coat pocket, writing in what looked like some kind of shorthand that included symbols, capital letter abbreviations, and hash marks.

"You'd need to pass my physical exam, an EKG, chest X-ray, stress test, blood pressure, and full gynecological exam for us to even consider it," Dr. Allen said matter-of-factly. "We do have some experience with advanced maternal age pregnancies. Last year we had a woman in our practice deliver at fifty-four."

I looked at my mother hopefully.

"There are some other things to consider," he said. "Did you say you live in Virginia?"

My mother nodded.

"You'd need to move here for most of the pregnancy," he said. "So we can monitor you closely. As the pregnancy progressed, I might recommend bed rest or even short stays in the hospital if blood pressure or any other issue arose. The blood volume doubles in pregnancy, more in the case of multiples—something to consider when deciding how many embryos to transfer."

I looked at my mother again but said nothing. We hadn't even begun to discuss those types of details.

"I realize that's jumping ahead a bit," Dr. Allen said. He leaned back in his chair and paused, resting his silver pen on his notepad, as if giving us some time to catch up with him. He cocked his head to one side and settled his sharp gaze on my mother.

"First, let's find out if your body can handle a pregnancy."

"You're considering taking us on?" my mother said, her eyes hopeful.

"If you pass all the tests to my approval, I would be honored to handle this," he paused for a moment, "mission."

My mother bounced her legs under the desk. I restrained myself from hugging Dr. Allen. He told us he could do the initial gynecological tests immediately and excused himself to prepare the examination room next door. When we assured ourselves he was out of earshot, we called Bill and cheered into the phone. "You will love this man," I said. "He talks like an army general."

My mother stood up while I was on the phone and had turned toward the door. I hung up the phone and walked to her, reaching my hand out. She turned and I dropped my hand. Her eyes were shining and wide. "I feel like the ostrich," she said. "I feel like I was made to do this."

While Dr. Allen examined my mother, I met with Pam, Dr. Allen's nurse practitioner, at the reception desk.

"My mother is in town for the next two days," I informed her. "I have Dr. Allen's list of tests here; we were hoping we could get them all done before her flight back to Virginia."

Pam jerked her eyes up from the desk.

"This level of tests usually takes several weeks," she said.

I attempted to keep my voice calm. My mother had made it clear that she wanted to attempt to become pregnant this fall.

"I've talked at length with your father," she'd told me in the car on the way to our appointment. "I'm fifty-nine already. If I'm going to do this, I need to do it now." Rachel at RMI had sent a heady typed list of items that needed to be completed before we even began treatment, with a note that the legal documents could take over a month to prepare.

"It takes longer than regular IVF," she'd said over the phone. "A minimum of two months." She went on to remind me that the legal documents could not be prepared until we had the medical okay.

"I just don't see how this would be possible," Pam said now, scrolling through the hospital's master calendar.

"If there is anything you can do," I said, laying my hands open on top of the desk console.

Pam set her hand on the phone. "Your mother's the one who offered to be your surrogate?" she asked. I nodded.

"As soon as Dr. Allen finishes with your mother, come find me," she said. "Be ready to run."

Over the next forty-eight hours, my mother and I flew through the halls of Evanston Hospital with Pam, sometimes literally running from one floor or wing to another, while my mother underwent the battery of tests.

More than once, the rapid train we were riding threatened to halt. The doctors in radiology said they would not perform a new mammogram without viewing my mother's most recent films, which were somewhere in an archive of some medical-records center in Alexandria. While my mother went to cardiology for her chest X-ray, I phoned four different doctors, tracing the paper trail from my her gynecologist to her primary care physician and ultimately to a medical-records center, where Tyrone, a saintly man, offered to personally go into the vaults, find the film, and FedEx them for same-day delivery.

The final item on the long list of tests was a glucose test—one I remembered from my own pregnancy. The test involved a blood draw before and after drinking a bottle of saccharine orange liquid to rule out gestational diabetes.

We reached the hospital's lab at four forty-five. In our haste, we did not see the blue-and-white placard on the wall informing

patrons that the lab closed at 5:00 PM. My mother had already managed to chug half the bottle of Glucola, when the nurse informed us
of the cutoff time. My mother's flight to D.C. was at eight o'clock
the next morning. "No, she cannot do the test at a lab in Virginia
and fax the results," the nurse told us when we asked. The tests
needed to be done as a unit, in one hospital—Dr. Allen's orders. We
would not be undone.

I called United Airlines and moved my mother's flight to two
o'clock the next day. She could come for the glucose test in the morning when the lab opened at nine, take the blood test by eleven, and
make it to the airport in time for her flight.

One week to the day after our meeting with Dr. Allen, Bill and I
received a letter by mail, with a note stating that a duplicate copy had
been sent to my mother's address in Virginia and another to Dr. Carolyn Colaum of RMI. The letter affirmed that my mother had passed
all necessary medical testing and baseline boards and was "approved
to begin fertility treatments with the intention of becoming pregnant
as the surrogate for her daughter and son-in-law."

There was a note from Dr. Allen himself, or perhaps from Pam,
that read: "We wish you the very best and please keep us posted as
you progress."

That night, my mother called and we celebrated this milestone.

"I am so grateful for my body!" my mom said.

"You should be," Bill said. "You're a marvel." I held the letter to
my chest and took it to bed with me, placing it on my nightstand. The
approval felt like a major validation. But lying in my bed that night, the
sound of Bill's breathing steady beside me, I felt doubts lurking in my
mind like shadows. The tests we'd just completed were only putting us
at a starting line. A surrogate pregnancy would be different, but we had
no more guarantees than we did starting any other IVF cycle.

Dr. Allen and Colaum were quick to remind us that we really didn't know how much age would affect chances of pregnancy and implantation as well.

In the morning I called Tracey to schedule our first "gestational host/IVF" appointment. We'd hoped to do an October cycle, but, based on the legal steps we still needed to complete our status, Tracey said the earliest we could start was November.

"And to make that, you're going to have to hustle," she said.

"We'll do November," I said, dialing my mother's number on my cell phone while I was still thanking Tracey on the landline.

Bill and I met with Stacy Jacobs, a reproductive technology lawyer, the first Monday in October. Her office was located in a large, stone, art deco–style building on a dense block of the downtown Loop in Chicago's financial district. Stacy wore a conservative brown wool suit and looked about my age, mid-thirties. She shook our hands and began to walk us through the legal document we would need to complete to be eligible for surrogacy.

"Your parents will need their own document," she explained. "It has to be prepared by another firm, but I can recommend someone if you'd like."

We told Stacy that we wanted to pay for the legal fees for both sides.

"That's fine," she said. "Most people doing surrogacy within the family do the same." She told us about other families she'd worked with, including an aunt-niece pair and sisters, who'd embarked on this very same process.

In the contract she would prepare, we'd be required to specify our decision if faced with a multitude of upsetting scenarios revolving around one core theme: What would we do in the event that we had to make a choice between the life of the baby or babies and the life of my mother?

In every case, we told Stacy, we would choose to save my mother's life.

When Stacy completed the exhaustive list, she asked about the number of embryos we intended to transfer, recommending that we be conservative.

The doctors always say the risk of multiples is low, but I've seen it so many times."

"Twins?" I asked

"And triplets," Stacy said.

The thought of my mother's becoming pregnant with triplets was sobering. Bill and my father were both advocating the transfer of one embryo. I felt comfortable transferring two. My mother said that she was on board for three, if Dr. Colaum would do it. When she said this, my father shook his head insistently at Bill, entreating him to be a tempering agent to my mother and me if he was not there.

"When do you start IVF?" Stacy asked.

I shared our November 1 appointment date.

"That's tight," she said. "The legal process is typically six to eight weeks." But she promised to prioritize our contract and aimed to complete the first round by October 10.

As she walked us to the elevator, Stacy said, "You picked a good state to do this. Illinois is one of the only states in the country that recognizes biological parents as the parents, regardless of who carries the baby."

If we were to have the baby in D.C. or Virginia, we would be required to file paperwork similar to that of an adoption.

"That *is* lucky," Bill said, as we rode the elevator down to the street level.

We stepped out into the sunlight that cut between the high-rise buildings and the press of morning commuters who populated the offices in this part of the city. At the crosswalk, I stood next to Bill in a sunny patch on the sidewalk and allowed myself to feel gratitude for this small blessing. If—or, I tried to think, *when*—our baby was born, my name would be the one on the line that read "Mother" on the official birth certificate.

My mother returned to Chicago again for the psychological evaluation and baseline ultrasound with Dr. Colaum. Although we were still waiting for our legal documents to be completed, my mother could start her precycle monitoring. Once we began officially, I would undergo the full IVF cycle of injections and oral medications, until it was time for them to retrieve my eggs. While my injections stimulated my follicles, my mother would start whatever combination of hormones Dr. Colaum prescribed to create a nice, thick lining in her uterus. We scheduled our ultrasounds the same morning and then had back-to-back psychological evaluations with Dr. Lee-Ann Kula, one of the approved psychiatrists on Dr. Colaum's list.

My mother, who had been therapy-averse most of her life, kept asking what I thought the psychiatrist would ask.

"We're not going for therapy," I reminded her. "I think she just has to verify that we're sane."

Normally, I would have been happy to speak to a psychiatrist. In my heart, and in our cozy discussions around our dining room table, I believed, the way my father did, that our vision was authentic and soul-inspired, but I also knew that to an outsider the idea could sound crazy. I hoped Dr. Kula was an open-minded sort of person.

We needn't have worried. Dr. Kula met us at the door to her office with open arms that turned into a full two-arm embrace. She wore a peasant-style skirt with a wide leather belt, and her office was adorned with hanging plants, swirling colorful artwork, and a jumbled bookshelf overflowing with self-discovery and therapy books.

She motioned for us to take a seat on a low white-leather couch and said, "I must hear how you came to this incredible idea."

My mother looked on guard. I wondered if she thought Dr. Kula's effusive behavior was a technique to get us to say something that would cause her not to approve us.

"I've been so excited to meet you," Dr. Kula continued. "I actually cried when I heard your daughter's phone message."

She sat in a well-worn chair opposite us and took a long sip of tea from a mug. "Why don't you start, Sara?"

Telling our fertility story was beginning to feel like singing a sad ballad from my first album, one that I hoped to grow beyond but that was always requested at concerts. Dr. Kula made loud *tsk*-ing noises when I came to the part about the twins' being stillborn and said "shit" when I told about the miscarriage. I was surprised and pleased by her transparent emotions. I decided I liked a therapist who swore. She also disclosed personal details about herself, telling us that she had tried to get pregnant for years, before, at age thirty-nine, adopting her son and then getting pregnant two years later. "My children have been my greatest gifts," Dr. Kula said.

My mother and I nodded, understanding why. As Dr. Kula continued, she unfolded her hands and placed her bag next to her on the couch.

"And now you, Kris," Dr. Kula said, turning her gaze on my mother. "How did you come to this vision?"

"It's interesting you should use that word," my mother said, seeming to release whatever reservations she had come in with. She told Dr. Kula about the vision workshop, her meditations at her rock in the woods, and the letter she wrote us offering to carry our child. She also said some things I had never heard before.

"I saw Sara suffering. And I thought, *I don't know if I can carry a baby, but I can get in there with her. She doesn't have to do this alone.*" She put her hand over mine. I couldn't bring myself to look at her directly. My throat tightened around a hard knot of tears.

"Mom," I whispered, starting to cry, not really caring what Dr. Kula thought or decided.

Dr. Kula handed me a box of Kleenex.

"I have another reason for doing this," my mother said after we'd re-grouped. "If I am completely honest, I want to have this experience for me." I felt a rush of gladness hearing my mother share this fact. It was something she'd shared with me, but it wasn't something I'd heard her say to anyone else.

"All my life, I wanted to be called to something heroic, but I could never think what," she said, her hands unclenching at her side.

"*This* is heroic," Dr. Kula said. "You'd be giving a gift, literally, of life."

For a couple of seconds, no one spoke. Dr. Kula looked between my mother and me, perhaps waiting to see if there was anything my mother wanted to add.

She looked at a digital clock on her bookshelf. We'd been in her office for close to two hours. She still needed to have a brief conversation alone with each of us, so we took turns waiting in the hallway while the other spoke to Dr. Kula alone. At the end, Dr. Kula hugged my mother while I wrote out her check.

"I'll be faxing my approval to Dr. Colaum's office and your lawyer's as soon as I speak to your husbands. Bill's appointment was the following day, and Dr. Kula had approved my father to do his consultation over the phone. "I especially cannot wait to meet your other half," she said to my mother.

"I passed!" my mother said as soon as we got into the car. I smiled as she recounted our discussions, but I had to struggle to concentrate on the road. I felt spent from the day of appointments, and the emotion of retelling about the stillbirths and miscarriage.

The afternoon traffic was heavy coming out of Evanston, and we slowed to a creeping pace. My mind poked at something Dr. Kula had told me during my individual consultation. During her attempts to become pregnant, she'd met with an unorthodox doctor from South America who was doing a new kind of fertility treatment. "He took the low bottom cases, those everyone else had written off," Dr. Kula had said. "When I went to see him, he put his hand on my shoulders, looked me in the eyes, and said, 'You will be pregnant within three months.' I had my second son later that year."

As I drove, I wished I could go see that doctor. I wished he could offer me that kind of assurance.

"You know what Dr. Kula said to me at the end of my session?" my mother said, interrupting my reverie.

"What?" I asked.

"She told me she thinks this is going to work. She said, 'This is going to happen.'"

My parents flew back to Chicago together for a "signing party" once our legal contracts were finally processed. We also scheduled our first IVF appointment at RMI that week.

My parents told us that they had shared the surrogacy idea with exactly one couple, friends of theirs for over twenty-five years. "Janine's first reaction was disbelief," my mother said. "When she realized I wasn't joking, she cried. And when she overcame her shock, she had so many questions."

She'd asked my mother if my parents thought it would be hard not to keep the baby after carrying him or her for nine months.

"I am so clear that this is Sara and Bill's baby," my mother had said. "What I want now, more than anything, is to be a grandmother."

Janine had continued to stare at my mother as if she were speaking to a stranger.

"There are lots of parents of grown children who want grand-children," my mother had said, trying to make a joke. "Maybe I'll start a trend."

"Don't count on it," Janine had replied, continuing to look at my mother in awe. "I don't think most of us would do it."

Meanwhile, Bill and I had told no one—not even Bill's business partners, Kaitlin, Amanda, or any of our friends in Chicago. We'd experimented in our previous IVF cycles, telling a lot of people, or very few. This time, I fantasized about waiting to share the news until the baby had arrived. "Hey, look! It worked. Meet our baby!" Or at least until we were seven to eight months pregnant, long past the twenty-two week mark, when the baby would be fully developed and capable of surviving on its own even if it were to be born that day.

On Monday morning Bill, my mother, and I drove to RMI to do our infectious-disease panels. We were thrilled to confirm (again) that we did not have HIV, syphilis, chlamydia, TB, or genital warts. We wrote a check for $15,000 and had an opportunity to show off our updated knowledge from the legal meetings, using the term "gestational host" instead of "surrogate." (In an email, Stacy informed us that a surrogate traditionally involves a woman's providing an egg and carrying the baby, while "gestational host" is the term used when a woman carries another's couple's biological child.) "I like it," my mother said. "I'm the host. It's like I'll be babysitting for nine months."

Bill waited in the reception area while Dr. Colaum administered my mother's and my ultrasounds. We decided to stay in the room for each other's examinations. "We're doing this pregnancy together," my mother said. "The group approach. Plus, we can save you a few minutes and some table paper each time we come."

Dr. Colaum shook her head and looked like she was trying not to laugh.

"You guys are funny," Tracey said from her post at the counter.

The exam was the first time my mother experienced an internal ultrasound. "Now, *that* is a fantastic uterus!" Dr. Colaum said, calling Tracey over to look. I tried to see what made it different from, say, mine, the only other one I'd seen on-screen. All I could tell was that it looked bigger. I felt a tug for a moment, a pang of grief that perhaps her body really was more suited to carry a child (even at her age) than mine. I continued to look at the screen and decided I liked the look of her uterus, too. Even in fuzzy black-and-white pixels, it looked inviting and safe.

"We're going to start you on estrogen pills, twice-weekly estrogen injections, and progesterone," Dr. Colaum said to my mother. "Tracey will give you your calendar, Sara. We're going to go for growing the maximum number of eggs."

I posted my IVF schedule on the side of our refrigerator with a magnet.

"You have so many injections," my mother said, comparing our medication charts.

"But you'll be doing them from transfer on, Mom," I said. "Believe me, if we get pregnant, you'll take plenty of shots."

This cycle, I administered all of the injections myself, taking Lupron in my stomach in the morning and Follistim at night, and even mixing the Repronex chemistry set every other night in weeks four and five.

November brought cool winds and crunchy brown leaves that carpeted the patches of grass and scraped the sidewalk as they blew past. When my mother was in town, Bill cooked hearty autumn meals: French onion soup, beef bourguignon, and oven-baked squash with brown sugar and butter.

When she saw that her IVF regime was so minimal, my mother flew home to Virginia for a week in the middle of the six-week cycle. My egg retrieval was scheduled for sometime the week of December 7. The transfer to my mother would be three to five days later.

"I cannot believe it only takes two weeks of medication to prepare me for a pregnancy," my mother said. "Two weeks to kick-start the uterus after ten years of dormancy."

Dr. Colaum had explained that really the primary thing necessary was a thick, healthy uterine lining, and the key ingredient the body needed to achieve that was estrogen. "Of course, we don't know what your body will do in response," Dr. Colaum said conservatively.

A week before the retrieval, my mother and I drove to Evanston for our next appointment. The outdoor lot that housed a summer farmers' market had given way to bales of golden hay heavy with pumpkins of varying sizes, dried cornhusks, and horns of plenty spilling over with knobby gourds.

"At first I was so afraid my body wouldn't respond at all," my mother said, looking out the window at the pumpkins. "Now I can feel it." She pressed her fingers into her lower abdomen. "Did you feel all bloated and puffy?"

"I usually did midcycle for a few days," I said, "but I was on all the other medications, too." My mother's mouth dropped at the corners.

"Do you feel okay?"

"I feel strange," she said. "Then again, I'm guessing my body is a bit perplexed. I imagine it's a bit of a shock to be called into active duty after being retired for ten years."

To distract our minds, we decided to play a game. We'd read *Eat, Pray, Love* and decided to do what Elizabeth Gilbert did before her divorce papers were signed: call to mind all the people who would be ecstatic if the surrogacy—or, in Gilbert's case, the divorce—worked.

"Your great-grandmother would get a real kick out of this," my mother said.

"Nana," I said, remembering my father's mother.

"Lissa!" my mother said. "And your father. He would get to forever say, 'It's all Lissa's fault.'"

"Nancy," I said, naming Bill's mother.

"For sure Nancy," my mother said. "You know, I dreamed the other night that she was helping to organize all of this."

I liked this notion. Bill's mother had been a skilled producer, orchestrating many media productions and, later, segments for the *Today* show. She was a woman who could get things done.

As I turned onto Ridge Road, I thought of more names: "Dr. Colaum, Tracey, Rachel, Lorelai, Lisa—everybody at RMI," I said.

"All the researchers, doctors, and nurses who have dedicated their lives to developing new fertility processes," my mother added.

"And Dr. Allen and Pam!" she continued. "They'll love having a great story to tell everyone about the *sixty*-year-old woman who successfully delivered a baby to term."

I saw a flash of an image of myself—like a memory, only of something that had not happened yet—helping my mother out of my car in the parking lot at Dr. Allen's office, her belly already bursting, seven or eight months pregnant. I could see her purple maternity top and tailored black maternity slacks. *Oh, please,* I thought, *please let this be real.*

In addition to checking my mother's uterine lining, Dr. Colaum needed to check and measure my eggs. I went first. Using the ultrasound, Dr. Colaum counted thirteen to seventeen possible eggs growing in my right ovary." More than we've ever had," she said. "Looking good, Sara."[1]

"Your turn," she said to my mother, who slipped off her pants and shifted herself to the end of the exam table. "Hmm," Dr. Colaum said, moving the wand back and forth to view my mother's uterus. Her smile had faded. I had only one leg in my jeans and dropped them to the floor, leaning over the chair with my legs and backside exposed. Dr. Colaum's lips were pursed tight. "There," she said to Tracey. I followed where she pointed. In the middle-left part of the screen, I could see a black shape that looked like an engorged comma filled with ink."

"What is it?" I asked.

"Fluid," Dr. Colaum said. "Have you been feeling bloated?"

My mother nodded, her lips pressed, her eyes wide and round. "Sometimes the uterus fills with some fluid in response to the hormones," she said. "We don't like to see that, because it can negatively impact successful implantation."

The room started to move like a carnival ride. I clenched the top of the chair.

"What does this mean?" I said.

"I don't think we should transfer this cycle. You're ready for retrieval; we need to get the eggs. So I suggest we retrieve next week, as planned, and freeze as many embryos as we get."

I didn't like this. I had the sensation of walking on a tightrope, a lone steel line, hundreds of feet in the air. I felt as if I might throw up on Dr. Colaum's floor.

"You always get great embryos," Tracey said to me in the hallway after I'd changed and she'd looked up dates for our retrieval. "They'll be safe until your mother is ready." I hadn't researched statistics about freezing embryos, but I thought I remembered reading somewhere in the RMI literature that the success rate for frozen-embryo transfers was lower than that of nonfrozen, and that not all embryos survive the thaw. With the extra $7,500 in medications for my mother and me, we'd spent almost $22,000 on this cycle already. I imagined $20,000 swirling down a large drain.

"Yeah," I answered glumly. My mother and Dr. Colaum met us in the hallway. I steadied myself by holding on to the counter and asked the question I feared: "If my mother got fluid once, is it likely to happen again?"

"We can't know for sure," Dr. Colaum said, giving us the only truthful answer she could. She turned to address my mother. "There's a good chance your body is just adjusting to this first round of hormones after ten years off. We'll give you a break over the holidays, retrieve Sara's eggs next week, and then we can start up again just after the first of the year."

I thought about my mother and the whispered dreams we'd started to voice—how synchronistic it was that it was our year to be together for Christmas and how sacred it would be to be newly pregnant, when the whole holiday was about a miraculous pregnancy and the birth of a baby.

Now, instead, we would be going to D.C. for yet another Christmas without a baby or a pregnancy, our embryos frozen in a solution of glycerol and sucrose. We could be hopeful, yes, but had no guarantees of what we would have when the embryos thawed and we attempted to bring about a pregnancy that was already going to require its own miracle of sorts.

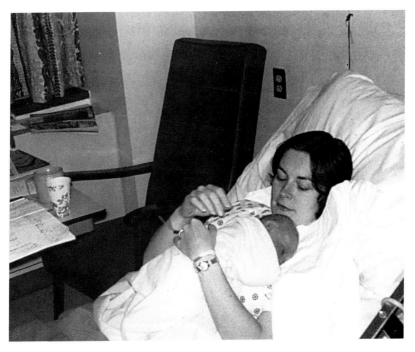

▲ Sara, 1 hour old,
February 25, 1975

◄ Sara, 9 months old

▲ Sara, spring 1976

▲ Bill's mother's
favorite baby
picture

Flying off the slide ▶
on Hickory Street

▲ Bill and Sara's wedding at Inverlochy Castle in Fort William, Scotland, May 2001

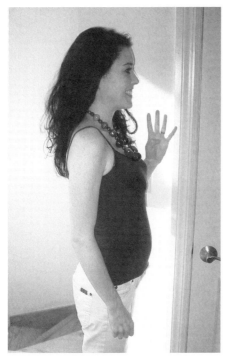

▲ Sara 4 months pregnant with twins, July 2007

▲ 5 months pregnant, one month before premature labor

▲ Kris surrogacy pregnancy,
3 months

▲ 7 months

8 months ▶

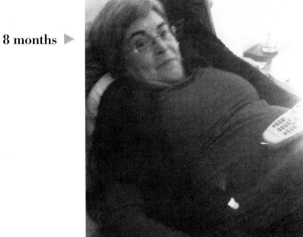

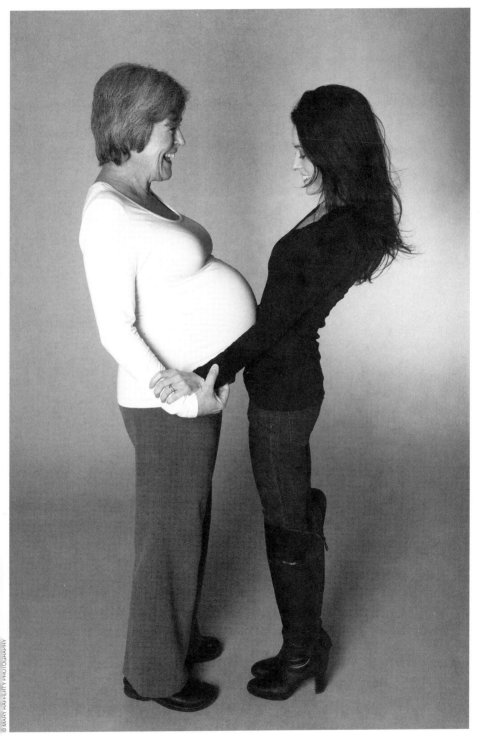

▲ **Studio photo of Sara and Kris**

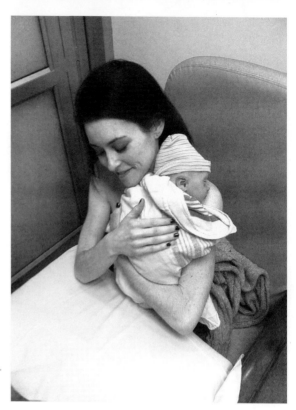

Cuddling after ▶
Finn's first nursing

Finn comes home! ▶

▲ Finn's "O" face, reading *Harry Potter* at Leavitt Street in Chicago

▲ "The Maestro," Finn's signature newborn move

▲ Writing *Bringing in Finn* while Finn naps

▲ Grandma's first visit after the birth, March 2011

▲ First visit to Grandma and Grandpa's, 4 months old, May 2011

▲ Finn on vacation, 9 months old, November 2011

▲ Celebrating Finn's first Christmas with family, December 2011

Chapter 8

On the day of retrieval, Dr. Colaum collected eleven eggs from my ovary. They looked strong, and of those fertilized with Bill's sperm, five embryos advanced in the lab. Carli from the lab called to tell us that two looked especially good.

"They'll be here for you when your mom is ready in January," she told me.

Bill was disheartened by the attrition rate. "It's the same every time, though. Ten eggs turns into two or three embryos. You think I'd be used to it."

We tried our best to focus on the positive. We had three good embryos. We reminded each other of the phrase we'd repeated consistently during other cycles: "It only takes one."

We flew to D.C. on December 23. Bill's stepfather, Roger, gifted us with three nights at the W Hotel on Fourteenth Street. The hotel décor was Mad Hatter mod, with angular black-and-white-striped rugs, oversize red and purple velvet chairs, and glistening chandeliers. In the lobby, gold and silver balls bobbed from white birch branches that hung from the ceiling. We made friends with the holiday staff and spent our days at my parents' house, wrapping gifts and baking the cookies that were my mother's classics: madeleines, pecan tassies, gingerbread men, and spritz. We didn't talk about the surrogacy.

"We'll make ourselves and everyone else crazy if we obsess," Bill had said the first day of our visit. My mother and I had agreed.

When Bill and I returned to the hotel in the evening, we'd take the elevator to the lounge on the top floor that offered a 360-degree view of the Washington Mall. On Christmas Eve, Bill ordered a single-malt Highland scotch, one made in a town that we'd visited on our first trip to Scotland, and we took turns taking little sips from the heavy crystal glass. D.C. was beautiful at this time of year; the Washington Monument, the National Christmas Tree, and the Lincoln Memorial twinkled like stars in the inky sky.

In January, my mother went to her gynecologist in Virginia to have a baseline ultrasound, the prerequisite for restarting her medications. Since it took only two weeks to grow the uterine lining, Dr. Colaum had taken her off the hormone medications during our break. Braun shipped the oral and injectable estrogen directly to her house. Midway through the cycle, she would fly to Chicago so Dr. Colaum could take a look at her uterus.

At the early-January appointment, my mother's uterus looked good. Not only good, but it had the desired thick lining. "Like a featherbed," Dr. Colaum said.

We were cleared to transfer in two weeks. I felt relieved but cautious. Waiting felt hard. With the eggs retrieved and embryos frozen, I didn't have anything to do. My mother decided to visit my grandmother in Nebraska for a few days while the hormones continued to take effect.

On January 29, Bill, my mother, and I arrived at RMI for transfer. Even though I had booked extra work each day and gone out with Bill or friends almost every night, the week leading up to this day had passed slowly—though not as slowly as the weeks we waited to find out if we were pregnant. During those, each hour felt as if it were being pulled through a lengthening device that made time as stretchy as saltwater taffy.

Now we were waiting in the patient waiting area, near the procedure room of RMI in the same curtained room Bill and I had sat in for many of our previous IVF cycles. I'd filled a two-liter bottle of water for my mother and kept encouraging her to drink more.

"Dr. Colaum wants the bladder really full for the transfer," I said.

Even when I wasn't pregnant, I would go to the bathroom every hour or two and had no trouble filling my bladder for transfer procedures. My mother was the opposite. She said her bladder was like a camel's. "If I need to, I can last almost a day without needing to go."

Bill grimaced.

"Sorry," she said, "too much information."

"Just getting used to it," he said. "Just never imagined I'd be privy to the details of my mother-in-law's urinary functioning."

Rachel arrived to our curtained waiting room and handed Bill a cup.

"What?" Bill said.

"Just kidding," Rachel said, amused at her joke. "Just didn't want you to feel left out."

"Ha, ha," Bill said. But when Rachel left to prepare the procedure room, he whispered, "Really, she loves me."

Dr. Colaum allowed me in the procedure room for the transfer. I sat in a chair and watched the team position my mother at the edge of the table her feet lifted up in the stirrups. The table was so familiar to me, I wanted to reach over and pat it with my hand.

Tracey rolled gel over her stomach and pressed into my mother's bladder. I tried not to think about the speculum, catheter tube, and urinary pressure. I wished I could do all the uncomfortable parts for her.

"I'm not getting a clear picture."

"Have you been drinking water?" Rachel asked.

"I've had half a liter or so," my mother said.

"It needs to be fuller," Dr. Colaum said. "Let Sara coach you. She's come in here every time at full capacity."

Tracey switched on the lights and the transfer team disbanded. My mother sat up on the table and began to chug water.

"I'm so embarrassed," she said. "I didn't think full meant about to pee on the table."

"Oh yeah," I said, "they mean bursting."

My mother's bladder was full thirty minutes later and the process started again.

Carli had shown us a photo image of the embryos when we arrived. She held the picture out toward us with long pale fingers. Two of the three had survived the thaw and were ready to transfer. I'd given the picture to Bill to hold during the procedure.

"Think good thoughts," I said as I kissed the image of each tiny life.

Dr. Colaum turned the flat screen toward my mother and I so we could watch the implantation. She'd asked me to describe the process to her in detail the night before. "It is majestic," my mother said now as we looked at the dark, vast terrain of her womb.

"Preparing two embryos," Carli called through the window from the lab.

"Ready," Dr. Colaum answered. "Transferring two embryos. Here we go, Kristine," she said, her hands guiding the catheter into position.

I watched the embryos shoot into my mother's uterus. They looked as they always did—like comets jettisoning through space.

"Perfect placement!" Dr. Colaum announced. I saw Rachel's shoulders drop. Two embryos had transferred, and landed. I let out an audible sigh.

I asked my mother if she wanted to rest alone in the room, but she invited me to stay. We sat without speaking, listening to the hum of the ultrasound machine, our eyes still fixed on the spot where the embryos had landed. I pressed my hands on her belly and she placed her hands over mine as we waited, our eyes never leaving the screen.

Two days later, my mother flew home to Virginia.

"Are you sure it's safe for her to travel?" I asked Tracey.

"Whatever has happened is done," she said. Now we just had to wait nine days before my mother could take the pregnancy test.

I tried to go about my regular life. I scheduled days of work downtown, meeting my clients at the Cultural Center near Millennium Park. I found the activity in the loop invigorating and I liked watching the stretches of people trudging along South Michigan Avenue. At two o'clock on the Wednesday of the week before our pregnancy test, I took a break and walked toward Lake Street and Michigan, where there was a breezeway lined with restaurants and cafés.

My mother and I had talked by phone every day, but we'd taken the previous day off, ostensibly because we couldn't schedule it, but really because we both needed a break. We would not know the results of the test for another week, and we found it impossible to talk about anything other than a potential pregnancy.

When I called my parents' number, my father answered on the third ring.

"Let's see if she can peel herself off the couch to come to the phone," he said.

"Is she okay?" I asked, feeling my heartbeat quicken.

"I'm feeling something!" my mother said, picking up the line.

Once my father hung up, she lowered her voice.

"I think your father is kind of freaked out," she said. "He came in from tennis and found me still sitting in the chair in the living room where I was when he left two hours earlier."

The skin on the back of my neck pricked.

"Of course I can't say for sure. It's been thirty years. But I swear I feel just like the other times. I am so tired I can hardly lift my hand off my leg. And my breasts are sore!" she said. Her voice shook slightly as she spoke. I pressed the phone harder into my ear. I heard Bill's voice in my head: "Don't read into anything. Don't assume anything until we take the pregnancy test."

I attempted a casual tone, as if we were discussing a recipe.

"I haven't wanted coffee either." My mother did not need to remind me of the meaning of the coffee aversion. I threw Bill's cautions aside. What my mother was describing was beyond what I had imagined. I wanted to hear about every twinge and sensation.

"It's the strangest thing," she said. "Like finding myself in a country I love but haven't visited in thirty years. It's amazing the way the body or psyche remembers the sounds, the foods, the smells."

Across the street, the time flashed on a digital clock on the side of a bank.

I had agreed to be interviewed at 3:00 PM for a documentary on women's health and nutrition, the project of one of my longtime clients. The film crew was set up at an office building, just up the street. The clock read 2:55, but I didn't want to get off the phone.

"I have to go, Mom," I said.

"Of course—I'm taking up your whole afternoon," she said.

"I would stay on the phone with you all day," I said, meaning it.

"I take the first pregnancy test at my doctor's office here on Friday, the official test Monday," she said, confirming the schedule we'd both committed to memory. "Tracey said she'd conference us both in to share the results on Monday afternoon."

Tracey called, by herself, Monday at 2:30 PM, with the results. I could hear my mother breathing on the other end of the line. Bill stood next to me, leaning into my cell phone.

"The HCG numbers are low," Tracey said. "I'm so sorry."

I shook my head, feeling confused. The air around my eyes seemed fuzzy, as if static had interrupted my vision. Just yesterday my father had taken the phone after I'd finished talking to my mother and told me that he thought she was pregnant. I'd taken his observations as truth. He was not prone to premature excitability or exaggeration. I heard the words but could not reconcile what Tracey was saying.

"Are you guys okay?" Tracey asked.

No one spoke.

I eventually said, "Yeah," and we hung up the phone.

Bill walked to the window. "Shit," he said. "Shit, shit." My mother was still on the line.

"Huh," my mother said, after another minute. "I really thought . . . I physically felt . . . Even now, I feel . . . "

"I know, Mom."

"Huh," my mother said again. Her voice sounded like a deflated balloon. We stayed on the phone, not speaking for another few minutes.

"I'll call you tomorrow," I said.

"Okay," she said.

Later that day I received a call from Dr. Kula, who'd heard about the test from Tracey.

"I'm here if you want to talk," she said, and left her office number. I threw the phone onto the counter without listening further. I'd brought my laptop to the kitchen to see if I could do some work, but I couldn't concentrate. I pushed the computer back on the counter, scribbled a note on an index card to tell Bill I was leaving, and stomped out of the house.

It was 5:00 PM, mid-February, and bitterly cold. I didn't care. When my friend's father died, she lost twenty-five pounds walking for miles a day, making a pilgrimage of her grief. I hadn't kept count of how many miles I had logged since we'd started trying to become pregnant, how many walks I'd taken when I was unable to bear the stillness of the house, the maddening inability to control our situation.

The sky was already shifting toward dark. I was warm inside the down parka I wore. The year before I'd splurged on a new one from North Face, a brown one with turquoise lining, that came down to the tops of my knees. I turned right on Barry Street and walked toward the lake, taking the same route I'd taken on that warm summer day when my mother had offered to be our surrogate. A harsh wind blew past, numbing my calves and fingers.

For some reason, I was most annoyed about the call from Dr. Kula. In our five years together, Dr. Colaum had never had a psychiatrist call us. My stomach clenched at the thought of being pitied or, worse, having become such a hopeless case that we needed unsolicited psychiatric support.

Before I'd seen Dr. Kula's number, I'd been feeling hopeful. Now I tried, through my heavy trudging, to return to that place. When we'd hung up the phone with my mother and Tracey the day before, Bill had reminded me that the way he looked at it, we had essentially started over with this round of IVF—a 33 percent success rate, a one in three chance. After five years of hating statistics, I now found them comforting. I didn't know for sure if my mother was up for another cycle, but if she was, we could try again.

When we talked the next week, my mother said she was open

to trying again but wanted to spend some time walking in the woods where she meditated.

"I was so sure this was an inspired vision, Sara," she said.

"It still could be," I said. My first coaching mentor in England always reminded me that just because something is inspired doesn't mean it comes easily. It was easier to see this for my mother than for myself.

My birthday came at the end of the month, and I asked Bill for an overnight in a small lake town, near the Wisconsin border. I wanted to go by myself and think—or, better yet, not think—and hike in one of the large national parks nearby.

Bill championed my request, sending me off with a Whole Foods bag of snacks and a couple of DVDs to watch on my computer if I felt lonely at night.

I drove to the small cabin I'd rented on a Friday night and woke Saturday to a startling light. Fresh snow had fallen in the early morning, and two feet of white shimmered on the ground. Snowplows had already cleared the major roads, and I found the state park easily, about ten miles west of the cabin. The parking lot was empty. I seemed to be the first and only visitor.

I chose a simple trail about three miles long. The path was feet-deep in snow, and my boots sunk in with each step. I hoped I would be able to see the green stripes that marked my trail. As I walked, the sun rose, and with it came just enough heat that I was sweating inside my coat by the end of the first mile.

I thought of pausing at a particular tree and asking the Divine Mother for guidance and some kind of sign. But as I stood there in the middle of the empty trail in piles of snow, the gesture seemed empty. I began to wonder if being in the park at all was a sane choice. I cleared my mind, the way I'd learned to do in meditation classes, and walked up a hill, following what I hoped was the trail.

"Please show me if we are on the right track," I said to the trees and the snow, unable to help myself from asking something of the vast nature around me. I asked, and then again tried to quiet my mind.

When I'd attended retreats in England, the facilitators had taught a technique for looking for signs: "Pay attention to the shape of a particular tree, an animal on the trail, a specific visual image, and interpret the message at the end of the hike. Notice anything that stands out, then allow the meaning to reveal itself through your mind," they'd instructed.

I heard and felt nothing of note, until I rounded the three-quarter-way point on the trail and caught sight of a dark green marker that affirmed I was on the way back to my car. I was cold again. The sun had dropped behind some clouds, and the sweat from the effort of climbing the hills was now chill and damp on my skin.

"Please show me if we are going in the right direction," I said. At the mouth of the trail, I saw a single branch sticking up out of the snow. I pulled off the large ski gloves I'd borrowed from Bill and reached for the stick, pulling it out from the top. It was thin and long, made of strong, youthful bark. The branch was a single stalk that opened into two smaller branches; it was the shape of a Y.

My mother and Bill also felt we should try again. RMI scheduled us for a spring cycle in May. My mother was happy that the May start would allow us to attend my cousin's (her nephew's) wedding in San Francisco. In early March, May seemed far off. This time, I was the one who wanted to start again immediately. Bill talked me around to seeing the extra time as a gift. We'd used up our insurance coverage three cycles ago and would again need to pay for this cycle, as we had for the last one, with our own means.

Bill took on a new client and sold another series of documentary vignettes. I increased my private-practice sessions and sold a few magazine articles. Thus far, we'd kept current with every IVF treatment, paying cash as we went. For the last cycle, though, we'd dipped into our savings. We hadn't contributed to retirement in five years. My parents said they would offer us an interest-free loan for whatever we didn't have by May 1, but I didn't like the idea of borrowing money.

"Most surrogates get paid for surrogacy," I said. "They don't front the money."

"I know you'll pay us back," my mother assured me. "We need to do the cycle this year, and your father and I have the money sitting in a long-term savings account. We don't need that money right now."

We agreed to accept whatever we needed to pay cash at the start of the cycle and repay any loan within two years.

"This is it," Bill said. "At least until we can pay them back."

"I don't know if my mother is up for three tries anyway," I said.

We flew to San Francisco on a Friday in May. The city was sunny and warm. We walked from Fisherman's Wharf to the Marina and through quiet, gleaming Pacific Heights and Lombard Street.

I felt expansive looking out over the bay and walking up the steep hills near our hotel in Nob Hill. At the reception on Saturday night, we were invited to share a wish for the new couple. The couple had laid smooth stones and Sharpie pens on a table near the entrance to the reception, next to a placard that asked people to write their wish on the long side of the stones.

"What did you write?" my mother asked Bill and me.

"Fertility," we said in unison. My sister looked surprised. She had been next to us as we'd written on the stones and had seen no discussion take place between us. Bill and I laughed.

"What else would we write?" he said.

The next weekend, back in Chicago, a musician friend of mine invited me to a church service where he was performing. We'd met in life-coaching training five years ago, and he now coached musicians on the days he wasn't composing. I had already taken my seat and was studying the program, when I remembered that it was Mother's Day. We had begun our new IVF cycle, and if I'd considered the day, perhaps I would have opted not to come.

Scores of children in frilly dresses and little suits and shorts sat primly, extra well behaved, next to their mothers. Behind the podium was a large banner bearing the message WE HONOR OUR MOTHERS. To the side of the pulpit stood a large vase filled with dozens of red roses. After his talk and my friend's trumpet solo, the minister asked all the mothers in the congregation to stand.

A pocket of pain arose underneath my ribs, spiky and barbed like a briar. The minister waved his arms, encouraging the mothers to rise. As women popped up out of their chairs, the rest of the congregation began to cheer and applaud. As more women stood, some of the men and children began to stomp their feet. The room sounded like a sports arena. I clapped along with them, genuinely honoring these women. But my movements began to feel forced, my face plastic and cold, like a mask. A well of anger churned in my gut. The woman to my left stood while her two young children reached out to touch her arm and cheered, "Mommy!"

I felt an impulse to stand. The words of the Divine Mother echoed in my head, competing with the applause: *You have been initiated.* The remembrance shocked me, and I stopped clapping. *Stand up.* The command came swift inside me.

Why not? I thought. The minister hadn't said, "Stand if your children are living." Was I not a mother to our twins, and even to the baby I'd carried for just six short weeks? Just because they had died, did it mean I was not really a mother? I stood. A rush of blood to my head muffled the applause that continued, now even louder than before. Ushers passed roses down the rows in baskets, smiling and prompting each standing woman to take one. The woman next to me selected her rose and handed the basket to me. I hesitated over the velvet petals, drops of moisture still resting on some of the folded buds. Standing was one thing, but I didn't think I could take a rose. I handed the basket to the usher and faced forward, avoiding eye contact with anyone around me. When the last of the roses had been delivered, the minister invited everyone to take their seats.

As I sat, my heart raced and I found it difficult to breathe. The act of standing had depleted me, and I felt as if the sound of the applause were pressing on my chest.

When it came time for the collection, the woman next to me leaned toward my seat and asked how many children I had.

"Two," I said. Saying it aloud calmed me for a moment and helped distract me from my racing pulse. Then, thinking of the miscarriage, I corrected myself. "Well, three." Her eyes looked to the seats beside me—looking for the mentioned children, I imagined. "Didn't stay," I said helplessly, searching for a nonmorbid answer.

Her eyes widened for a moment, and then she tilted her head, regarding me with curiosity. I realized that I'd confused her. She probably now thought my children had died in some kind of accident or illness, or that I was insane. I regretted having stood up at all.

"And you?" I said, hoping to change the focus. "Two?"

"Two," she said. "But four total. Two here and two that didn't stay."

She understood. I looked at her stunning children, smiling and robust with life, with blue eyes and long lashes that looked like hers. I felt a stab of something dark in my chest. I didn't want to envy this woman, but I did. She'd had losses but was now mothering the way I wanted to be, while I stood looking at a crevasse I did not know if I would ever fully cross. I wished then that I had taken a rose. I would have pushed a thorn into my finger; the physical pain would have been a welcome distraction.

I walked fast toward the atrium the minute the service ended. I wanted to congratulate my friend on his performance and leave quickly. As I exited into the front hall, I felt a hand touch my arm. The woman from my row was standing beside me, her eyes and face wet.

"It would never have occurred to me today to acknowledge all the children I carried," she said. I forced myself to meet her eyes. I didn't want her to see my jealousy, or my sadness.

"It really moved me," she said. I nodded and dropped my eyes. "Thank you," she said, and pressed her rose into my hand.

By the time I returned home, I no longer felt like sticking my finger with the thorns. Something had been transmuted in the exchange with the rose. I held the flower in my hand. It was beautiful, soft, and just beginning to open. I put it in a small vase in the kitchen next to my IVF medications. I felt emptied out from the service but opened as well, opened up for something good and new.

When my mother arrived for her baseline ultrasound a week later, Bill called a family meeting. We were about halfway through the IVF cycle, roughly three weeks from retrieval and transfer. I had taken my evening injections, and my mother and I were sitting at the island in the kitchen while Bill cooked.

"I've been thinking," Bill said, lowering eggplant cubes into a flour mixture, "that maybe this round we can bring in some lightness. I don't mean half-assing anything with our medications or appointments. I'm talking about lightening up our conversations and watching funny TV shows at night—that kind of thing. These cycles can feel so intense."

My mother and I agreed to the new intention. We made a few other family decisions as well.

"This time, I'm going to stay in Chicago from retrieval all the way through the pregnancy tests," my mother said. We all thought waiting for the ten days after transfer together might feel excruciating, but we wanted to eliminate the variable of plane travel.

"I know doctors say there's no way travel that early can impact a pregnancy," my mother said, "but I want to give this cycle every chance of success."

We did not discuss what we would do if we were not pregnant this time. I felt, though it was not explicitly stated, that this cycle could be our last try.

My mother's age aside, I didn't know how many more rounds of IVF my body could take. I had purposely not counted the number of cycles, injections, and shots I'd subjected myself to. Presurrogacy, each time my mind had reached to make a calculation, I'd forced myself to stop, fearing a quantifiable number would send me into despair. When I focused on one cycle at a time, the regime felt manageable. Logistically, I'd become so accustomed to IVF cycles that I no longer even thought about the medications between injections. I could administer an intramuscular shot into my buttocks with one hand. Still, my stomach and behind looked like the surface of the moon—bruised and indented—and I lost a few pounds with each cycle that I never could quite put back on between rounds, so I had a slightly starved and pinched look about the face.

As this cycle progressed, we stayed true to our intention and looked for opportunities for distraction and fun. People in Chicago became exhilarated the minute the weather turned warm, rushing outside, flooding restaurant patios as soon as they opened. The path along Lake Michigan was dotted for miles with bikers, runners, and people playing beach volleyball in sand.

Bill cooked inspiring meals, and we watched Will Ferrell movies and comedies on TV. We found an Italian restaurant that made a macaroni-and-four-cheese lasagna that my mother fell in love with. To her delight, they delivered.

"I'd better become pregnant this time," my mother said, "as I am apparently already eating for two."

I worked most days but looked for opportunities to go out with my mother. When I could take time off, we went on adventures. We spent a day in Evanston exploring the lakefront and shops and made periodic visits to the Spice House on Wells Street in Old Town (her favorite store). We tried to carry our intention of lightness into Dr. Colaum's office. We baked cookies for the staff and spent our time in the waiting room wishing for success for every couple there with us.

Bill seemed relieved by the humor and lack of intensity. He looked more relaxed than he had in several years. My father surprised my mother by flying to Chicago to be with her during the week between our procedures and the pregnancy test. The day of our retrieval, Bill and I urged my parents to go out together. It felt right that we would go on our own: as the hopeful parents, there for the big-bang moment when—we hoped—our child or children would be conceived.

As profound as we knew that moment to be, we remained true to our intention of lightness on the retrieval day. Bill loaded his iPod with Bill Maher podcasts. We arrived at RMI in good humor.

The clinic was booked that day, and Rachel told us they'd run out of patient rooms in the back area. "We've made up a temporary space for you here," she said, walking us to the wall across from the curtained waiting areas. The staff had draped a sheet over a hanging rack in front of two black office chairs.

"We wouldn't normally ask this, but we thought you two could handle it. You're veterans."

We told Rachel we didn't mind. She rolled the hanging rack in front of the chairs, handed me the set of hospital clothes, and told us to take a seat. I changed quickly and sat back in the chair. The sheet curtain didn't quite cover our seating area, and we could see the staff coming and going. I set the paper surgical hat aside and Bill turned on a podcast. At one point I laughed and heard the sound echo across the room. I clamped my mouth shut as Rachel walked a couple into the first patient area, the one Bill and I had been in for our procedures for every other retrieval and transfer.

The woman of the couple had a round body and crinkly hair. Her partner was a tall African American man in a striped shirt. Before he pulled the curtain shut, I saw him reach out his hand to help her unwrap the gown and scrubs.

"I can do it," she snapped, her voice as rigid as her jaw.

"First-timers," Bill mouthed to me. I nodded and silently wished them a successful outcome.

We continued our game of people watching from behind our curtained-off area. While we waited for the anesthesiologist, Rachel stopped by again. She took in Bill Maher playing on Bill's nano.

"You guys have come a long way," she said.

Within the hour, a female anesthesiologist whom we'd not met before started me on an IV. She had cool hands and stuck the needle into the vein with one try.

Rachel walked me into the procedure room, and she and Tracey began to count backward from ten. I counted along with them. By four, I was out.

Afterward I was groggy but felt relaxed, even chipper.

"Anything interesting happen while I was gone?" I asked Bill.

"I delivered my donation," Bill said. "And Dr. Colaum reported that she retrieved thirteen good eggs," Bill said. "Nine look strong for fertilization."

"Nine is good," I said.

Once Rachel cleared us to go, I got dressed and we stood at the edge of the room, waiting for Lorelai or Tracey to take me down in the wheelchair.

Tracey permitted me to walk from the front door to the car as long as Bill held my arm and we walked slowly. While we walked, Bill told me that he'd seen the man from across the room go and return with his donation.

"He looked so miserable," Bill said. "I wanted to tell him that part gets easier. I was sure I would not have wanted someone to say that to me then, though. So I gave him a salute."

"You saluted him?" I asked.

"I did," Bill said.

We arrived at the car, Bill assisted me into the front seat, handing me the seatbelt and waiting until I clicked the buckle before shutting the door and walking around to his side.

In the car, he continued the story.

"You know my friend Alan, the one who worked on my account at the agency?"

I remembered Alan, a boisterous man who'd been known as a gunslinger within the agency.

"He and his wife did IVF a few years ago. And he told me that to keep his spirits up he started doing this thing called the victory lap."

"That sounds like Alan," I said.

"After every donation, he would run through the office and gave a high five to the entire staff at the clinic."

"I'm sure they hoped he'd washed his hands," I said.

"Do you want to hear this?" Bill said. I nodded.

"He made the victory lap every time he gave a donation—I mean, he really hammed it up. On his fourth cycle, though, the doctor came out and stood in the doorway during Alan's run. He was afraid he'd gone too far and was going to get himself and Cindy kicked out of the practice, but he had to do something to take the pressure off. I could relate. When I saw that guy looking beaten today, heard his wife all cranky and scared, I wanted to do something. I remembered how I felt at the beginning. A high-five lap isn't me, but a salute seemed fitting. I raised my hand and lifted my chin and nodded to him—in solidarity."

I turned in my seat so I could see Bill's face. Even in profile, I felt as if I could see both the scars and the gifts of our journey. We'd vowed repeatedly through the past six years to let what we faced bring us closer. If what we experienced was going to change us, we would look for ways for it to strengthen, not distance, us. Looking at the square of his jaw, his hands holding the wheel capably and confidently, I felt proud of him. Proud of us.

The day of our transfer, three days later, dawned warm and bright. Bill, my mother, and I went to RMI together.

Carli had called the day after retrieval to tell us we had three strong embryos. Our procedure was scheduled for Tuesday at noon. This time, my mother brought her own liter bottle of Evian and chugged the water with devotion as we sat in the waiting room.

The procedure area was calmer than it had been when we'd come for retrieval, and Tracey ushered us to the first patient area, which we'd come to think of as our own. Rachel had rolled in an extra chair so the three of us could sit together. Bill stepped outside the curtain while my mother changed into her gown and paper cap and I pulled scrubs over my clothes and shoes. Dr. Colaum allowed me into the room again.

The procedure room was soothing and tranquil, the institutional white walls and medical equipment fading into the soft glow when Tracey dimmed the lights. Carli appeared in the square window in the door to ask my mother to state her name. Her blonde hair was pulled into a ponytail, and her nails were painted pink. When she saw me, she waved.

"Are you sure we're doing two?" Dr. Colaum asked, winking at my mother. "We have three great-looking embryos."

"Two," I said firmly, honoring my promise to Bill and my dad. We'd already filled out paperwork to have the remaining embryo frozen and stored in the RMI lab.

"Ready," Dr. Colaum said. Her pink cheeks and light hair beneath the blue surgical cap gave her the look of Mrs. Claus.

"Transferring two embryos," she said as she wove the tube up through my mother's cervix into the uterus. I heard a flick and saw the embryos rocket into the uterus. My mother let out a "wow" as we watched the display on-screen. I never tired of this moment.

The RMI team left the room. My mother and I waited again, in silence at first; then I sang the lullaby chant I'd sung after my first transfers, while we imagined the little life/lives searching for a spot to implant.

My mother held her bladder until Tracey came to relieve her and escort us outside. Bill drove the car around to the front of the building. We offered my mother the front seat and suggested she put her feet up on the dashboard to maintain an inverted position for the drive back into the city—the same way I had done on our first cycle, when I became pregnant with the twins.

"I'll stand on my head if it increases our chance of pregnancy," my mother said. "I'm going to go right back to your house and into bed. This time, we're not taking any chances."

Two of my mother's friends drove from D.C. to Chicago to entertain her the following week. They were interested in Frank Lloyd Wright houses and stopped in Ohio to visit a few properties along the way. On Friday, they drove with her to RMI to take the first blood test, and then drove west, to Oak Park, to take a Frank Lloyd Wright house tour there. After the tour, my mother tracked down the walking labyrinth she'd read about at Grace Episcopal Church, a gothic structure on the corner of Lake Street and Forrest Place. Her friends decided to find a café and have an iced tea while she walked to the church. Happy to be alone, she told me, she placed her feet at the start of the labyrinth.

"I cleared my mind and asked to truly surrender. But I couldn't. The most honest thing I could do was say that I wanted this pregnancy with my whole heart, being, and soul—wanted it desperately, in fact, which is exactly what's not advised in any spiritual practice, no matter what religion or philosophy you read. I decided to walk the labyrinth anyway and asked it to tell me whatever I needed to know."

She kept her mind poised on the sounds around her, the step of her foot on the grass, the wheels of a car on the road nearby. She tried to push away all thoughts and remain calm as she followed the winding path. When she reached the grassy center, she stopped.

"I planted my feet in the ground and waited. When a few minutes went by and I didn't feel or hear anything, I started to cry. I thought for sure I would feel some direction, some sign, once I reached the middle. I looked around to make sure I was alone, and then began talking.

"We've done everything we could do," she said to the labyrinth, the surrounding trees, and the sky. "My uterus is strong. The embryos were transferred. We've come all this way.'"

Then, she said, a calm feeling came over her, as if a great wind had stopped blowing, leaving her ears and skin still tingling from its force.

"I heard something," my mother said, saying the words slowly, watching my face for my reaction. "Not out loud, like regular speech, but inside my head."

"What did it say?" I asked, remembering the day in my bedroom with the Great Mother.

"*You're right where I asked you to be,*" my mother said. "That's what I heard.

"I wanted to hear, *You're pregnant* or receive some kind of affirmation or sign to that effect," she continued. "But I was gobsmacked that I heard anything, actually. It was an incredible moment."

I thought again of that day on my bedroom floor after the twins died. I hadn't heard what I'd wanted to hear, either. And yet what I had heard had resonated with me as real and sustained me many times over these long three years.

"That's my experience of those kinds of messages, too," I said.

"I guess the Universe wants us to wait and find out like everyone else, at the pregnancy test," my mother said.

The sky had grown dark outside the window of the guest room where my mother and I had been snuggled on the bed. The moon was full and cast white light into the room. I turned to look out the window and attempted to bat away a thought that had been lurking as my mother recounted her experience in the labyrinth, and probably ever since she had made the offer to be our surrogate.

Maybe the whole purpose of her vision was for us to get to this place, a place of love and appreciation for each other, of unimagined intimacy and closeness. If that was the purpose, it should be enough, I told myself. Bill and I would survive. Even though we wanted deeply to be parents, we didn't need a baby to live a complete life. I told this to myself, but I didn't fully believe it.

Just like my mother at the labyrinth, I could not totally surrender my desire. I shrugged and smiled at her, and we went downstairs to see if Bill wanted help with dinner.

On the morning of the official pregnancy test, I drove my mother to Dr. Colaum's. Bill had a preproduction meeting for his next shoot and would be in a suburb of Chicago for most of the day.

"It's probably better that I'm not there," he said. "I'm so jumpy."

My mother didn't look anxious. She held a small water bottle in one hand and a banana in the other. There was no trace of uncertainty. My heart pumped hard as we turned onto Ridge Road and pulled into the RMI parking lot.

I turned away as a new nurse on staff administered the blood test. I restrained myself from double-checking the vial to ensure she'd accurately marked my mother's name and date of birth, our phone number. In the last regular IVF cycle we'd done, I'd had nothing to eat or drink before the blood test and had been shaking so forcibly that even Tracey had had trouble getting any blood out of my vein. I looked to see if my mother was having any difficulty and realized my own hands were shaking.

"Cell phone or landline?" Rachel asked me, not needing to go over any other protocol for the day.

"Cell," I told her and rushed out of the office with my mother, my hands and body still trembling a bit.

It was only ten o'clock. I hadn't scheduled any work for the day, and we had hours before the results would be in.

"Let's go to Jerry's," my mother suggested. Jerry's was a hipster lunch place in Wicker Park that I'd taken her to once before.

I had practice waiting for pregnancy tests, I told myself. This was just one more. I'd committed myself to walking through this day with calmness and courage. But I grew more anxious each mile south that we drove. It was as if a giant clock were ticking in my ear, slowly counting down the minutes before someone from RMI called. My throat and breath felt tight and I fought back tears. I parked the car and brushed the corners of my eyes. My heart fluttered the way it had after the twins died. The sensation was not comforting.

We walked through a few boutiques, and I ran my hands numbly over the clothes, commenting on one or two dresses my mother held up.

"It's going to be okay, Sara," she said, pulling my arm into the curve of her elbow. I knew ultimately it would be. I repeated what I had so many times to myself on the day of these tests: Bill and I could keep trying. We could pursue other options. We would not live or die by the results. And yet I felt the steel wire of that tightrope, plummeting space on either side.

We walked toward Jerry's. The sun had reached its height and the day was warm, seventy degrees with a breeze. Most of the tables were full of people eating avant-garde sandwiches and salads out in the sun.

My mother stopped me by my arm again a few feet from the entrance. "I have a good feeling, Sara," she said.

I did not have any feeling aside from mounting anxiety. I had refused to be hopeful about any pregnancy symptoms my mother might feel, not wanting to repeat the false expectations from the previous cycle. Whatever would be would be when Tracey or Rachel or the whole RMI team called with the results.

I knew in some part of my brain that a positive pregnancy test did not mean we would for sure have a baby. But I also knew a positive test was the only chance we had of having one now, and in the moment, every mental faculty I had was focused on the results of that test.

When our lunch arrived, I pushed the food around my plate, poking cucumber slices with my fork. My mother seemed to be relishing her turkey Reuben, eating the sandwich in long, savoring bites. I had no idea how she could be so calm. She glanced at a tray being delivered to a table next to us.

"Those sweet-potato fries look good," my mother said. "Will you have some if I get us an order?"

"I don't feel hungry," I said.

"Well, I am having a lovely lunch," my mother said. "I am feeling extra hungry today. Ravenous, in fact." She pulled a piece of turkey from the sandwich and took a large bite. Ignoring my silence, she continued the conversation in monologue.

"Maybe because of all the activity of the transfer," she said, staring me in the eye. "Or maybe because I feel so pregnant."

"Mom!" I said again. I could not believe she was being so flip.

"I'm trying to hold on to my sanity here," I said.

"Then trust me," she said. "This is going to be good."

My cell phone screen lit up. RMI's number.

"Oh, god," I said. "It's them."

"Pick up!" my mother said, dropping her sandwich onto her plate.

"Not here," I said, glancing around at the crowded tables, hearing the clinking of utensils on ceramic plates. I picked up the phone and asked Tracey if we could call her right back.

"I'll call you," she said, her voice giving away nothing. "Five minutes?"

I flagged our waitress for our check. My mother and I half-ran to the car. I tapped Bill's number into the screen of my phone.

"Sweetie," I said, breathing hard, "Tracey is calling us in about two minutes. Can you take the call?"

"Conference me in," he said.

My mother and I loaded ourselves into my car. There was a lot of street noise, so I pulled into a convenience store parking lot, hoping for a quieter spot. Before we had a chance to park, my phone screen lit up again. I looked at the dilapidated fence with peeling wood and the Dumpster on the side of the convenience store—not the desired ambience for this potentially epic moment.

I answered and asked Tracey to wait while I conferenced Bill in.

As we waited for Bill to pick up, I focused my ears on the RMI line, trying to discern if Tracey was alone.

"I'm here," Bill said. He sounded wired.

"And your mother's on the line, too?" Tracey asked. Her voice came through clear. No background noise at RMI. Just Tracey. My shoulders threatened to collapse forward. I checked that the car was in park. My hands were shaking again.

"I'm here, Tracey," my mother said. I put the phone on speaker and placed it on the seat next to my mother's thigh. I wanted to hold her hand but also keep mine free in case I felt the need to leap from the car.

"We have the results," Tracey said. "I made sure we looked at yours first."

And? I thought.

"The HCG numbers are high," she said. My mind raced to compute this information. I heard some commotion on one end of the line and wondered if the crew on Bill's set had found him.

"Sara, Bill, Kristine," Tracey said above the voices, *"you're pregnant!"*

I screamed. My mother waved her arms above her head, saying, "Oh! Oh!" Bill yelled something I couldn't even make out through the phone. We heard Rachel's and Carli's voices from the lab.

"The whole team is here," Tracey said. "I won the bet to make the call, though. Dr. Colaum is in with a patient but sends her highest congratulations."

Tracey told us the numbers. "On Friday you were a twenty-eight point two. As of today's test, you're sixty-nine point one. As you know, anything above a five is positive for pregnancy, and the doubling shows strong advancement." I also knew the numbers indicated a single pregnancy, versus twins. "Kristine, congratulations—you and Sara and Bill are really, truly pregnant."

We hung up with RMI and I jumped out of the car. My mother followed me out and we spun around in the parking lot. My mother let out a loud whoop, opened her mouth like the picture of the ostrich, and jumped up into the air. Bill cheered through the phone. My mother stopped suddenly to steady herself against the splintery fence.

"Maybe I shouldn't be jumping," she said.

"Right, because we're—you're—pregnant!" I squealed, running to her and kissing her stomach through the front of her shirt.

My mother confessed later, much later, that she'd gone to CVS Pharmacy that morning and taken a home pregnancy test. Bill and I were shocked. Rachel reminded us every cycle that home pregnancy tests were forbidden, and we'd come to regard the rule as inviolable.

"I had a feeling," my mother said, "and I just had to know."

Chapter 9

The first person I told we were pregnant was a mentor of mine, another therapist. My mother had flown back to D.C. for a brief visit with my father before our next prenatal appointment. In her absence, my old pregnancy fears surfaced like hungry sharks.

Dr. Richards specialized in trauma recovery and was known for giving unorthodox assignments to his clients. When I described my anxiety, he asked what I would do if I was not afraid of losing the baby.

"I would read to the baby," I said. "I would read or sing to the baby every day."

"What would you read?" he asked.

"*Harry Potter,*" I said, surprising myself by having so ready an answer.

"Then do it," he said.

I wrapped my arms around one of the mohair pillows on Dr. Richards's couch.

"I expected you to say to wait until the second trimester, to hold off on that kind of thing until we see how this progresses," I said.

"For what reason?" he asked.

"If I start reading to this baby, I will get attached. I will already fall in love."

"As if you could prevent that," he said, his eyes boring into me over his wire-framed glasses. "As if you aren't already."

He was right.

I drove straight home and, without removing my sweater or putting down my bag, walked to the bookshelves in my bedroom. I squatted in front of the bottom shelf, where I had been amassing a children's-book collection for the past seven years. I located the first Harry Potter book, *The Philosopher's Stone.* The price sticker from Waitrose Bookstore in London, where I'd purchased it, was still stuck to the cover. I pulled the book from the shelf, dusted it off, and put it under my arm.

The day was warm and the June breeze was gentle. I walked toward Hamlin Park and made my way to the center, where three small pear trees stood in a row. It was the same spot where I used to lie in the sunlight during our early IVF cycles. I sat down beneath the center tree, resting my back against its trunk, and dialed my parents' number in Virginia.

"Sweetie!" my mother said. She sounded tired but excited. My father had told me she'd hardly been out of bed since she'd arrived home.

"It's a good thing she's shipping back out to you next week," he'd said. "She says you are much better at giving her the injections, and all she wants to talk about is the pregnancy."

"I'm calling to see if you and the baby would like to start having story time," I told my mother.

"Well," she replied, "I don't know for sure about the baby yet, but I am always up for a story. Maybe it will take my mind off the nausea."

I hated thinking of my mother being nauseous and knowing I couldn't take away her symptoms. I wished there were some way for her to carry the baby but not have to do any of the hard parts. In certain moments, I worried that the sacrifices she was making were too much, but she affirmed over and over again that she was giving this gift willingly, and I could feel the veracity of her words.

"I never forget what I'm doing this for," my mother said during our early calls. "I feel so honored. I just think about the vision."

I did my best to focus on it, too—on my mother's vision of fulfilling her calling, and Bill's and my vision of having children. We wanted this baby to come out alive and thriving in the world like we wanted to keep living.

"Have you picked out a book?"

"*Harry Potter,*" I said, holding the book up to the phone as if she could see it.

My mother and I had read *Harry Potter* several times already, but this series about magic and a world in which natural laws are not limited to those we know in regular human life felt right for the moment, and reading it to our baby was the purest form of love I could offer. When I read, my fear and past experiences were blotted out and I could establish a direct connection to my child.

"Hogwarts!" my mother said. "The baby approves."

"Okay, then, baby," I said, the word "baby" making my heart thump like a kettle drum, "here we go."

"I'm putting the phone on speaker," my mother said. "We're snuggled on the yellow couch in my auxiliary bedroom." I took a moment to imagine them there. My parents had converted my childhood room to an annex of their master bedroom, with a comfortable sleeper sofa, built-in bookshelves, and a window seat. It had become a reading room. And on one shelf, also near the bottom of the bookcase, she'd stacked the family library of childhood favorites: *Pippi Longstocking, A Wrinkle in Time, A Little Princess, The Secret Garden*—ready, my mother said, for when her grandbabies came to stay.

I touched the screen of my phone for a minute. Then I tucked it back against my ear and opened *Harry Potter* with both hands.

"Chapter one," I said, and stopped. My mouth was open, my lips already poised to read the first sentence.

"What is it?" my mother asked.

"It's the title of the chapter," I said. "It's been so long since I read this, I'd forgotten . . . "

"I don't remember either," my mother said. "What is it called?"

"Chapter one," I said, feeling like white water dropping over a cliff, "is called 'The Boy Who Lived.'"

My mother flew back to Chicago on Monday. I picked her up from the airport and we had lunch at Jerry's again, before heading back to the house. When Bill came home from work, he found us in bed in the guest room. I was curled around my mother's body in a half moon, both our hands resting on her belly. *Harry Potter* lay on the duvet next to us, and I was reciting some Shel Allenstein poems I still knew from memory.

Bill looked at my mother, whose skin was slightly green-tinged and pale. Her eyes were half closed and her body folded in on itself as if she were the one gestating in the womb. "Whoa," he said. "This is real."

After dinner, before my mother headed back to the guest room for the night, I handed her a bag of ice for her backside and drew a syringe of progesterone for her injection.

"How long do I take these?" my mother asked.

"I took them for the first nine weeks. I think Dr. Colaum keeps the shots going for most of the first trimester," I said, remembering the soreness and occasional radiating pain. My mother turned her back to me and I felt around for the coldest spot.

"I wish I could take them for you," I said.

"You've taken enough," my mother said. "Besides, the way you do it, I hardly feel it."

We had planned on seeing Dr. Allen for the pregnancy, but my sister had convinced us to meet with Maternal-Fetal Medicine (MFM), the high-risk specialist team at Northwestern, where she worked.

"Prentice is one of the top maternity hospitals in the country," she told us. "It's ten minutes from your house. Please have your baby there."

Prentice, the women's hospital of Northwestern Memorial Hospital, was built to handle the delivery of 13,600 babies a year. The building took up the good part of a city block and looked more like a museum of contemporary art than like a hospital. The delivery rooms contained sleeper sofas for partners and flat-screen TVs with iPod docking stations. Friends reported that delivering at Prentice was like giving birth at a luxury hotel. As long as we would be somewhere different than where we had the twins, I was happy to go where my sister recommended.

"I just want to have a baby," I said. "If you think Prentice is best, we'll go to Prentice."

As much as I understood that MFM would be an excellent choice for us, I still bristled at the term "high-risk." We'd been high-risk in our first pregnancy, and that had not gone well. I kept thinking of Dr. Baker's always worried face, the label of "incompetent cervix," the failed cerclage. I'd liked that Dr. Allen's practice in Evanston handled the whole spectrum of pregnancies, so we would be just another member of the family, as we were at Dr. Colaum's practice. Whatever I felt, though, I understood the best care for our pregnancy was more important, so I called Northwestern for a consultation.

A receptionist put me through to a physician's assistant, who offered us the next available appointment with a Dr. Gerber that coming Friday.

"Can you be here at eleven?" she asked.

I told her we could.

Maternal-Fetal Medicine was on the fourteenth floor of Galter Pavilion, two blocks from Prentice Hospital. The waiting room was small and institutional. A seasoned-looking receptionist with lined skin and a gravelly voice sat behind a long counter. She introduced herself as Francis.

My mother and I took seats in two vacant chairs. A very pregnant woman sat across from us, reading *Fit Pregnancy* magazine.

"Kristine," Francis called out. We met her at the front, and she walked us down a short hallway into an examination room.

Dr. Gerber appeared several minutes later. She looked like my sister: fair skin, freckles, and blue eyes that looked cut from tourmaline stone. She took a seat across a table from us and spoke rapidly, as if we were a couple of old girlfriends who had dropped by for tea.

"So lovely you know Brooke," she said, mentioning my sister's colleague who had called on our behalf. "We adore her. Haven't met your sister yet—she's in sports medicine; is that right?"

My mother and I nodded, but Dr. Gerber had already moved on. "So, tell me how you came to pursue this unusual surrogacy." She gestured for my mother to begin.

The mood shifted in the room. Dr. Gerber pulled back in her chair and studied us through slightly squinted eyes as my mother spoke. I started to worry that she thought we'd taken an unconscionable risk. I was hoping she would embrace our pregnancy, as Dr. Colaum and Dr. Allen had. This consultation was not a guaranteed entrée into the practice, however—it was more of an interview.

"How far along are you?" she asked.

"Almost eight weeks," my mother said.

Dr. Gerber placed her hands in front of her on the table. She was quiet for a moment. She drummed her fingers on the metal desk for a moment, considering.

"We'll take you," she said reinstating eye contact. "We can work with a doctor in D.C. or Virginia for the first part of the pregnancy. But we'd want you here full-time by week sixteen. Preeclampsia can show up around then, and we'd need to have you local if we need to prescribe hospital visits or bed rest."

When we returned to the waiting room while Dr. Gerber filled out some paperwork, my mother and I analyzed the meeting. "She seemed on the fence for a minute, and then warmed up."

"I'm just grateful she took us," I said. I liked the quietness and order of the waiting room, Dr. Gerber's succinctness, and the coolness of the hallways, which gave the impression of an elite operation.

"I think we're in with the A-team," I said.

We attended our final appointment with Dr. Colaum the following Wednesday. The baby was growing. It now had a clear heartbeat, a little head, and a body that curved along its spine like a freshwater shrimp.

When Dr. Colaum said that my mother could stop the progesterone shots, my mom let out a "Hallelujah!"

We celebrated the end of the injections that evening with non-alcoholic beer and lasagna.

As I packed her bag and printed out her boarding pass, I asked, "Are you sure you feel okay to fly?" Aside from her doctor's visits and the short walks we took together in the afternoons, my mother spent the majority of her time in bed, feeling nauseous and tired.

"Dr. Colaum wasn't kidding about the fatigue," she said. "I feel like I'm being held under a truck, and this baby isn't even an inch big yet."

"I don't want to be away from you and the baby," I said. When we were together, I felt almost pregnant myself. I felt the connection when we were apart also, but it wasn't the same. I knew the baby would be fine. In fact—although I didn't feel ready yet to say this out loud to anyone—part of me thought the baby was better off snuggled inside my mother, where the paralyzing anxiety I'd experienced in my last pregnancy couldn't touch him or her.

Still, physical distance was hard. Being day-to-day in the same space, my mother was so available, I truly felt as if we were doing the pregnancy together as one, the way she said she'd envisioned it on her rock.

"We'll see you in D.C. for the twelve-week appointment," my mother said. "We'll have story time every day. I'm basically just babysitting."

She wasn't, of course, but the idea lifted me and sparked an image of a time, maybe a year or two in the future, when Bill and I might want to go away for a day or two and could take our baby to stay with my mother. What we were doing now didn't feel so different. I liked it.

"I just get to start nine months earlier than other grandparents," my mother said.

I put my hand on her belly then, feeling better and wondering how soon it would visibly swell.

Before she left for the airport, I bent down to my mother's stomach and placed my hands on her right and left sides. "I'll see you in ten days, baby," I said, pressing my face into her sweater and kissing the place where I imagined the baby was curled into a ball.

At eleven weeks, according to BabyCenter, our baby was the size of a fig and about one and a half inches long. In the ten days since I'd seen my mother, I had called to read *Harry Potter* every afternoon. Sometimes I would call from my office after my sessions were over for the day. Most often, I would call from the guest room where my mother stayed during her visits. When my schedule was hectic, I would pack the book into my bag, protecting it with a section of silk fabric I'd found at a store in Glastonbury years before. When the weather was agreeable, I'd take the book with me on a walk and read over the phone as I wove through the streets.

My mother would always tell me where she was in the house, along with any new foods she'd discovered that did not make her feel sick, and she'd report on any new pregnancy symptoms (though they were mostly always the same ones: nausea and exhaustion).

When we came to the end of chapter one in *Harry Potter*, I cried.

"J. K. Rowling is deep," I said.

Our twelve-week ultrasound was scheduled in the middle of July in D.C., with a Dr. Aiken, an OB-GYN in Georgetown.

My father picked me up at Reagan Airport.

"I don't know how your mother seemed when she was with you in Chicago two weeks ago," he said, "but she is a sad sack right now."

The car swerved as my father changed lanes two or three times. I was grateful she was not in the car for this ride. Even I was nauseous.

"She sounds good when we talk on the phone," I said. She hadn't mentioned anything more than the nausea and the fatigue, which Dr. Colaum told us would subside in the second trimester. I felt sick at the idea that something more serious could be going on, with her or the baby. My stomach lurched as my father took a sharp turn to the exit ramp off the highway.

"Have her symptoms worsened?" I asked, though part of me didn't want to know.

"No," my father said. "She's just wiped out. She goes out in the morning with her walking group and then gets back into bed or lies on the couch for the rest of the day. She hasn't done a thing in the house since she got pregnant, not even sitting up to have a proper dinner."

I'd never experienced my father as a complainer, and I couldn't tell if he was worried or just needed to vent. I felt pained that the surrogacy was disruptive for him.

"That sounds hard, Dad," I said. "What can I do?"

My father's face cleared. His shoulders dropped a few centimeters. "I just want to make sure she's okay," he said. I continued to study his face. He wasn't upset about needing to be the one to wash the kitchen floor; he was worried about my mother's health.

"When you go to the doctor tomorrow, make sure she tells them honestly about the severity of her symptoms," he said.

My trepidation joined guilt as I walked toward the house. The temperature had climbed into the upper nineties, with a humidity that hit like a wall the moment you stepped outside.

My father walked ahead of me with my suitcase and opened the door with his key. A blast of cold air hit my face as we walked inside. He rushed me in and shut the door quickly with his body, as if the heat were an intruder he was trying to keep out. I removed my shoes at the top of the entryway stairs and in bare feet walked down the hall toward the annex where my mother now spent most of her time.

I found her asleep on the yellow couch. She lay on her side, her legs curled up into her stomach. A small TV was tuned to some interior-design show, with the volume turned down low. The room had been recarpeted in a soft blue since the last time I'd been home; the walls and built-in bookcases were painted white. My mother's vision board with the ostrich hung on the wall. I walked over to look at it. There was the image of the healthy woman exercising and the words WOMEN AFTER MENOPAUSE HAVE A CHOICE. There was the young woman with her new baby, next to which she'd written, "Sara's baby," and the ostrich's quivering mouth stretched open into a giant yawp of excitement.

"You're here," she said, stirring. She opened her eyes in a squint. "I wanted to come to the airport, but"—she smiled and swept her hands across the couch—"I needed another nap."

"Dad says you've been feeling awful," I said.

"Your father isn't used to seeing me so inactive. And I think it scared him. I haven't been taking care of the laundry and all the things I normally do. I've been going to bed for the night at seven," she explained. "But I am fine. Honey," she said, shimmying her shoulders back and forth until I smiled. If she was making jokes, things couldn't be so bad.

"I'm fine," she repeated. I scanned her body. Her eyes were clear and her cheeks were their normal-looking shade of peach. I lowered myself to the floor next to the couch.

"Dad is a trouper for putting up with this," I said. "I want to help while I'm here. Put me to work."

"What I'd love," my mother said, "is for you to take me shopping for some maternity clothes."

"It's not as noticeable when I'm lying down," she said stretching the black cotton of her shirt over her belly, "but I think I'm beginning to show." I looked at her belly from every angle from my position on the floor. I couldn't see a bump. My mother let me search for a minute and then began to hoist herself to sitting.

"Don't get up, Mom," I said. "I can see later."

"I'm getting up so we can go shopping," she said. I helped her to her feet and agreed, with a thrill, that I could indeed see just the tiniest convex curve forming in her abdomen.

"*Wow,*" I said, continuing to stare.

"You can look while we shop," she said. "I am designating you my official maternity stylist."

We found a small wardrobe at a boutique maternity store in Old Town and rounded out the collection at Old Navy and the Gap. When we returned home, we laid out my mother's new clothes on the yellow couch: one pair dark denim jeans; two thick wool sweaters ("for when I come to Chicago," she said); two cotton V-neck tops, one purple, one black; three extra-large bras; and my favorite purchase of the day: a soft, bathrobe-style fleece jacket in black.

She patted the elastic top of her new maternity jeans. "What relief."

I remembered the moment I'd surrendered my regular jeans in my pregnancy with the twins. The soft fabric extension had both contained me and allowed my belly to expand. I was grateful that that pregnancy gave me a way to identify with my mother now. She made an exaggerated *ah* sound, and I laughed at her delight. She put her hand to the waist a few more times, marveling at the advancement.

"When I was pregnant before, the style was to show nothing," she said. "We basically wore muumuus."

My father came into the room to investigate the hilarity. My mother modeled her new jeans for him, showing off the low waist and expandable cotton attachment. "Let's go out to dinner," she said.

"Out to dinner!" my father said. "You haven't made it to the dinner table in our house in two weeks."

"I'm feeling rejuvenated," she said.

"It's just because Sara's here," he said, pushing his shoulder into mine. He looked relieved to see a familiar scene, my mother and me shopping and conspiring about clothes.

I felt a giddiness rising in my body. I searched to remember a time when I had felt so happy. That night in the car, before we went into the restaurant, I hugged my parents over the back of their seats, pressing my head into the space between theirs, the way I had a vague memory of having done when I was very little, recalling the way my dad would say, like a radio announcer, "Family huuuug."

"I'll drive you right home if you feel nauseous," I said when we stepped inside the foyer of the restaurant. We'd chosen a place less than a mile from the house, an upscale bar and grill that specialized in seafood. But my mother said she felt great. She ate two jumbo crab cakes and an ear of corn. "Maybe I'm turning a corner."

The next day, my mother and I drove to Georgetown for the first-trimester genetic screening test and consultation with Dr. Aiken, an experience that left much to be desired. The offices were cluttered and spilling over with patients. The waiting rooms reminded me of Dr. Bizan's office from many years before. The office had no record of our files' being sent from Dr. Colaum, even though I had sent them via registered mail and had received a confirmation notice.

The genetic-screening blood test took so long that we nearly missed our doctor's appointment. The staff began closing up the office at ten minutes to five, and the hallways and rooms looked deserted by the time Dr. Aiken came into our exam room at 5:01 PM. He was a pasty-looking man and wore a sour expression.

"I'm not sure what I can even do for you," he said after we explained we'd be there for just two appointments.

"Whatever you do for the twelve- and sixteen-week prenatal appointments is great," I suggested.

"Well, we really don't do anything," he said. "As long as there aren't any problems."

I prodded my mother to tell Dr. Aiken about the fatigue.

"I feel extremely tired," my mother said. "Exhausted, actually. And nauseous."

"You're sixty years old and pregnant," he said in a monotone. "How did you expect you would feel?"

With that statement, Dr. Aiken left the room.

I waited until I heard the *click* of the door before speaking.

"That was weird," I said.

"Did we offend him in some way?" my mother asked.

I couldn't imagine how.

I offered to contact another doctor for the sixteen-week appointment, but my mother said she was content to see Dr. Aiken again. "It's just one more meeting."

It turned out to be two.

I returned to D.C. for our sixteen-week appointment. In the three weeks since I'd seen her, my mother's belly had swelled to a distinguishable bump.

"The second trimester is great!" my mother said.

"She's still really tired," my father said.

"I think he's anxious about me leaving for four months," my mother said when he left the room. My father said he'd be fine, and truthfully, he was so immersed in the mediation techniques he'd learned from the conference held earlier in Chicago that we knew he would be engaged and entertained. But I also knew he'd miss my mother.

"I wouldn't want to be away from Bill for that long," I said. "Let's invite him to come to the appointment."

The day was sweltering. If July was a wet mop of heat, August felt like someone was holding a blowtorch over the city. When we arrived at Dr. Aiken's, his nurse-practitioner, Aimee, told us he'd been called away to deliver a baby. She gave us the most thorough prenatal checkup we'd had to date and was able to confirm that we were in the lowest-risk group for genetic abnormalities. Because we'd used my egg and I was under thirty-five, no further genetic testing was needed.

"I'm so impressed," Aimee said as she weighed my mother on the digital scale. "You've only gained three pounds."

At the end of the appointment, she let us listen to the baby's heartbeat. Afterward, my parents and I went to lunch and walked around the cool floors of the Georgetown Park Mall until we got a call from the office that Dr. Aiken had returned and could sign off on the sixteen-week exam.

"I'm going to try and warm him up," my father said while we waited in the exam room. He prided himself on being able to get a laugh out of anyone with a rough exterior, and was usually successful. But Dr. Aiken retained his dour demeanor and had nothing additional to request of us. He asked if we had any questions, and my father cleared his throat. I braced myself for some kind of antic. My mother turned her head to the side so she wouldn't catch my eye.

"What advice do you give to the spouse of a sixty-year-old pregnant person? You must see this kind of thing all the time."

"I do not," Dr. Aiken said, without cracking a smile.

We passed the seventeen-week mark. Then eighteen. As we neared the twenty-week mark, I gave myself a kind of mental scan. After the twins died, Dr. Baker had told me to plan for the twenty-week mark of my next pregnancy to be challenging.

"When a woman loses a baby late-term," she'd said, "the old emotions of that loss, along with heightened anxiety and grief, can surface—similar to what people experience on the anniversary of a death."

I wondered, as the day approached, if this would be true in a surrogate pregnancy. I didn't notice increased anxiety as we rounded the twenty-week mark, nor did I feel a decrease in the levels of anxiety that I'd now accepted was part of the pregnancy experience for me. From the beginning, fear would strike erratically. I would feel peaceful for several days and then find myself being pounded by uncomfortable chest flutters, or a fit of spontaneous crying that would last for a few minutes and leave me feeling vulnerable and tense.

Nighttime was the worst. One night, when I was sleeping in the basement during the sixteen-week visit, I heard the floorboards squeaking upstairs. My mother had gotten up to use the bathroom, but by the time I'd raced up the stairs I was convinced I'd find the lights blaring and see bedclothes soaked in blood.

I charged toward the bedroom and almost bowled into her in the hallway. She jumped in her cotton pajamas and put her hand to her chest.

"Honey!" she said. "I am just going to the bathroom. You have *got* to calm down."

Back in Chicago, I thought about what I could do to relax. I began doing relaxation meditations morning and night. A colleague, Angela, who'd gone through coaching training with me, told me about a woman she worked with who'd given birth to a stillborn baby at full term. "During her second pregnancy, she bought a heart rate monitor so she could listen to the baby at home," Angela said. "And she created a mantra: *It's different this time. It's not the same as the first one.* She repeated it many times a day."

I wished the mantra would work for me, but my mind did not feel calmed by "different." "Different" didn't equal live birth. Different left too much space for possibilities.

I invented my own mantra: *The anxiety I'm feeling has nothing to do with this pregnancy. It has nothing to do with this baby.* I tried it for a few days, and the words sung like truth in my bones.

The following week, my mother unknowingly provided a key to allow me to lighten up. We'd begun book two of *Harry Potter,* and when I began a new chapter, she yelled for me to stop.

I had no sense of what was happening on the other end of the phone. I stopped and waited, the seconds counting themselves one by one in my head.

"Now read the next line!" she said. I remained perplexed but assumed she and the baby were okay if she wanted me to continue.

I resumed where we'd left off, speaking slowly.

"He kicked!" my mother said. "The baby kicked! He's kicking at the sound of your voice!" I attempted to continue, but I couldn't concentrate. I'd worried secretly sometimes, mostly at night, that the baby wouldn't know me, that I would be a stranger after nine months inside someone else. And yet here he was, ostensibly recognizing, or at least responding to, me—my voice.

"Has the baby kicked other times?" I asked.

"Nothing like this," my mother said.

My mother referred to the baby consistently as "he." She said she meant it as the universal pronoun, to avoid saying having to say "he-she" or, worse, the impersonal "it" for nine months. Bill was convinced we were having a girl and used "she" if ever a pronoun was needed. I'd intended to think of some kind of gender-neutral nickname, but since early on—I think ever since we'd started reading *Harry Potter* and "The Boy Who Lived"—I'd had the feeling the baby was a boy.

The next day when I called, my mother placed her iPhone on her stomach while I read; she thought the baby would hear better that way. This time, the baby kicked the phone so hard that it bounced off her stomach and onto the floor. I heard a *thunk* and then my mother's laughter.

The following Monday, my mother sent me a text to call her right away. Again, nothing emergent was happening with the pregnancy.

"You will never believe what I found," she said when I reached her. In one of her TV marathons, she'd come across a show called *Pregnant at 70.*

"It's one of those low-budget reality shows, like *A Baby Story,*" she told me. "And, okay, most of the women are in their fifties or sixties, but one woman from India was over seventy—and these are all people who are planning to parent. They're not surrogates! I've watched every episode I can find. I even made your father watch with me. Can you imagine—seventy and pregnant!" she said. "I feel so young!"

Although Dr. Gerber had told my mother to move to Chicago by week twenty, we negotiated another plan as a family in October. My mother would fly out for the twenty-week ultrasound, and if all was well with the pregnancy, she would go home for one more month and move to Chicago near the first of November. My father was happier to have another month with her, and I think we all felt relieved to have thirty more days of our regular routine before we moved in together for the final trimester.

The night before my mother flew to Chicago for the twenty-week appointment, I received a package from my friend Sandy in Santa Fe.

Out of a large packing box filled with tissue paper, I pulled a box hand-painted with swirls of copper and gold. Inside were two pacifiers, one pink and one blue. An accompanying note explained that if we were planning to find out the baby's sex, we could bring the box to our twenty-week ultrasound and have the technician put the pacifier that corresponded to the baby's gender in the box. I liked the idea, and Bill and my mother thought it would be fun to bring props.

We arrived at the ultrasound appointment with the pacifier box and in a state of high anticipation, eager to find out the exciting detail about who was inside.

We gave the box to Kenisha, the technician, and asked if she would hand the corresponding-colored pacifier to Bill once she confirmed the gender. Kenisha, a new mother herself, seemed amused by the request.

I'd forgotten how many images and measurements the doctors required. As Kenisha swiped and clicked her mouse around the screen, my excitement gave way to trepidation. I forgot about finding out the baby's gender and began to pray that our baby was simply alive and developing normally. Bill's hand clenched mine as we looked at the screen.

My mother lay turned toward the screen. I could not see her face or know what she was thinking. Ten minutes became twenty, and Kenisha was still quiet, angling the roller along the baby's image from seemingly infinite angles. Bill's hand began to sweat. The moisture ran onto mine. I remembered the same sensation the day of our wedding, when Bill's hands had grown slick against mine in the chapel in Scotland where we'd said our vows. I'd saved the gloves I wore; the leather bore a salt line from his hands.

Bill broke the silence and asked Kenisha directly if the baby was okay.

"I've been told I look very serious when I take the images," she apologized. "The baby is just fine. Would you like to know the sex now?"

Bill fell back into his chair; relief pooled at my feet. My mother turned from the ultrasound screen and looked at our shaken faces.

"I so wanted this to be easier on you, since I'm carrying the baby," my mother said.

"It is, Mom," Bill said.

"Yeah," I said. "Think what shape we'd be in if you weren't."

Kenisha mimed a drum roll on the side of the machine and then held both pacifiers, pushing one and then the other out in front of Bill several times. She extended the pink one almost to the tip of his hands and then switched fast, delivering the blue pacifier into his upturned palms and saying, "You're having a boy!"

Bill and I shrieked in the exact way I imagine we would have if we had heard we were having a girl. Our baby was okay, and we now knew it was a he. Bill went into the hallway to call our brother-in-law and his business partner while my mother changed. She did not get up right away. She lingered at the screen for another moment, looking at the center, where Kenisha had saved a length-wise image of the baby.

"A boy," my mother said, marveling. "I kept saying 'he,' but part of me thought the baby would be a girl, since that's what I've always had."

"You finally get to carry a boy—as a grandmother," I said.

My mother continued to stare at the screen, a look of amazement on her face.

We walked together to our next appointment, where we were scheduled to meet Dr. Julien. MFM aimed to have each patient meet all the doctors in the practice by the end of the pregnancy. If the action had been even remotely appropriate, I would have done cart-wheels down the hall.

Dr. Julien was a sturdy woman with a good sense of humor who informed us she was four months pregnant herself.

"But I look seven," she said, and made a joke about her size.

She reconfirmed that everything was progressing ideally with our pregnancy and that she had embarrassingly few things to check at the appointment.

"I *will* check your blood pressure," she said, strapping the black cuff to my mother's upper arm and squeezing the rubber pump at one end.

"Incredible," Dr. Julien said. "You have lower blood pressure than most nonpregnant thirty-year-olds."

I felt like early snow melting onto a warm sidewalk. Muscles I didn't know I'd been tensing relaxed. For the second time that morning, my body flowed with relief. For the moment, everything was fine. My mother could return to D.C. for a month. And in a period of weeks, we would enter the place where we were banking on my mother's body's being able to do what mine had not: carry our child to term.

More emotions would come. For now, though, I felt only sincere, depthless gratitude and the greatest hope I had known since we became pregnant with our twins.

It was the gratitude that ameliorated the separation pangs I felt at the thought of so much distance between my mother and the baby for the next month. My bond with our child felt as strong to me as it ever had with the twins. Having seen the baby so vital on the ultrasound screen allowed me to trust more. I also knew it was the last time we'd be apart. When my mother returned to Chicago at the end of October, the three of us, along with Bill, would be together until the birth.

During what we came to call our bonus month, my parents rented a house on the Outer Banks of North Carolina and spent a week at the ocean with friends. Bill and I went to Arizona with his father and stepmother, to a resort built into a red desert mountain.

"It's your babymoon," they said, waving to us as they dropped us at a private cabin on the property and told us they'd see us at dinner, if we wanted to come.

"We want you to fully enjoy your last trip as a couple before the baby arrives."

We swam in the pool, I went to yoga, we hiked in the mountains surrounding the resort. The place was holistic and soothing. Still, I found it difficult to let go for more than a few minutes. My attention gravitated constantly to my mother and the baby. I felt a pull to them, tethered by an energetic umbilical cord. It was often only after I called for story time, my feet dangling in the tepid water of the pool, having heard my mother's voice and a report on the baby's kicks, that I would allow myself to jump into the water or take a nap or make love with Bill in our cool desert cave of a room.

By the end of the week, I felt as if we were (sort of) like any other couple expecting a baby: excited, hopeful, and certain that life as we'd known it was about to change.

"I think I really did relax, finally," I told Bill in the car on the way to the airport.

"Good," he said. "Because we need to get ready. Your mother moves in on Sunday."

My father was attending a conference in Boston, so my mother's friend Lissa, the one *responsible* for this whole thing, as my father liked to say, drove with my mother from D.C. to Chicago.

They broke the trip into two days, stopping to see my cousin in Hudson, Ohio. When my mother revealed the reason for her trip, sweeping aside her coat to reveal her basketball-shaped baby bump, my cousin and her husband were stunned and thought she was pulling some kind of prank. My mother said she enjoyed the looks of shock on their faces as the fact that she was actually carrying their second cousin inside her that very moment took form in their minds.

"It kind of brought me back to the beginning of the vision," she told me later. "I've grown so used to the idea, I'd kind of forgotten there was anything unusual about what we're doing."

My mother and Lissa estimated they would arrive at about five o'clock in the evening on October 30. It had rained briefly that afternoon, and our front walk was wet and matted with red, yellow, and orange leaves. Bill made a fire of birch branches and twigs, and the air smelled of chicory and spices.

Any apprehension I'd had about living with my mother for four months had dissipated, but I felt a twinge of nervousness as I tidied the last of the pillow shams and towels in the guest room and straightened the stack of books and movies I'd collected to entertain her during her stay.

"I would lose it within a week of living with my mother," a friend of mine had said as I was preparing for my mother to come. "Aren't you worried you'll drive each other crazy?"

I thought about how I would have thought the same thing five years earlier, how the entire situation would have seemed a ludicrous impossibility. I remembered Bill's and my forty-eight-hour rule: no visits longer than two days. When I thought about my mother's arrival now, however, the overwhelming emotion I felt was joy. Of course, my mother and my baby were inseparable at this point. I ran the vacuum cleaner one last time over the rug in what would now be my mother's bedroom and thought about the conference we'd attended in Albuquerque and the afternoons we'd spent making art and reading sections of books together over the past three years. I would have been excited to have her come live with us for four months even if she weren't carrying our child.

My friend Jane seemed to find this fact as incredible as the surrogacy. "When I met you, you never spoke about your mother at all," she said one afternoon when she'd stopped by for tea. "If anyone asked about her, your face clouded over and looked pained."

"For a time, I felt separate in the relationship," I said. "I felt lost."

"It means there's hope for all of us," said Jane.

The doorbell rang. I ran to the door. I flexed my arms preparing to help carry the "half a carload of stuff" my mother had warned me she'd felt compelled to bring. My mother and Lissa stood on the doorstep, wearing turquoise T-shirts and matching teal-sequined gangsta hats that looked like they belonged in a rap video. They both stretched the fronts of their shirts down so I could read the words they'd bedazzled on themselves in glitter paint. My mother's read: I AM CARRYING MY SON-IN-LAW'S BABY, and Lissa's read: IT WAS MY IDEA, with an arrow pointing toward my mother. They gave me a moment to read the messages and then doubled over, my mother holding her belly and Lissa slapping the side of my mother's arm with her hat.

"We needed some entertainment after all the hours on the road," Lissa said. They'd found the sequined hats outside of Gary, Indiana, Lissa continued, and the inspiration had just flowed from there. "We've been laughing for three hours."

Bill was amused by the shirts and began taking in armloads of my mother's things from the car.

"I'm so embarrassed," my mother called to Bill as he returned from a seventh trip. He'd brought in a TV table, a quilting frame, a photo scanner, grocery bags of DVDs, and a large duffel bag full of books.

"I brought lots of projects to keep me busy during the day," my mother whispered to me as Bill took everything up the stairs to the guest room. He's probably afraid I'm never leaving."

"You're carrying our child, for god's sake," Bill said, when we'd emptied the last items from the trunk and my mother had apologized again. "You can take over the whole house, as far as I'm concerned."

Lissa flew back to D.C. the next afternoon. Bill, my mother, and I handed out candy to trick-or-treaters in the neighborhood. Bill made chicken soup from his own stock; the smell of garlic, carrots, and leeks hung in the air. I carried the bowls to the dining room table, and we sat for a moment, waiting for the soup to cool.

"This baby is so lucky to be coming into a home where he gets to eat like this every day," my mother said.

"Cheers," Bill said, holding up his glass. As of that week, we were now farther along in a pregnancy than we had ever been before. And each day that passed brought us a day closer to this baby's actually being born.

Our twenty-three-week appointment was uneventful. We met Dr. Grobman this time. He was the youngest member of the practice and had full pink cheeks that reminded me of a cherub's in a Renaissance painting. He asked if my mother had moved to Chicago yet, and we nodded yes, grateful that he did not ask the precise date of her arrival.

My mother's blood pressure was low to normal—about 100/70, the place it hovered for most of the pregnancy.

"You have good genes," Dr. Grobman said. My mother's belly had grown to the appropriate girth for five and a half months, and Dr. Grobman could think of nothing else to discuss.

"You feel good?" he asked.

"Just tired," my mother said. The fatigue had lifted significantly, yet many days she lay in bed, as she had done at her house in Virginia, rolling from side to side, logging hours of home-makeover shows on TV.

Before bed each night, I would walk down the hall to the guest room and read *Harry Potter*. We were halfway through the second book, and Harry, Ron, and Hermione were on the brink of discovering the entrance to the Chamber of Secrets.

I loved being close to the baby just before we went to sleep, lying in the dark with my mother for a moment, before returning down the hallway to my room, where Bill was reading in bed. I knew it was supposed to be strange that my mother was carrying our baby, but to me it felt natural now.

When we had first contemplated the surrogacy with my mother, Bill had said it would be the next-best thing to my carrying our child. In quiet moments at night, after I read *Harry Potter* to the baby, I would slip underneath the duvet back in my room and wrap my arms around Bill's chest. I did not feel as if this pregnancy constituted a "second-best." Maybe "different" did not have to mean "lesser," I thought. Or perhaps I was just trying to convince myself that what we were doing was as good as a traditional pregnancy because I was so tired of feeling broken and inadequate.

All I knew as I lay in the dark, listening to Bill's breathing, was that this pregnancy felt positive and hopeful and right. And I knew that the nightly ritual with my mother—story time, my face resting on the place where the baby kicked—felt like a real pregnancy and it felt holy.

At five months, we started seeing the OB every three weeks instead of every month. At six months we would increase our appointments to every two weeks. In a typical pregnancy, women see their doctor two to three times total before the thirty-week point. At five and a half months, we'd been to the OB eleven times, counting the early prenatal appointments with Dr. Colaum. The frequency was standard in high-risk pregnancies.

"The primary symptom we're still looking for is preeclampsia," Dr. Grobman informed us at the twenty-six-week appointment.

My mother asked if there was a particular reason they were so focused on preeclampsia. Her blood pressure that day was 100/70.

"Even though your blood pressure has remained low, the blood volume will close to double as the pregnancy continues," Dr. Grobman said. "At any moment, we may need to intervene with bed rest or closer monitoring in the hospital."

"I can't imagine what difference bed rest would make," my mother said that evening, helping herself to another of the crab cakes Bill had made for dinner. "I've been on self-imposed bed rest since week one."

We saw Dr. Julien again. She was now five months pregnant, and her round belly bumped up against my mother's as she leaned over the exam table to measure her stomach. She asked if my mother was seeing floaters or having interrupted vision, knife-edge-painful headaches, or any intense cramping—new signs of preeclampsia that could emerge at this stage.

"You look good," Dr. Julien said. "At our staff meeting this week, Dr. Gerber said she wished she had tolerated her pregnancy half as well as you have; she was on bed rest for months."

"Oh, I'm doing bed rest," my mother said. "Let me be clear: I had all of these grand intentions of exercising, making photo albums and a quilt for the baby, reading a book a week, but I haven't touched a thing. I am the definition of sloth."

"Yeah, Mom," I said. "You should really be out accomplishing more. Just think: All you do all day is sit around being pregnant at sixty years old. You're quite a slacker."

Dr. Julien laughed and handed my mother a pamphlet with some stretches she could do in case her low back started hurting.

"I'll just call in my live-in masseuse if that happens," she told Dr. Julien. "Do you know I have a live-in personal chef and a reflexologist in the house? These kids really know how to take care of me."

"When can I come over?" Dr. Julien asked.

A week before our six-month appointment, I went to see my mother in her room. I'd finished with client sessions for the day and had brought *Harry Potter* with me for an early story time. My mother was sitting blankly against the pillows on the bed. The skin on her face was blotchy, and she looked as if she had been crying. I dropped the book on the floor and approached the side of the bed. She scooted over a foot so I could sit down next to her on the duvet. The streak of light that had illuminated the sky a moment before was now gone, having dropped below the horizon line. The room was dark.

"I'm probably just hormonal," she said, wiping the corner of her eyes with her sleeve. "I feel fine physically. But I'm so tired and I feel so consumed with the physical experience of this pregnancy that I haven't done a single one of the projects I brought with me. I feel isolated and cut off."

"It makes sense that you're lonely, Mom. You're here away from Dad and your routine and your friends. What can we do?"

"Talking about it helps," she said. "I wondered if you had a colleague you could recommend, someone I could see for some coaching?"

I felt my neck tilt back and my eyes widen. I righted myself, doing my best to conceal my surprise. Even though my mother had come to one of my workshops and we now shared an interest in personal growth, she still, to my knowledge, remained skeptical of individual counseling. My heart brightened at the idea of her having special, dedicated support. I'd longed to suggest the idea before, especially in earlier years when she'd talked about her struggle to find a passion and a calling in her life.

I imagined the less I said at that moment, the better. I scribbled down the names of a few colleagues, both coaches and therapists I thought my mother would like. As we ate dinner that night, Bill joined in to brainstorm ways my mother could feel more supported. We planned a lunch date with her at least once during the week. I suggested we try for a joint artist date on Friday afternoons as well.

"I will come up with things to do on my own, too. I'm not really as infirmed as I've been acting," she confessed.

When I came in to say hello the next morning at eight, my mother had showered, packed a bag and a book, and put on a new purple maternity turtleneck and sweater. She'd already called one of the coach-therapists I'd recommended and had an appointment that morning.

"I already feel better for having something to do," she said.

That night, I walked upstairs after my last session, surprised to feel trepidation. I fought with my desire to ask about my mother's session with my colleague. I suddenly feared that she would discover that she regretted her decision to carry our baby, or need to spew about how awful it was living with Bill and me. The worry struck me as ironic. When I'd asked to go to therapy my senior year of high school, my mother had seemed cagey and upset. "Did they ask about the family?" she said when she picked me up from the first session. "Did they ask about me?" She'd seemed so concerned that a therapist would fault her for any problems I might have. At my next session, I had told the therapist that I'd decided not to continue.

Now, I resolved to respect my mother's privacy and committed to honoring any feelings she chose to discuss or keep private. I found her sitting in her usual spot on the bed, surrounded by little squares of fabric. She waved me over to the bed.

"I had a great day," she said. The heat had been turned up high all day, and the room was warm. My mother's cheeks were pink, and she looked happy. "It was so wonderful meeting Joelle," she said. "I think seeing her is really going to help me.

"Let me tell you about my session," she continued. I interrupted. "That's for you Mom, I don't want—"

She cut me off: "I'll just share what I want. Not all the things I said about you." I felt a tremor of insecurity and then, seeing the grin on her face, started to laugh. If she needed to vent about me, that would be okay. Our relationship could take venting.

"I actually told Joelle I love that I can share what I really feel with you and Bill," she said.

"I feel really able to be honest with you, too, Mom," I said. "If you do ever want to work through anything, I want to be available to do it together or in a session."

"Thanks, sweetie, but today the focus was on what I am going to do with myself for the next three months. This, for instance," she said, pointing at the squares of fabric on the bed, "is the material for the quilt I started for your cousin's baby, who, as you know, is coming up on nine months old. I have to finish this one so I can make one for this baby." She poked a finger at her belly.

"It's beautiful," I said, lifting a few squares of the woven black-and-white fabric that would make the border.

When my father called for his nightly check-in, my mother put the phone on speaker. "I'm doing my coaching homework!"

"What have you done to your mother?" my father asked me, laughing. Previously, my mother had expressed the same reservations about counseling to him as she had to me. My mother shrugged her

shoulders, as if she couldn't imagine what either of us was so surprised about, and began stitching the next square onto her quilt.

October became November.

We hadn't seen snow yet, but the sky was heavy with chalk-white
clouds the day we drove to Northwestern for our six-month appointment. Other than her belly's protruding a bit more, my mother felt
just as she had at the five-month appointment: steadily low blood
pressure, fatigue, and what she called laziness. Her only new symptom was that her feet had begun to swell in the evenings.

The levels of the parking garage at the Northwestern Medical
were marked by old music legends. We parked on level five, Tammy
Wynette; the sounds of "Slow Burning Fire" drifting through a
speaker in the ceiling kept us company in the elevator bay. We discovered that we could make our way to MFM without going outside
if we exited at the second floor and took the enclosed walkway into
the Galter Pavilion.

"This will be handy moving forward," my mother said, eyeing
the heavy sky.

"Yeah," I said. "This may be the best weather we have for the rest
of the pregnancy."

It began to snow during our appointment. From the windows in
the corridor that led into Maternal-Fetal Medicine, we could see fat
white flakes falling in spirals through the air.

Patricia, who went by Pat, was our nurse that morning. "We
all vie for who gets to be your nurse," she said, as she walked us
to our exam room and helped my mother onto the table. She took
a seat next to my mother and me. The MFM team never treated
me as an insignificant member of our party. They fawned over my
mother, which I loved, but they also asked me questions about how
I was feeling. When they talked about the baby, they addressed me

as the mother and my mother as the grandmother and patient. They seemed as delighted to support a team pregnancy as much as they did a traditional one. In their presence, I felt like a whole and complete mother-to-be.

My mother now looked unmistakably pregnant, her winter coat now pulled wide at the front zipper when it closed. My sheer gratitude that we were moving toward actually having a child was now mixed, on certain days, with a poisonous firing of thoughts that I didn't deserve this gift—that if I couldn't have a baby on my own, the "normal" way, I didn't deserve to have one at all. People earn a baby by carrying one; the sacrifices of pregnancy make you worthy. My mind offered up this thinking in a kind of serpent-like tongue.

My father had given me a CD a couple of years earlier of a talk by a progressive Catholic priest on the subject of worthiness. "To our human mind, we won't ever be worthy," the priest said. "When my mind tries to trump me with my inadequacies, I tell it, *You're right. To you I'll never measure up. Good thing you're not the authority here.*

"We are worthy because we are here," he went on to say. "If there is any human sin, it is in forgetting that we are already whole." I tried to imagine the idea of wholeness as a light inside me that I could hold on to when the darker thoughts came.

Pat's pager buzzed on the counter in front of her, and I jumped.

"The doctor will be right in," she said. My mother looked at me from the examination table, raising her eyebrows as if to ask if I was okay. I nodded and found myself smiling. She was wearing the black maternity pants we'd ordered, a Pucci-inspired top with swirls of purple and black, and a stylish new pair of black rubber boots. I couldn't remember ever having seen her look so confident or expressive. I remembered her saying once that she'd always been afraid of standing out. Now, I wondered if her opinion may have changed. If

I'd seen her on the street, I would have been intrigued. I would have thought she was fascinating.

"I need a urine sample," Pat said, interrupting my thoughts. She handed my mother a plastic cup. My mother knew the way to all the bathrooms on the floor. Once she was out of the room, Pat told me she could not believe how great my mother looked.

"From the back she doesn't even look pregnant," Pat said.

"I'm sure she'd love to hear that when she comes back," I said. "She says she's starting to feel huge."

When she returned, Pat showed my mother her weight, pointing out that most people would have gained fifteen to twenty pounds by this point and that she had gained only twelve. She checked my mother's blood pressure and placed a thick paper strip with color squares on it into the urine sample to check for proteins.

"Protein in the urine is another sign of preeclampsia," Pat said. "We start checking around the third trimester." She took a seat on the wheeled stool next to the exam table where my mother sat. When the test was ready, she recorded that my mother's urine was negative for offending proteins and made a note for the doctor to check on the swelling in my mother's feet.

Dr. Socol, the cohead of the practice, was our doctor that day. He was tall and lanky and reminded me of Alan Alda as Hawkeye on *M*A*S*H*. He affirmed that everything was progressing well. He said the swelling in my mother's feet was textbook and asked Pat about the results of my mother's glucose test. Pat sifted through the papers in my mother's file to discover that the test, usually given between weeks twenty and twenty-four, had been overlooked somehow. Dr. Socol looked concerned and called the lab to put in an order for my mother to take the test immediately.

We took seats in the waiting room outside reception, as instructed, to wait to be called for the glucose test. Conversations in the waiting room were infrequent, but when they did take place, they had the air of a veterans' meeting at a VA: We might not have known each other or ever see each other again, but we shared a common bond. These women had also been initiated by the Great Mother, and I guessed that pregnancy for many of them was like it was for me—less a scenic canoe ride than walking a tightrope every day—a cold thin steel wire hundreds of feet in the air, where life existed on one side and death on the other.

An attendant in a lab coat brought my mother a clear plastic bottle filled with fizzy orange liquid and returned an hour later to escort her to the lab for a blood test. I remembered Dr. Baker's giving me the same type of bottle to take home with me after my twenty-week appointment. I'd actually been scheduled to take the test the week after I went into premature labor with the twins; the orange liquid had stayed in our pantry for at least eight months, until I went on a cleaning spree and forced myself to throw it away.

While my mother took the glucose test in the lab, I picked up an issue of *Vogue* and attempted to read. The waiting room was empty, aside from a young woman with caramel skin and fleece-lined boots that were wet from the snow. She was heavily pregnant. She filled a cup of water from a tank on the end table and lowered herself carefully back into the chair.

"I am high-high risk," she said to me. "I lost my first pregnancy at twenty weeks—incompetent cervix. They did a cerclage for my second pregnancy, and it didn't work. I had my son at twenty-four weeks and spent the better part of four months in the NICU."

"God," I said.

"He's fine now—Jarell. He's a fighter, one of the tallest kids in his class. He just gets colds more often than some kids, from having been born so premature. Other than that, he's like any normal three-year-old."

I felt dizzy, as if I'd taken a strong drink. My gut burned with knowing. I had never trusted the cerclage. "I can't believe you went for it again," I said.

"I didn't, until we found a doctor who does transabdominal cerclages, with almost a 100 percent success rate. His practice is here in Chicago. It was a three-hour procedure and not pleasant," she said, flicking her fingers in front of her for a moment, as if she were trying to shake off the memory. "But it worked. My cervix is closed tight. Now I have preeclampsia, though."

"I lost twins at twenty-one and a half weeks," I said, wanting in a way I never did in ordinary conversation to voice what had happened in my first pregnancy. "They were stillborn."

Outside this room, I felt defective or bereft when I talked about the twins. I had yet to speak of their death without a painful tensing of my throat or crying. In here, with another woman who'd been through a similar fire, I spoke with my face lifted. In this conversation, I was not a victim, but simply a warrior who'd seen battle.

"So you know," she said, holding my gaze steady.

"Yeah," I said. "I know."

The next day, we received an email from BabyCenter: "Congratulations, you've officially entered the third trimester!"

"Don't you think it's time to start telling more people about the baby?" my mother asked me when I came to see her after finishing my sessions for the day. I cleared off the bed so I could give my mother a reflexology treatment. I propped her legs on a pillow and began to massage the sides and then the soles of her feet. The skin was soft and white, puffed just slightly on the top of the foot and ankles.

"Oh," she said, "that feels so good." She closed her eyes and nestled further into the pillows. I ignored my mother's question. I imagined she could guess our reasons for keeping the pregnancy mostly to ourselves, namely fear.

"Hi, baby," I said, trying to beam my thoughts into the womb instead. "This treatment is for you, too." My mother opened her left eye a slit, like an alligator, and lifted her head up to look at me.

I continued to focus on her foot, making long, slow strokes and then pulling the toes at the top.

"Sara?" she said, her eyes opening and closing again.

"Okay," I said. "I know." I wanted to wait a couple more weeks, until we reached viability, a clinical term I didn't like but still thought of constantly. It was the point after which the baby could survive on its own outside of the womb—somewhere between thirty and thirty-five weeks. My plan was to stay hunkered down with my work, sock away as much money for my maternity leave as possible, and then start telling people sometime in the seventh month.

My mother confronted Bill and me at dinner later that night.

"Okay, you two," she said, narrowing her gaze first at Bill and then at me. "You have some important preparations to attend to for this baby. I want to talk about baby showers and my accommodations. I know you offered to keep the guest room intact until the baby is born, but I think that is unnecessary. I will be comfortable downstairs, and I want to help put together the nursery. If you are too scared to do it for yourselves, do it for me. Just because I am also the gestational host doesn't mean I don't want the full experience and excitement of being the expectant grandmother."

Bill and I looked at each other. I felt scared and superstitious, and I'd been stalling. The baby items we'd been given for the twins had haunted me for years. I think some part of my mind still believed we could have done the first pregnancy differently. That we could have prevented what happened. I thought that maybe if I hadn't loved the twins or prepared for them, we wouldn't have lost them. Or, if we had, the loss would not have hurt so much.

I looked at my mother, her brown eyes light and full, her belly rounded to the size of a small watermelon. We had no guarantees this time, either. But I took her urging as a sign that it was time to take the next emotional risk.

The week before Thanksgiving, Bill and I spurred ourselves into action. My father flew out to Chicago for the holiday and to celebrate my mother's birthday, on December 2. Bill and I used the time while she was with my father to start on Prentice's series of recommended classes for first-time parents: Infant Care 101, Baby and Child CPR and First Aid. We registered for baby items online. We chose a date for a couples' shower: December 11. As we went through our week, we began sharing our news with friends and clients. People who knew us well mostly cried, even one of Bill's friends. When I told my friend Mark Anthony, the head of the center where I led many workshops, he said many times he'd wanted to offer to carry our baby himself and would have done so if he had been in possession of the right equipment.

After client sessions and dinner, looking at baby names became our nighttime activity of choice. We combed through books on mythology, my Shakespeare collection, and baby-name websites.

"I thought this would be easy for you two—both creative types," my sister said when she stopped by after work one evening and saw our pile of books and lists of names on loose-leaf paper. It was more likely that because we were both creative people, name choosing was a more involved process. As a writer, I cared about the sound of the name and the meaning.

My sister picked up our master list and scanned the page now marked up with circles and stars. Choices Bill and I both would consider included Fletcher, Hunter, Austin, Jasper, and Finnean. Finn was the name that had been in my heart since the sixth week of our pregnancy, ever since I had thought we might be having a boy. Finnean Lee. The middle name was decided; Lee was Bill's mother's middle name, and it worked with everything.

My mother told me later she liked Finnean best as well but wanted to stay out of the discussion. "I don't want to play the mother-in-law-who's-carrying-your-baby card and swing the vote either way."

"I like Finnean, but I'm not 100 percent," Bill said. "What about Bradley?"

My sister and I both made a face.

"I'll tell you what," Bill said, crossing the living room to put two more logs in the fireplace. "If our child has light hair, his name is Finnean, Finn for short." I told him I didn't want to name our child on a bet.

"Suit yourself," Bill said, coming back toward the dining room table and punching my bicep with a light tap. He looked smug, like he'd made a bet he couldn't lose anyway.

"I have light hair," my sister said, lifting her hands to the side of her head as evidence. Her hair had remained the same strawberry blond it had been since childhood.

"You're the only one in the family," Bill said. "Sara and I have almost black hair. And light hair is recessive. What are the odds?"

My sister smiled cryptically and shrugged.

As we neared the thirty-week mark, I began to unclench my jaw, which had felt locked ever since we had become pregnant. My brother-in-law told us at dinner one Sunday that he had been born premature—around thirty weeks. I looked at him: broad shouldered, athletic, very much alive. He had followed his passion for sports and now worked as a physician's assistant on the surgical team for the Bears. Thirty weeks. We were not far.

We sent out printed invitations for our shower. I began to tell more acquaintances and friends that we were expecting. On the eleventh, thirty people piled into our house, shaking snow off their jackets and boots. Bill's father and stepmother drove in from Cincinnati, bringing us two strollers (regular and travel), bedding for the crib, and a faux-sheepskin rug to place on the floor in front of the crib in the nursery. From friends, we received a car seat, bottle systems, baby clothes, burp clothes, swaddle blankets, a baby monitor, and a high chair. My parents bought us a traditional white crib with wooden panels that we'd picked out at the Land of Nod.

I wasn't sure I could keep breathing as the gifts piled in a stack next to us. Having a baby was already so much. Our house was now full of equipment and accoutrements. Our friends and colleagues knew. There was no going back.

At the end of the shower, Bill made a toast.

"They say it takes a village to raise a child," he said, lifting a glass of sparkling water in thanks. "In our case, it's taken a village to have a child. Our child is so blessed to be born into so much love. Thank you. You are our village."

By mid-December, we were going to Maternal-Fetal Medicine every week. The week of December 14, Dr. Socol, whom we'd now seen three times, added a stress test to the weekly agenda.

"The name is misleading," Dr. Socol said. "It's really more of a nonstress test. We want to see the baby being active while you're resting."

Katie was the nurse assigned to us that day. She wore bright pink lipstick, and her hair bounced with large curls that looked like they had been set with hot rollers. She was the most talkative of the MFM nurses and put me at ease.

She escorted us to an examination room with two La-Z-Boy recliners and said, "We'll hook you up to a heart monitor for thirty minutes. When we see three distinct periods of movement with elevated heart rates, you're done."

Something about the size and whir of the machines bothered

me. Or maybe it was the brightness of the fluorescent ceiling lights. Katie offered me the second La-Z-Boy but then asked if I could sit on one of the rolling stools instead, because another pregnant woman was due to take her test in ten minutes. I felt brittle that morning. As my mother reclined in the chair, a stab of longing surged through me, like a kick. For a flash of a moment, I wanted to be the one sitting in the first chair. I wanted to feel the baby moving in my body.

I swallowed a dry lump in my throat and reached for the stool. The baby had grown so big inside my mother now that her belly was wide through the middle and took up most of the tape Katie used to measure the length of the bump. My mouth contorted into a smile. I remembered a colleague, a recovering alcoholic in a twelve-step program, saying he always watched in meetings for the moment when addicts became grateful for their addiction because it brought them to a new way of life, a life that bore gifts beyond breaking the habit that had brought them in. "It always comes for people who are open to the idea," he'd said. "There are gifts in everything."

I was not unconditionally at a point where I felt grateful for my body's inability to carry our children, but our path had already revealed undeniable gifts. I was experiencing a physical intimacy with my mother that I had likely not had since I was inside her womb. The love I felt seemed to burn away what had caused us pain, through misunderstandings of the past. I'd heard clients speak of experiencing such relational transcendence when they were with a parent as the parent died. Yet we were being given this experience while bringing in a life.

Katie and my mother were still chatting.

"I like to think of the baby as being in Sara's old room," my mother said, making Katie laugh.

"I want to take you home with me," Katie said.

She invited me to roll my stool over and put my hands on my mother's belly while she set up the stress-test apparatus. She stuck white plastic sensors to my mother's stomach and sides. Once the sensors were attached, they snapped into a blue Velcro belt that went around my mother's middle. Katie switched on the machine and we waited and watched, trying to discern activity and a heart rate on the belt of paper flowing out of the machine's mouth.

Around the ten-minute mark, Katie came back into the room and stood looking over the tape. She motioned for us to be quiet. After another moment, she nodded and told us everything was normal.

Dr. Socol put his stamp of approval on the test.

"You're so close," he said. "You're viable. Now we want to do everything we can to get this baby into the world alive."

The fact that any other outcome was still possible continued to torment me at night. We did our best to keep things light on the days of our stress tests, singing Christmas carols on the drive downtown and joining in on the ballads of whatever crooner was piped through the speakers on our floor of the Northwestern parking garage.

At our last appointment before Christmas, my mother and I sat next to each other in the La-Z-Boys in the stress-test room and listened to the sloshing sounds of the baby's movements through the sensors. My mother sipped heated soy milk while I read her an article from a magazine someone had left on the chair. A moment later, Katie and Pat hurried into the room with Dr. Socol. My mouth went dry. I rushed over to my mother.

"Is something wrong?" I asked, my mind racing and wild.

"We're just checking," Dr. Socol said, his voice even but short. His shoulders hunched as he bent over a paper printout on the machine. I focused my attention on the sound of the baby's heartbeat. I wasn't sure, but I thought it sounded fainter than it had on other days. The inside of my body went cold, like river water under ice.

"Just keep an eye on it," he said to Katie. "Bring me the results at the end of the half hour." The doctor, Katie, and Pat shuffled out. Katie returned two minutes later. My mother's face was pale. My hands and arms were shaking.

"It's probably fine," Katie said. "We don't want to scare you."

Too late for that, I thought.

"What's the issue?" I asked.

"The baby's heartbeat sounded irregular," she said. My mind raced to grasp on to anything I might have read about that would show up in the seventh or eighth month. My brain offered up a blank screen.

"We just want to see if it happens again. We'll know in a few minutes." My mother gripped the side of my hand with her fingers.

"How about we pray?" Katie suggested. She launched into an impassioned prayer of thanks to and faith in "the Lord God" for protecting this baby and my mother; all was well with this baby now, and his heart and every other organ in his body were expressing only the full perfection and wholeness of life.

"God gave you this vision," Katie said to my mother. Then she turned to me. "Now we trust God to fulfill it."

Dr. Socol determined that the irregularity had been a fluke, probably caused by the machine.

"Still, let's have you come twice a week from now on," he said before we left.

"Whatever we need to do," I said. My mother nodded.

Quite a prayer," my mother said in the car on the way home. The sky was heavy with clouds, and although no snow had dumped on the city that week, meteorologists were predicting a white Christmas.

"I'll take every prayer anyone wants to give us," I said.

We stopped at a raw-food restaurant for lunch. My mother said she wanted something healthy and small. She tried the raw ravioli, and I ordered a nonpizza pizza with olive tapenade and fresh spinach over a "cheese" made from macadamia nuts. I offered my mother one of the small triangles of my pizza, and she agreed it was a preferable choice. Outside, we watched snowflakes fall in white lumps and start to pile on the sidewalk outside the café.

"I can go to some of the appointments on my own," she said, "now that we're moving to two appointments a week. You and Bill have a lot of work booked in these next two months."

"I want to go to all of them," I said. I put my fingers around a glass bud vase on the table and began moving it back and forth across the tablecloth.

At the beginning of the pregnancy, I had vowed to be at every appointment—partly to support my mother, but also for myself. I felt that I was more of a participant in the pregnancy if I went to every appointment and every meeting. As I would have if I'd been carrying, I found ways to be flexible in my work. I opened up more sessions in the evenings, when we wouldn't have OB appointments scheduled. I booked workshops and talks on weekends. I saved every extra dollar in a maternity fund. If we went full-term, I would have three months of my salary saved in the bank by February 1.

My father and youngest sister came to Chicago for Christmas. We decorated a tree with blue balls and clear glass ornaments and ribbons of the tartan from Bill's ancestors in Scotland. I stayed up late watching movies with my sister, both of us reciting the lines to *When Harry Met Sally* and *Elf*.

At our Infant Care 101 class that month, we sat in a room with ten couples to practice dressing, bathing, diapering, and feeding a doll. My mother came along. From the minute we arrived, I felt prickly and on edge. The instructors eyed our triumvirate quizzically, and I hurried to the closest available table, sitting with my shoulders hunched, not wanting to take off my coat. I cast a glance around the room. Every other woman swelled at the belly and looked strained in her very pregnant body.

"They all look miserable," Bill said. He glanced at my mother, who was eating a banana. She looked entertained and content. "You are such a pro," Bill whispered to her across the table.

I said nothing. The women did look miserable; two of them were bloated in the face and appeared seasick. A blond woman who told the class she was thirty-nine weeks and six days put her head on the table for a nap, and the wife in an Indian couple behind us snapped at her husband, before sending him to the cafeteria to get her some pizza.

And yet their bodies all did something mine could not: They all carried their babies to term. I kept my coat over my lap for the first hour and spent the remainder of the class feeling jealous.

My antidote to the jealousy, when it arose, was to focus on my mother and the baby. When I was sitting with them, running an errand, reading to the baby, I felt at peace. In a surrogacy, it was easier to remember that I was not in control of this or any other life. In the presence of my mother and the baby, I connected to love.

As we entered the eighth month and the threat of premature labor disappeared, I fantasized about being able to tag into the pregnancy. I watched my mother slow down just a bit, panting sometimes after walking from the car or up a flight of stairs. I wanted to relieve her of the strenuous final stretch. Having now made it to full viability stage, I felt empowered and could imagine myself successfully participating more.

The night of the baby class, I dreamed that my mother and I were in the stress-test room at MFM. The fluorescent ceiling lights had been replaced with blue tubes, and the room glowed indigo. The wall behind the Lay-Z-Boys melted into a small operating room with tables and trays of surgical equipment. Two nurses I didn't recognize were there in scrubs, and Dr. Socol was washing his hands at a sink.

"We're going to transfer the baby now," he said, motioning for the nurses to lift us onto adjoining operating tables. My mother rested on her table, and I felt Dr. Socol attach a cord from her uterus to mine. I felt a flood of anticipation as I realized the baby was about to come into my body. My belly inflated as Dr. Socol cut through my midsection and peeled back my skin to make space. I experienced no pain, only a singing note of elation, as I felt the little body settle into the cushion of my womb, our hearts, mine and the baby's, beating as one.

In the eight month, the longing continued to lift when I was with my mother. Her energy remained high, and we kept our commitment to regular outings and artist dates. One Friday in January, we drove to Vogue Fabrics in Evanston to pick out material for a quilt for the baby. Another day we loaded up on specialty ingredients at the Spice House and baked Mexican wedding balls and quadruple-ginger cookies. She came along on errands with me, just to get out of the house. Later that week, my friend Krista, who had a ten-month-old named Oscar, invited us over for tea.

"What's been the best part?" she asked me when my mother went to the bathroom, "besides that you are having a baby?"

"The intimacy with my mother," I said.

"And the hardest part?" she asked.

"Not carrying the baby in my body," I said.

"I know it sounds crazy," I continued, voicing something that had only just occurred to me after the dream, "but something I'd really, really love would be to nurse." We had walked from the living room into the kitchen, where Krista had put on some hot water for tea. Krista shifted Oscar to her left hip and walked to her laptop over the kitchen table.

"It's not crazy," she said. "I am sure the woman who taught my birthing class mentioned that adoptive and surrogate mothers can nurse."

"What?" I said, stunned. How had I not come across this in all the reading I'd done? The kettle began to sputter and screech. I snapped it off the heat and moved it to a cool burner.

"The process had some name—I'll give you the instructor's card," Krista said. "She is also a lactation consultant."

Krista found the card, and I held it in both hands as if it were a golden ticket.

On the drive home, I daydreamed about nursing. I wanted the physical, primal connection with my baby. My body had brought forth milk once before. Maybe, even without having the baby physically in my body, it could again.

Bill was not enthralled with the idea of consulting another expert. We stood in the kitchen talking after my mother had gone to bed. In the past month, we had become organization freaks, clearing shelves in the pantry, emptying cupboards and closets, working our way through the house, slowly, slowly, toward the room that would become the nursery. I placed the hand-washed pots back in the cupboard.

"I just want to try," I said.

"Okay," Bill said, "but if they so much as mention the term 'herbal tincture,' we're out of there."

The lactation consultant, Jamie Simms, came to our home the next day.

"We'll need total commitment and to work quickly if we're going to get milk," she said. She wrote out the protocol for induced lactation, which involved taking a medication called domperidone, a drug created for gastrointestinal irregularity but that had the side effect of lactation in some people. I would also need to start pumping with a breast pump six to eight times a day for the six weeks leading up to the baby's birth. At the end of the appointment, she recommended an herbal blend called Mother's Milk that was available from Whole Foods.

"Thin ice," Bill whispered in my ear, as I wrote out a $75 check for the consultation.

"You'll need a prescription for the pump from your doctor," Jamie said. "Prentice rents them out on a month-to-month basis."

The second week in January, my mother accompanied me to my annual visioning workshop. Twice during the afternoon I stole into the bathroom and pumped while the workshop participants created their vision boards. At the end of the afternoon, I invited my mother up to the front of the room to share the story of her vision board from two years earlier. As she reached the point where she had offered to be our surrogate, she pulled her shirt close to her body and swiveled to each side, providing a lateral view of her belly.

"So, be really conscientious about what you put on your boards," my mother said. "You could end up pregnant with your grandchild." Even though she was attempting to be funny, several people in the room had begun crying. One woman, a photographer who worked out of a studio in Ravenswood, asked if she could do a portrait of us.

"I'm doing a mother-daughter project," she said. "Yours is exactly the kind of story I want to shoot."

The twice-weekly stress tests at MFM became routine. The baby's heartbeat was regular, and he usually finished the three periods well before the half hour was up. I toted the breast pump to and from appointments, affixing the plastic cups to my breasts as the baby kicked in the chair next to me.

The doctors and nurses in the practice were all very interested in the process.

"Any milk yet?" Katie asked whenever I saw her. I shook my head.

"The lactation consultant told me it would take six weeks minimum—just in time for the baby," I said.

"Does it hurt?" Katie asked.

I described the sucking motion the machine made and then acquiesced that it was in fact painful for the first ninety seconds or so, until my nipples became slightly numb.

"Just like nursing," my mother said.

Every time the doctors checked the baby's position, he was head down. Dr. Socol, whom we seemed to see most often, was delighted by this news and never failed to mention that it was optimal for delivery. The doctors were all excited about the likelihood of a vaginal delivery.

We met Dr. Peaceman at our thirty-seven-week appointment. He was a short, energetic man who was on the faculty of Northwestern's Feinburg School of Medicine.

"I'm going to check the position of the baby," he said, pressing hard into my mother's belly.

"Ow," she said, and shot up from the table. I jumped.

"This baby is head up," Dr. Peaceman said.

"We had an ultrasound four days ago," I said. "Dr. Socol said he was head down."

"This isn't good," he said. "They can't turn again after thirty-seven weeks. If he's breech, we'll have to do a C-section."

"That's okay," my mother said. "We just want to get the baby here safely."

Dr. Peaceman didn't cite my mother's age as an increased risk, but he seemed averse to a C-section, so I had to wonder.

"Whatever is safest for my mother," I said, still standing.

"If the baby hasn't turned by Friday, I'm going to try to turn him manually."

We looked up instructions for a manual turning procedure on the Internet that night. My mother grew distressed as she read. People on the website reported it to be painful and said the procedure could bring on immediate labor. "Go with your bags packed," one website said.

"It seems extreme," my mother said. "Are we sure this is what he was talking about?"

At the bottom of the page, the website listed exercises women could try to turn a breech baby. My mother knelt on all fours and rocked back and forth, the way we saw in the pictures. I dug my reflexology book out of a box in my office to confirm the point on the foot that was said to make a baby turn. I worked the reflex on the side of the pinky toe by pressing my thumb into the skin and massaging the point with my knuckle and then thumb.

When I woke up the next morning, my mother was sitting in the kitchen, sipping a cup of tea.

"I felt something," she said, her face hopeful. "I don't know for sure if he's turned, but at two in the morning he was moving so much that I wondered if I was going to start having contractions."

Dr. Peaceman ordered an ultrasound.

"He's head down," he confirmed, as he slid the ultrasound roller over my mother's belly.

"Whoo!" I called out.

"Wow!" my mother said. Dr. Peaceman handed the ultrasound roller back to Kenisha, the same technician who had performed our twenty-week ultrasound, and said he would meet us in the regular exam room to finish our appointment as soon as Kenisha finished measuring the baby. As soon as Dr. Peaceman left the room, my mother said she was convinced the baby had turned on request.

"I told him last night to do whatever was perfect for him, but said if going head down was just as good, Grandma would so appreciate it."

"The baby looks good," Kenisha said, moving the roller around to try to give us a 3-D view from the front. My mother and I watched the screen together. The baby was scrunched up in a ball with his hands up, covering his face, like a boxer.

"But *whew*," Kenisha said, letting out a low whistle.

"What?" I asked, startled. I relaxed my hands, which had been clenched. I was not going to feel calm until this baby was out, breathing, healthy, and in my arms.

"He's all good," Kenisha said. "But that baby is *big*."

"Now I'm nervous," my mother said, as we walked from the ultrasound room to meet Dr. Peaceman. "I read that the baby gains half a pound a week from this point forward. I don't know if I can push a ginormous baby out of this old body."

"Weight tests can be a pound or two off in either direction," Dr. Peaceman assured her. "Don't worry about his size."

When he checked her cervix, it was high up in the back, closed tight in a thin, straight line, like a clam.

"With so little precedent for delivery at your age," Dr. Peaceman said, "we just don't know if your body will go into labor on its own. We assume so, but if you haven't started by week forty-one, we'll do an induction."

"Forty-one!" my mother said, aghast. "Dr. Gerber told us we wouldn't go beyond thirty-eight when we met with her."

"That was in the first trimester, before we saw how well you've tolerated the pregnancy," he said. "You have yet to express a single troubling symptom."

As much as I wanted our baby out with us, I was grateful, right there at the end, for a little more time. "We still have so much to do," I told my mother on the way home.

"Well, you'd better get on it," my mother said. "I want this baby out by February twelfth."

The next week, we had the fire department professionally install a car-seat base in both of our cars, something my mother thought was ridiculous (how hard could it be?) but that the teachers of our Prentice classes had implied was the only nonnegligent action to take. We attended the remaining CPR and infant first aid class, and the next night moved my mother's things to the basement, where we'd outfitted the new guest room with a featherbed mattress and favorite items from our travels that we hoped would give it a feeling of luxury and warmth. And the last weekend in January, we finally did the nursery.

We invited my sister and brother-in-law over for a decorating party. Bill put together the changing table and the crib. I vacuumed the carpet, washed the floorboards, and stacked linen shelves in the closet. My mother informed us that we would need to prewash all the baby's things with a special detergent before he came home.

Taking the tags off all the clothes and folding them into the drawers and closet shelves called up my old fears again. As the crib went up, I fought the urge to grab everything and put it back in the closet. My mother started a marathon of laundry, washing multiple loads of onesies, burp clothes, swaddle blankets, sweaters, and a quilted zip-up sack with a hood, a splurge from Nordstrom that we thought would be warm and ideal for the baby's trip home from the hospital.

I stacked our children's-book collection on the bookshelf, a cheap, white IKEA basic, my own from my old bedroom at my parents' house. It was the first piece of furniture I had bought with my own money and the one piece I had moved to college and then to my first apartment, to England, and all the way back to this nursery. I wanted our baby to have it now, a place to house his favorite books.

By six o'clock, Bill had assembled all the large pieces, the green patterned sheets were on the crib, and I'd switched on the Japanese paper lamp Sandy had sent from New Mexico, which projected images of trucks and bicycle riders on the ceiling.

My mother went to the kitchen with my sister to decide on something to order for dinner. I walked around the room, straightening the books, running my bare feet over the furry rug and the pile of blankets stacked six high on the changing-table shelves.

"Do you still feel scared?" Bill asked.

"No," I said. Sometime in the course of the ten hours we'd been at work, I'd experienced a shift.

"I love this room," I said. "And you know something?"

Bill sat down on the gray, modern foldout chair that we'd purchased so one of us could sleep with the baby whenever we wanted. He waited for me to continue.

"This room now feels like it is what it always wanted to be."

On February 1, Bill and I surveyed our living room, which now contained a baby swing, a high chair, and a bouncy seat.

"I think we're close," I said.

"Good thing," Bill said, craning his head toward the dome window, looking at the sky. "The Weather Channel predicted a big snowstorm this weekend."

The snow came on Saturday night and dropped hard—two feet in one night and another foot the next morning. Only the roofs of the tallest SUVs were visible along the streets. My mother's car, a Toyota hybrid, was buried completely.

"I guess that's one good thing about the baby not coming early," she said, looking at the spot on the street where her car was parked. "No need to go anywhere today."

For Christmas, Bill's stepfather gifted us with an overnight at the Elysian, a sumptuous hotel in Chicago's Gold Coast neighborhood. When Dr. Peaceman told us that we might well go to forty-one weeks, we planned to do our overnight for February 11, the week in between our two birthdays.

"Don't wait that long," Roger said. "I want you to have one more fabulous night out before the baby arrives. Once he's here, you won't be going out for a long, long while." Mostly to appease him, we decided to move our stay to February 7, the Monday after the snowstorm. I worried about leaving my mother at home on her own, but she was convinced the baby was going to be late and that the doctors would make her stay pregnant through week forty-one.

"Not a single one of you was on time," my mother said, giving Bill the statistics of her deliveries and our lateness: me (five days), Laura (one week), and Ellen (two and a half weeks). "None of them wanted to get out. And now this little guy is staying put, too. I thought for sure a boy would come sooner."

"That's why you're the gestational host," Bill said, as I propped a pillow behind my mother's back. "Your uterus is like the Four Seasons—no one wants to leave."

I peered out our living-room window, stretching my neck up to see the sky. The streets had been plowed and no new snow was predicted, but I still felt protective.

"Go," my mother said. "We don't all need to be here, twiddling our thumbs. I'm going to order mac 'n' cheese lasagna and watch romantic comedies all night. If by some wildness I go into labor, I can walk the half block to the fire station and they will get me to Prentice sooner than you could."

As I carried our single overnight bag to the car, I ordered a taxi to take my mother to our OB appointment in the morning.

"I'll meet you at MFM at nine fifteen," I said. "We'll have our cell phones on at all times."

"Now," my mother said, waving her hand at me and pushing Bill by the back toward the car.

Our room at the Elysian was a decadent suite with two fireplaces, a king-size bed, and an enormous tub big enough for two.

"Thank you, Roger," Bill said as he opened the closets and sniffed the neroli hand lotion in the bathroom. With the precipitous weather, the Elysian wasn't full and the staff seemed happy to have guests to dote upon. The concierge sent the chef from the hotel's restaurant to our room to ask if we'd like him to prepare a special tasting menu for dinner. The maître d' sat us at a cozy table in the corner and delighted us with Dover sole, lobster with chestnuts, and a charcuterie plate that almost made Bill weep.

"I can taste the grass from the pasture the goat grazed on to make this cheese," Bill said.

We reminisced about our days at the advertising agency and how we used to come to restaurants like this with clients on huge expense accounts.

"Tonight feels like when we first started dating," Bill said to me. "I love you now more than ever."

The next morning, we slept in until eight. Bill got ready quickly for a meeting, and I took a bath. The room phone rang just as I sunk into the water. I fumbled for a towel and answered the bathroom phone, water falling from my body into a puddle.

"Honey, it's Mom. I'm sorry to bother you. I'm completely fine.

But the taxi still hasn't come." I pulled back the curtain in the bedroom and saw that it had started to snow again. Even without inclement weather or traffic, I would not have made it to my house and down to Prentice by nine fifteen. And Francis had reminded us to be on time, as the office was booked solid for the remainder of the day.

I pulled on a sweater and the pair of jeans I'd worn the day before and threw my dress, nightgown, and cosmetic case into my bag. I called down to the hotel concierge to have the car brought around.

"I'm on my way," I said.

"I'll call and tell them we'll be late."

I drove as swiftly as I could through the streets. Flurries had begun again by the time I reached the house. My mother saw the car from the window and climbed down the front steps, taking care on the steep cement. I helped her into the passenger side of the car.

"Drive safely," she said. "Just because we're late doesn't mean we need to be in a panic." I calmed myself, taking the turns slowly and staying off the smaller streets, which had become ice sheets underneath powdery snow. We parked in the Northwestern garage and took the pedestrian walkway to Galter Pavilion.

Pat met us in the waiting room and said they had been able to shift some patients around to fit us in.

When we walked into the ultrasound room, Kenisha was there, ready to go. "I feel so big I can hardly move," my mother said, grunting as she climbed onto the table. "I just don't know if I can take another three weeks of this."

"You may not have to," Kenisha said, watching the screen. "The amniotic fluid looks low." She tilted her head from side to side and squinted.

"The baby's fine," she said quickly. "It's just that if the fluid goes below a certain point, they take that as an indication that the baby is running out of space."

"What's the cutoff?" my mother asked in a hungry tone.

"More than five," Kenisha said. "Under five, they usually induce."

"And what's my level?" my mother asked.

"Four point nine." My mother looked at me, her eyes hopeful.

"I'll let the doctors know you're right on the border," Kenisha said. "They may not want to do anything."

Kenisha sent us to the stress-test room, where the nurses had set up my mother's station. They had just begun stretching the band around her belly when Dr. Gerber burst into the room. We hadn't seen her since our very first consultation with MFM. She wore a thin headband and a pressed white lab coat with the MFM seal.

"Your amniotic fluid is lower than we like to see," she said, glancing at the chart.

"Are your bags packed?" My mother and I looked at each other. *Our hospital bags?*

"What I mean to say," Dr. Gerber said, pausing, seeming to enjoy the drama of her announcement, "is that you're having this baby today."

Chapter 10

We did not have the baby that day. When we heard Dr. Gerber say that we would, however, my mother and I squeezed each other in a ferocious hug, the fronts of our bodies pressed together, the baby in a warm cocoon between us.

"Call Bill!" my mother said as we released our grip.

I ran to the fourteenth-floor lobby, where I could get cell phone reception, and punched Bill's number into my phone.

I paced a strip of gray carpeting near the windows, feeling as if I might rocket out of my body. I imagined Bill in the middle of a meeting, similar to the day we had found out we were pregnant. Even though we were only a week from our due date, we'd talked about how—to some part of our brains—the idea that we were actually having a baby still felt abstract. The journey we'd taken had made us expert waiters. We had waited for this day for nine months—six years and nine months, if we counted from the beginning.

Part of me still worried that something would go wrong. "You won't know for sure until you're holding the baby in your arms," a woman had said at the fertility support group I'd attended several years before. But for the moment, I was attached to the part of me that believed we had a really good chance. I wanted to enter the hospital in this spirit, in faith.

The phone line crackled and took a minute to ring. I caught my reflection in one of the large windows and was startled by my appearance. I looked wild, with my hair loose and unbrushed, wearing yesterday's now slightly rumpled clothes, bouncing up and down on alternate legs.

Bill answered, but the connection cut in and out and he couldn't hear me well.

"We're having the baby today!" I nearly yelled when he asked me to repeat myself for the third time.

"Baby?" Bill asked.

"Our baby!" I said. "*Today!*"

The line cleared and Bill sputtered, "Oh my god. Right now?"

"Dr. Gerber said today. We're going to Prentice now."

"Oh my god," he said again. "How's your mom? Do you think I have time to pack up our bags?"

My mother caught up with me in the lobby. She was carrying the breast pump and her down coat. Two pink spots had appeared over her cheekbones. I put the phone on speaker so she could talk to Bill.

"I'm not even in labor yet," she laughed. "They're going to induce me. We have plenty of time."

"Okay." I heard him draw a ragged breath. "I'll check in every ten minutes."

I put the phone back to my ear so I could say goodbye to Bill. I wished I could touch him through the phone to feel his heartbeat on my chest, the way I did when we hugged.

"Our baby!" he said.

"We're having our baby!" I said, holding my hands against the glass to steady myself.

My mother and I walked the two blocks to Prentice. We stopped just outside the main entrance so she could call my father and tell him to get on the next plane to Chicago. The day was chilly but bright, the winter sun splashing the sidewalk between the large buildings with pale light. I watched my mother: one hand on her belly, her feet in black rubber boots, legs bent in a slight squat. Her short hair, which she'd let go natural during the pregnancy, had turned salt and pepper. To me, she looked like some kind of modern fertility goddess. I felt an urge to document the moment. I pulled my phone out of my bag and began shooting video.

"How do you feel?" I asked when she hung up her phone.

"Ready," she said. "Excited and scared."

"Me too," I said. "This is it."

Anticipation churned in my stomach. I reminded myself to stay in my body.

We waited one more moment before entering.

My mother reached for my hand. I slid my arm protectively through hers and we walked through the revolving doorway together, into Prentice's mammoth lobby.

Our entrance was anticlimactic. The lobby was quiet and airy, with just a few clusters of people sitting at the café and perusing the elegant flower shop, whose orchids and towering arrangements rose up toward the three-story-high ceiling. We'd neglected to find out from Dr. Gerber where we were supposed to check in once we arrived and walked around for fifteen minutes before we found someone who could admit us.

Once we'd registered, a staff administrator took us up to the eighth floor and admitted us to a room directly across from the nurses' station. The room had polished hardwood floors, wood-paneled walls, and a plane of windows that offered a vista of skyscrapers and a sliver of the lake—the same view as the one the million-dollar condos nearby had.

A young nurse named Lindsey handed my mother and me identification bracelets and a name badge for me that read MOTHER. Seeing the word stung my throat. My eyes watered, and I had to make several attempts to secure my mother's bracelet on her wrist.

Despite the constant reminders in our birthing classes that early labor was uneventful and long, I think I still expected the movie scene: Woman goes into labor; doctors and nurses race her down the hall to a delivery room with bright lights; baby arrives!

Lindsey was in no rush, nor was anyone else on the floor. Both the room and the hallway had an ethereal quality, as if time did not exist. Lindsey waited for my mother to change into a hospital gown and entered some additional information into a computer in the room. She activated a fetal monitor and turned the volume up so we could hear the baby's heartbeat. Her prework done, she left, telling us that someone from Anesthesiology would be in within the hour.

At our thirty-seven-week appointment, we'd met with Dr. Peaceman and an anesthesiologist from Prentice to create our birth plan. The Maternal-Fetal Medicine team remained enthusiastic about a vaginal delivery. They were thrilled to hear that my mother had had three successful vaginal births, and almost refused to discuss other options.

At the birth-plan meeting, Dr. Peaceman asked if my mother would also like to attempt natural childbirth, since she'd done so successfully before.

"I'm doing this so that Sara and Bill can have a child," she'd said, "not for the *birthing experience*." She told the anesthesiologist to sign her up for the drugs.

When the anesthesiologist looked at me for confirmation, I pointed to my mother. "Are you kidding?" I said. "Whatever she wants."

When I was pregnant, I thought I would try for natural childbirth and be ready for an epidural should I want one in the moment. I'd worked with many clients as they considered birth plans and did not believe in there being a *right way*. I heard women at parenting classes, at yoga, say things like C-sections weren't *real childbirth*, that epidurals were cheating. These kinds of comments were similar to what I would later hear about mothers who didn't breastfeed or who worked outside the home. I wondered if these women had ever lost children in utero or otherwise.

I didn't give a rat's ass which way our baby came out. As long as he arrived alive, with my mother healthy and okay, that was all that mattered. Loss had simplified some things for me.

As we waited for the anesthesiologist to arrive, we explored the room. Along the window was a cushioned seat that pulled out into a bed. The room had an in-suite bathroom with an oversize shower and two sinks, and a flat-screen TV, a DVD player, and an iPod docking station synced to a central entertainment system. The medical machinery, hung tastefully on a wood-paneled wall behind the bed, like art, seemed almost an afterthought.

"Whew," my mother said, when we'd taken a full loop around the room. "Things have changed since I gave birth to you."

Three miles north, Bill entered into a frenzy of activity, taking on the completion of every task remaining on our baby to-do list in the span of four hours. He raced through the baby outfitters on the north side of Chicago like a dervish, procuring Pampers, wipes, three kinds of formula (in case my milk did not come in), and liners for our diaper disposal system.

When I finally caught up with him, his voice sounded garbled, as if he were having trouble pronouncing certain consonants. He explained that he had a screwdriver in his mouth and was in the nursery fixing a shelf that had come loose.

"You don't have to do everything today," I said.

"I keep thinking of things," he said, grunting as he jimmied the shelf back into position.

He went on to tell me that he'd washed three more sets of burp cloths and blankets, and then, in a fit of inspiration, he'd driven across town to a store where we'd seen a stunning African-style baby wrap. In the store, I'd buried my face in the woven crimson fabric and commented that I thought I could feel the wisdom of the women who'd made it. We'd told ourselves it was too expensive and that we'd be just fine using the blue cotton one a friend from my yoga class had lent me.

"I wanted you to have it," Bill said.

For the second time, I choked back tears. The wrap had become for me a symbol of my realization of motherhood, and Bill had sensed this. We'd read about the "fourth trimester," the baby's first three months of life. Experts in the theory recommend skin-to-skin contact during this time for long periods each day. I needed no further invitation. I planned to start the moment our baby came out of the womb.

"Just a couple more things," Bill was saying. I wanted to tell him to drop it all and come, but I stopped myself. I understood something, too: that the maelstrom of activity was Bill's own form of labor, his way of fulfilling his role as provider for his child.

"I just want everything to be perfect," he said.

"It will be," I said, praying that what I was saying was true.

I told him the doctors were only just preparing to start the induction and there was no real hurry. "Come soon," I said anyway. I wanted him there next to me to count down the minutes as our baby's birth approached.

At 3:00 PM, Dr. Socol started the induction process.

"I'm administering a low dose of Pitocin," he said. "We want the cervix to dilate and kick-start the body into labor."

Bill arrived at four o'clock, heaving into the room, his arms and back straining under the girth of our hospital bags, laptop computers, and air mattress and sleeping bag he'd thought to bring from the house. He dropped the pile onto the floor in the corner of the room and went straight to my mother.

"How are you feeling?" Bill asked, taking a seat on the chair next to the bed, where my mother sat up smiling, chewing on ice chips.

"Great. I haven't even needed an epidural yet. When I gave birth to Sara, they wouldn't even let me have water," she said, crunching down on a nugget of ice. "Then again, I'm not really in full labor yet."

Dr. Socol returned. Since they'd begun the Pitocin drip, my mother had dilated only three centimeters.

"The Pitocin can only do so much," he said. "We're trying to get your body to participate."

My father arrived during Dr. Socol's consultation. He looked calm for a man whose sixty-one-year-old wife was in labor. He shook a dusting of white flakes from his coat. He wore a blue sweater my sisters and I had given him for Christmas a few years before. The curls on his head were wet where snow had melted. I hadn't even known it had begun snowing.

"I can see the resemblance," Dr. Socol said, looking between my father and me. I guessed he and my father were about the same age.

"You have a quite a wife," Dr. Socol continued, clasping my father's shoulder before leaving the room.

My father leaned over the bed and kissed my mother on the forehead. "I most certainly do," he said.

"Thank you for coming," she said. She looked more relaxed now that my father was here, as if now all the pieces were in place and she could focus fully on the labor.

"This was the thing I asked him for," she said to Bill and me, holding my father's hand. "To be with me on the delivery day."

"I am here at your service," my father said.

An observer would have perhaps thought that my father's behavior was expected and lovely, but I knew that his devotion was also an act of atonement. It was well known in our family mythology that when my mother went into labor with me, my father asked if he could go to his business school final before meeting her at the hospital, because the professor had told the class the only excuse for a student's absence would be his or her own death.

My mother had replied something along the lines of, "That could be arranged." My father, rousted by her tone, jumped in a taxi and arrived at the hospital in ample time to see me born.

"I was, in a word," my father said, directing his comment to Bill, "an idiot."

My mother did not disagree.

Another hour passed. Bill had begun to yawn in the corner, catching himself as he fought sleep. I still felt jittery with excitement, but disconcerted by the hospital ward's silence and the strange floaty quality of time inside it. The only sound for minutes at a time was the *whoosh* of our baby's heartbeat. The anticipation mixed with waiting started to grate on me. I offered to give my mother a reflexology treatment.

"Oh, yes," she said, pulling the blanket off her legs. My father and Bill asked permission to get some coffee at the café on the second floor. "I'm not doing anything tonight without asking first," my father whispered to Bill on their way out. "Not making that mistake twice." My mother waved them on like a queen, both of us amused at my otherwise type-A father being so deferential.

As I massaged my mother's feet, I kept one ear tuned to the noise that blipped out of the fetal heart rate monitor. I'd listened already for so long that occasionally the sound would appear abnormal, like a word that begins to sound strange after one repeats it many times in succession. The machine was designed to set off an alarm if the heart rate accelerated or dropped, but I still kept a close eye and ear to the screen, vowing to hear any change or fluctuation that might require attention.

My father and Bill returned and entered the room cautiously, looking to see if my mother was asleep. My father was carrying a pitcher of ice.

"I forgive you," she said, as he returned to the chair next to the bed.

"Whew," he said, miming wiping sweat from his brow. "Thirty-five years, and I'm absolved."

Dr. Socol came again to check my mother's cervix. "I'm going to up the dosage of Pitocin," he said. "You're still only three and a half."

Every doctor check-in was the same: My mother needed to dilate more.

At 8:00 PM, she had dilated to four centimeters and could feel frequent, but faint, contractions. Bill's father and stepmother had driven through the snow from Cincinnati to be there. They entered the room flushed and excited, dressed in wool sweaters and big coats to buffer themselves against the frigid night. The temperature had dropped twenty degrees since the morning. I took in the sight of them with joy. My sister and brother-in-law arrived straight from work, and the room now took on a festive atmosphere, everyone cheering my mother on and speculating about when the baby would be delivered.

At 9:00 PM, Dr. Socol sent everyone home, saying it was unlikely the baby would be born before early morning. Bill's parents left for a hotel nearby, and Ellen and Chris went home to their condo in Logan Square, making us promise to text the minute the labor became active.

"Try to rest," Dr. Socol said. "Our resident, Miranda, will page me the minute we're ready for action."

The higher dose of Pitocin did little to increase my mother's contractions. The night began to feel like a repetitive dream. No one felt like sleeping.

My father unearthed his newspaper and read in one of the chairs. I sat by an outlet near the window and plugged in the breast pump, covering my chest with a sweater. I winced as the machine pulled at my nipples. I'd forgotten to pump in the commotion of the day, and my breasts were sore from not having been pumped for six hours. In the light of the chair lamp I watched a thin film of white, like snow, appear against the plastic pump cups. The white was probably colostrum—the viscous premilk substance that contained nutrients for the baby. The lactation consultant said colostrum was a good sign, but it did not ensure full lactation.

I felt restless when I finished, and I stepped into the hall. The wall clock read 10:20 PM. At the nurses' station I saw BABY CONNELL on the monitor, but the view didn't comfort me, as I'd hoped. I felt as if our baby were hooked up to an oxygen tank with a limited supply of air, and that with every hour that went by, his reserves were being depleted.

When I returned to the room, my mother had inclined the bed and was sitting upright again.

"Can't sleep?" I asked.

"Too much adrenaline," my mother said.

Bill and my father stirred at their posts, too.

"I know," my mother said. "You could decide on a name."

We welcomed the task. My father, Bill, and I pulled chairs

around my mother's bed, and I pulled out our short list, which I'd been carrying in my phone for the past month.

My mother refilled her plastic cup with ice. Bill switched on one of the overhead lights above the bed.

It took us an hour to take the list down from five to two names. At the end of the hour, Bill and I had decided. Our son would be either Jasper, meaning "treasured one," or Finnean, "mythical warrior poet."

"I want to meet him in person to make the final decision," Bill said.

I agreed. My mother said the activity had made her sleepy and she was ready to try and rest.

We arranged ourselves in various positions: my father on the sleeper couch, Bill and I on the floor on the air mattress. Within seconds I heard the sounds of heavy breathing from Bill. I felt alone. I struggled not to feel scared. It had been fun to talk about names. It made it feel certain that we were really having this baby. But I felt drained from the years of uncertainty. And still, we were hanging in a place of "maybe." Instead of feeling closer to the baby, I started to feel as if I couldn't connect to him at all, even though he was right in the room. I remembered the way it had felt as though the twins had left my body right before the doctor said they would die. I tuned my ears to the heart monitor in the corner of the room. Steady.

I imagined I was running toward our baby from a great distance. I believed he was coming, running to meet me as well, but I still couldn't see him. Again, I had the irrational fear that he might run out of oxygen while we waited for the induction to achieve labor. My mother said later that she felt the pull, too. If the doctors had asked either of us, we would have opted to go for the C-section.

In the moment, no one was offering anything except the option that offered no relief: *Hold on. Not yet. Wait.*

Somewhere around 1:00 AM, I fell asleep. I awoke to see Dr. Socol's resident, Miranda, and another figure enter the room. They approached my mother's bed, their bodies looming and dark. Miranda woke up my mother, who looked groggy and confused.

"You still haven't dilated past four," Miranda said. "We need to take the next step. Annie is here to break your bag."

I tried to see the time on the wall clock, but the overhead lights were still switched off and I couldn't make out the numbers. I guessed it was about 2:30 AM.

"That doesn't sound fun," my mother said. She blinked in the glare of the exam light Miranda had positioned at the end of the bed. Their movements looked tense and hurried.

Miranda said the procedure should take just a few minutes and that Annie was the best bag-breaker at Prentice. My mother said she hoped the procedure wouldn't hurt.

Neither doctor answered her question; instead, they busied themselves with a tray of instruments on a table they'd rolled next to the bed. I took a step closer. The moderate surge of protectiveness I'd felt during OB appointments with my mother now swelled to a roar. If I could not carry this baby myself, I could at least protect her. If they hurt her, I would stab them with their own instruments.

I wondered if the aggression was easier to feel than guilt. My mother wouldn't be in this position if Bill and I hadn't needed help.

"Are you prepared to see your mother in pain during labor?" Pat had asked me at one of our final OB appointments.

"We're having an epidural," my mother had replied, keeping the tone light. "We're going for pain-free."

I'd felt Pat still looking at me and I'd pretended to find a speck of dust or paint on the wall fascinating. I was not comfortable seeing my mother in anguish.

Thinking about my mother in pain was only a short skip to

How would I feel if my mother died? Ironically, it was easier for me to talk myself down from that thought than it was to think about her in pain. I think because we'd talked about it once, my mother and I, when I'd forced myself to bring up the subject with her, at the very beginning of this process, right after she'd made the offer to be our surrogate.

"I am sure you'd feel really, really sad if I died," my mother had said. "That would be awful. But that's no reason not to pursue this vision. First, because I don't think I am going to die. Second, because doing this is my calling. You know the worth of that—you talk about it in your workshops. I live my callings now. Period."

In the OB appointment with Pat, I had finally muttered that I would think about it so she would stop looking at me. I knew that physical pain would be involved in delivering our child. I'd found a way to make peace with seeing her tired and nauseous and swollen and sore during the pregnancy; I told myself I would be able to do the same in delivery *if* the issue arose.

The sight of those instruments now and my intimate knowledge of their destination were causing me to bristle like a cornered cat. I squared my body between the bed and the doctors.

"Breaking the bag is necessary to advance toward delivery," Miranda said, as much to my mother as to me. "We need to take greater measures to trigger the body into full labor."

Bill poked his head out from under the sleeping bag on the floor and then ducked down again when he saw my mother's legs in the stirrups. My father was curled under his winter coat, either asleep or pretending to be asleep on the sleeper couch at the window.

"We'll try to be as gentle as possible," Miranda said.

I fixed my eyes on my mother, and Annie scooted herself closer to the bed. Miranda handed her a thin stick that looked like a knitting needle.

I gripped the chair next to the bed as a feral screech emerged from my mother's mouth—it was an awful sound, somewhere between a moan and a cry, the sound of a wounded animal.

Bill sprang from his place on the floor and grabbed my hand, keeping his eyes averted from my mother's body. Annie bent over my mother, maneuvering the stick. My mother moan-cried again, sounding more human this time, and I lurched for the bed.

"Are you almost done?" I asked.

"We just haven't quite been able to break it," Annie answered, her voice sounding strained.

Miranda stepped in and gave one final torque of the needle, and my mother yelled again. I heard it before I saw it—water, spilling out over the medical pads under my mother and onto the polished wood floor.

Annie and Miranda looked relieved. A nurse came in to clean up the station. My mother told her to let the doctors know she would take that epidural now. With the water released and the epidural ordered, my mother revived quickly. She was like a rescued ship-wreck victim, who now, out of peril, was eager to share the tale. She took a long swallow of ice water, and I took in large gulps of relief. My father, who'd remained crouched on the sleeper sofa, approached with trepidation. Bill stood closer, next to me, by the bed.

"You know something?" my mother said, slapping her palm on the mattress. "This baby is incredible! The only reason I was induced was for low fluid. I think he really took those *Harry Potter* books to heart." She looked at the three of us to see if we were following her. "He performed an illusion—by hiding the water at the ultrasound." I nodded, with her completely.

Bill and my father looked pale and disturbed. My father wiped the sides of his face and his forehead with a handkerchief. He let out a low sigh and then sank into the chair, shaking his head at my mother.

"This is what we get for letting the two of them hang out every day," he said to Bill.

Once he was sure my mother was fine, Bill went into the hallway to "get some air," he announced, "and probably have a nervous breakdown."

On his way back to the room, he overheard Annie describing the bag-breaking incident to the some of the nurses at the station.

"You should have seen it in there when the water broke."

"Big one?" one of the nurses asked.

"It was like Lake Michigan," Annie said.

Dr. Socol returned at seven in the morning. My mother had still not dilated past four centimeters and had now been in labor for sixteen hours. We were hoping for another doctor from the practice, thinking someone new might offer alternatives. Dr. Gerber stuck her head through the door to say good morning and that she would be back at the hospital again around 6:00 PM. "But you'll probably have had the baby by then," she said, giving my mother a wink.

"I certainly hope so," I said, looking at the clock on the wall.

My mother brought up the issue of a C-section.

"We're still very optimistic for a vaginal birth," Dr. Gerber said, as if this were an athletic event and she and Dr. Socol were sports commentators.

"We do whatever we can to avoid unnecessary surgery," Dr. Socol said, giving the boilerplate answer we'd already heard from the staff.

The baby's heart rate was strong, and my mother's blood pressure and vitals were steady. She continued to be free from contraction pain, thanks to the epidural, but was starting to show signs of fatigue. Her hands shook now when she reached for the ice pitcher. She'd mostly stopped drinking water. I worried about her energy; she hadn't eaten in twenty-four hours.

"When does surgery become necessary?" I asked.

"When the life of the mother or baby is endangered, or there are no other alternatives. We see people go eighteen, even twenty-four, hours and then kick into full labor," Dr. Gerber said. Then, having completed her pep talk, she left the room.

"You'd think being sixty-one would give you some special treatment," Bill said once she'd left.

"Seriously," my mother said.

The sun rose orange in the sky. Streaks of light poured into the room, so much that we lowered two of the shades. The hours unfolded at a protracted pace. Each time someone came to check on my mother's progress, they said the same thing: "More Pitocin. We'll check in again two hours."

"It's not as if we can perform the C-section ourselves," my mother said, though I thought I could hear wistfulness in her voice.

It was eleven in the morning, and no one besides my mother had slept for more than an hour during the night. We laughed at things that weren't funny: the stick-figure icons on the TV menu; the terrible production quality of the educational videos on the in-house birthing channel.

Punchiness gave way to impatience. Adrenaline and lack of sleep distorted my reality. The hallways started to look elongated and bendy, like a fun house's. My reflection in the mirror looked unfamiliar.

Bill's parents stopped by again to show support. Ellen and Chris returned after an entire next day of work, incredulous that my mother was still laboring. I felt claustrophobic. The jovial atmosphere I'd enjoyed in the room the night before now felt distracting. I felt even further away from the baby and grasped to make some connection. The staff's lack of urgency or concern began to feel robotic and disturbing. Part of me questioned whether our baby was even still inside my mother: Would he ever actually be brought out, or would we continue indefinitely in this limbo?

We won't go later than midnight," Dr. Gerber said when she arrived to check on us again. "If you haven't gone into full labor by then, we'll move to cesarean." At least we had an end point now. My mother and I had been in the hospital for thirty-three hours. She'd been in induced labor for twenty-eight. The next scheduled check-in was at 9:00 PM.

I felt a resurgence of energy. My mother encouraged Bill and me to go out for something to eat. She felt comfortable with my father sitting with her and would welcome an hour to rest. Based on the way the past check-ins had gone, none of us anticipated anything much would change at nine.

I wasn't sure if I could eat, but my stomach rumbled in response to the idea of food and I reached for my coat. My sister said she would join us and suggested a sushi place one block north. We bundled ourselves into coats, hats, and gloves and walked into the night. The sky was inky black, and our breath looked like white smoke in the air. The wind hit like a wall. It was so strong that we had to hold the side of the building to stay upright.

I felt strange being outside the hospital. Prentice had become an insulated pod. Out on the street and even amid the cozy warmth and tinkling of ceramic spoons against bowls of soup at the restaurant, I felt thrust into the ether.

We set our phone timers for eight fifty, giving ourselves ten minutes to return to the room. "No need to run back, though," Bill said, eyeing his phone. "I'm sure they're going to tell us we're going until midnight."

While we ate, my sister described the cesarean, a procedure she'd participated in during her obstetrics rotation.

"The ones I've seen are pretty fast," she said. "It only takes maybe ten minutes to get the baby out."

I was usually the one engrossed in medical discussions with my sister while Bill reminded us such conversations tended to ruin a meal. Tonight, however, Bill was riveted and I hummed a song in my head. I didn't want to hear too much detail. As much as I endeavored to focus on this as a new experience, images of my own cesarean pushed themselves forward when I thought about the operating room.

I didn't care to add any visuals to those already flooding my mind. I turned to the side and saw a wall of water running down a large slab of slate near the entrance to the restaurant. The fixture reminded me of the water feature in the solarium of our house. It was likely our baby was going to be born via C-section that night, and I was going to do everything in my power to be all there—in the OR and in life—for him.

"I'm more worried about them continuing the labor than I am about the C-section," my sister was saying. "Thirty-two hours is long, even for a young person."

I looked around the room for our waitress, with her long shiny hair and pressed blue-and-white kimono. She was taking a long time bringing the check. I eyed my phone, wondering if I should run back to the room and let Bill finish and pay.

"There's no hurry," Bill said. "I'm sure we'll go until midnight."

I tapped my foot under the table and tried to restrain myself until the check came.

At three minutes past nine, we rounded the corner toward the nurses' station and I saw a mob of bodies outside the entrance to our room. The door swung open, and more doctors and nurses in lab coats and industrial scrubs swarmed the room like bees.

"Oh my god," I said, racing toward the door.

I pushed through the crowd and slid on the polished floor. The room was unrecognizable. Glaring lights shot down from the ceiling, and Dr. Gerber was standing in scrubs by the head of the bed. At least fifteen people, including the resident who'd been on duty the night before, were moving about, checking monitors, hanging another IV bag.

"We're going to section," Dr. Gerber announced, a triumphant smile on her face. My mother was sitting up, radiant.

"It's time!" my mother said.

A hospital attendant instructed us that we needed to move our things to the postdelivery room on the fourteenth floor. Another barked that whoever was going into the OR needed to change immediately into scrubs.

My body tried to catch up with my cognitive process. *We're going into the OR for a C-section.* Our baby was, in fact, finally about to be born.

"This is happening," Bill said. He grabbed my shoulders from behind. I turned to face him. Years before, the first or second year we lived in England, Bill had awakened me after having a powerful dream. We had only just been married and I was still on the Pill, still years from even trying to start a family.

"I met our child," Bill said. "She came to me and said, 'It's going to be okay, Daddy.' She took my hand. It didn't feel like a dream, Sara. She was so real."

We'd talked about the dream once or twice in the beginning of our fertility endeavors. Sometime after the twins died, though, we'd stopped. Trying to convince ourselves it had been a prophesy or assurance that we would have children became too painful. We had to find a way to move forward knowing that there were no guarantees.

Neither of us had mentioned the dream in a long while, but I thought of it now as we moved toward our son's birth. I pressed myself against Bill's chest and squeezed hard. In six years, we'd held to our promise to not turn away from each other. We had never fully lost faith.

"Only one of you can come into the room," Dr. Gerber said.

Bill and I joined my father at the foot of my mother's bed. The doctors had been pressing so hard for a vaginal birth that we didn't even know the hospital protocol for C-sections. I had not really considered that we wouldn't all be allowed in for the birth. How often did a sixty-one-year-old woman give birth to her own grandchild?

Now, I wanted with all my soul to be in that room. I was sure Bill and my father felt the same.

The three of us cleared more space around my mother's bed. Around her was the din of a pre-OR circus. I felt a pull inside my own body, a palpable connection not just to the baby, but to my mother as well. I felt a wave of calm. Whatever she decided would be fine. A tall, angular male nurse cut through our circle and extended a set of scrubs. "We need to know who's coming," he said. "You need to decide now."

"Sara," my mother said, her eyes on mine. "Bring the Great Mother with you."

I looked at Bill, wanting a moment with him, to find out how he felt. He smiled at me, and the nurse pushed the scrubs against my rib cage.

"Now," he said. Dr. Gerber called to the team that it was time to move. After the creeping pace of the past thirty-six hours, action felt accelerated.

Bill and my father threw our belongings into bags. I could see Bill almost at the door, his shoulders stooping just a bit under the weight of the large duffel bag and our laptops. I ran to meet him, standing on tiptoe and grabbing the sides of his face so I could kiss him.

"Big picture, right?" I said. It was what we'd said to each other when we'd faced other obstacles or delays. "Big picture" was having our baby.

"Bring him in, Sara. Bring him in safe," he said.

It wasn't fair that Bill didn't get to come with us, but I'd seen the futility of arguing against hospital policy. I swept aside the guilt I felt and pulled the gray scrubs over my clothes. I promised myself I would be in the room for both Bill and myself.

By the time we left the room for the OR, every member of the surgical team was covered top to bottom in gray. We walked en masse down the hallway. The mood of the entourage was focused, as if they were all feeling, with my mother and me, the significance of our mission.

The OR was gleaming and white. Bulbous lights beamed onto the operating table. Michael, the primary anesthesiologist, began to administer pain medication through the same tube used for the epidural. I again tried to untangle myself from memories of my previous visits to the OR.

All I could see of my mother was the strip of her eyes between her surgical cap and gown. I was afraid to ask if she was scared, but I forced myself. In what she was about to do, I believed my job was to support her and be present for the birth of our child.

She only nodded at first, yes to feeling scared.

Later she told me she was praying: *Please don't bring us all this way and leave us.*

I squeezed her shoulder.

The surgical team assembled at the base of the bed. A nurse lifted a tall paper sheet and fastened it to a bar, separating my mother's head and our view from the rest of the room. I heard a loud sucking sound as a machine came to life. Dr. Gerber called commands to her team. Michael went to work, flicking his finger on the tube of an IV that would deliver numbing medication to my mother's body. A nurse pulled a chair next to my mother's head and told me to sit beside her.

As my mother answered Michael's questions about what, if anything, she could feel below her waist, my brain finally worked out the calculation that I had been resisting for six years: two years of acupuncture, six IVF cycles, three hundred injections, two still-births, a miscarriage. I bit down on the side of my cheek. It had all led to this moment.

"I'm beginning," Dr. Gerber announced.

"This is it," my mother said. I offered up a prayer to the Great Mother.

"Please," my mother added, "please finish this in joy."

I began to cry. A tear ran down the side of my mother's face. Then she jerked and grimaced.

"I'm in," Dr. Gerber said.

"Does it hurt?" I asked, forcing myself to ask this question.

"No pain," my mother said. "But I can feel them pulling."

"Should she be feeling anything at all?"

"You'll feel slight sensation," he said. "But no pain. Just before the baby comes out, I am going to tell you to push."

I squeezed my mother's shoulder again. Our baby was almost here. As the doctors worked, I pulled my mind into the room, tuning my ears for a specific sound—the one sound I'd been anticipating for the nine months of this pregnancy, for the 208 weeks since the twins had died: our baby's first cry.

Minutes passed. The operation was taking too long. My sister told us it took only minutes to get to the baby.

I looked pleadingly at Michael.

"Nonemergency C-sections take longer," he said. "Everything is going well."

"We're almost there," Dr. Gerber said.

Waves of recognition of what was happening broke over me.

"One more minute," Dr. Gerber called, her voice rising. My brain flooded.

"This is it," my mother said. "This is the vision—you and me together, doing this."

I cried harder.

"Okay, Kristine," Michael said. "Get ready. In just one minute I'm going to tell you to push."

"Ready now," Dr. Gerber said. "I see him." I felt as if I had been lifted up to the ceiling, stretched beyond my body. I held on to my mother's shoulder and the side of her arm.

My breath became rapid and shallow. The room began to feel otherworldly. I locked eyes with my mother and for one second I saw something beyond our bodies, this arrangement of mother and daughter. For a moment, she and I melded and I saw only one.

I came back to my own body, buzzing with electricity. I wondered if other parents felt this sensation. It was if something had reached inside me and swirled its fingers through my essence. Some part of who I had been was no more. Who I would be now, as a mother, was yet to be revealed.

"He's here," someone called out. I hunched over the chair, coiled like a spring. I strained for the sound. The seconds felt stretched and hung in the air. I sensed movement but still I heard nothing. My fingers on my mother's shoulder went white. Where was the cry?

Then it came, his first rasping sound—a wonderfully strong, hoarse little voice that filled the room. More cries came, and I heard them like the crescendo of a symphony. I saw an arm and a foot being lifted and a wriggling form being handed to the pediatric team. I reached for him, even though I'd been told he would not be passed to me until he'd been checked and cleaned off.

At the side table where the pediatric team worked I saw his foot, an exact replica of Bill's father's foot: wide in the middle and big, with long toes. That was all I could see of his body through the cluster of doctors and nurses: his grandfather's foot, in miniature, on his long but tiny leg.

The team bent over our baby, moving him, poking, producing another cry. Every sound was an affirmation, a trumpet. I sat on my hands; I wanted to go to him so badly.

My mother looked agitated. She said later she felt disoriented from the medication. "I could not relax until I saw you hold him," she said later, in the recovery room. "That's the image I've held to through all of this."

"They'll bring him to you soon," Michael said, attempting to soothe us.

A nurse called out stats as the team continued to surround the baby.

"Born: baby boy, February ninth, 9:47 PM."

"Seven pounds, three ounces."

"Eighteen inches."

"Is he okay?" I finally called out.

"He is perfect," the pediatric nurse said, swaddling him in a hospital-issue blanket with blue and pink stripes. "He's just a little pale. We're going to keep him under the lamp for another minute."

I waited, hardly able to contain myself. The doctors had begun the restorative part of the cesarean and were now putting my mother's insides back in position, one layer at a time. Every few minutes she cringed as the doctors tugged or applied the next row of suturing. I tried hard not to picture the activity on the other side of the curtain. I placed my hand on the top of my mother's head and focused my attention on comforting her.

Finally, the pediatric nurse checked something on a clipboard and began moving toward me. "Stay where you are," she said as I half-rose from my chair. "I'm bringing him to you."

I turned in the chair, wanting to keep some contact with my mother as the baby was brought to us. The nurse lowered him gently so we both could see. "Look at all his light hair," she said, and she placed the baby into my arms. A low, tear-soaked moan came out of my mouth. I kept him as the nurse had placed him and sank into the chair.

He was awake! He looked up, blinking his eyes in the glare of the lights. The room became a vacuum for a moment—all I could see was myself and this baby, my baby. I rolled these words on my tongue for the first time, tasting their sweetness. His eyes were the color of blue sky over the ocean, a shade close to my father's and mine. My mother said I had been seven pounds, five ounces, at birth. It was hard to imagine that life started this small.

I turned more toward my mother. I held my baby firmer now, securing my arms under his little body, cradling his neck in the crease of my arm. The baby-blue knit cap they'd placed on his head kept scrunching upward and threatened to fall off. He kept his eyes open for a longer stretch, looking up at me, I imagined, and then to the sides, around the room.

"He's just like you were when you came out," my mother said. "Alert and looking all around. He is so beautiful, Sara. He's perfect."

I looked down at my son and agreed.

"This is what I wanted," she said, closing her eyes. When she opened them, tears streamed down the side of her face. "You with the baby—your baby—in your arms."

I was crying again, fat tears falling onto the swaddle blanket.

My mother had often lamented the way many spiritual teachers talked about spiritual awareness coming only through experiences of great pain. "Kind of invalidates those of us who haven't had some kind of big trauma," she said.

I'd felt cracked open by our fertility challenges and the loss of the twins. But as I felt the baby move in my arms and saw my mother's body opened and laid out in sacrifice for the deepest dream of both our hearts, I was cracked open again. Perhaps knowing this feeling was part of the point of the vision.

"Wide open, Momma," I said without context. "Wide open."

My mother seemed to recognize the reference. She laughed, and then we were crying and laughing at the same time.

Then I did what I had wanted to do since the nurse handed our baby to me. I pressed his body against my chest, my tears wetting his blanket, and breathed him into my heart.

The pediatric nurse sent a runner to the visitors' lounge to give a report to the family. Bill had spent the fifty-six minutes of the cesarean in the five-by-ten-foot square of the elevator bank outside the visitors' lounge. He'd walked in circles, counting each loop he made of the perimeter—150 circles—until he'd reached the forty-five-minute mark, whereupon he broke his private vigil. He found my sister's eyes through the lounge window, his anticipation now having transitioned to terror, overtaken by memories of the night he thought he'd lost me along with the twins. My sister, gripped with her own memory of that night, did not move, but held his gaze in solidarity.

Bill saw the nurse first, walking in her pink teddy-bear scrubs with a stethoscope dangling from her neck. He nearly tackled her.

"They're all okay: Mom, baby, Grandma," the nurse reported. My father and Bill's parents let out a loud whoop of relief.

"They're finishing the cesarean now," the nurse said.

"Anything else you can tell us?" my sister asked.

"The baby is a beautiful, healthy seven pounds, three ounces," she announced. "With a head of light blond hair."

"Sonofabitch," Bill said. The cheering stopped. Bill's father looked at him, appalled.

Bill burst into a kind of relieved, hysterical laughter.

"He's Finn," Bill said. "The baby's name is Finn."

When the surgery was complete, Dr. Gerber's team swarmed my mother and me with hugs. She, Miranda, and the nurses who'd been in the room for the surgery were all wet-faced and crying. The team escorted us to the recovery room, where, for the first time, now that her arms were free of the OR straps and bindings, my mother could hold Finn.

"I'm a grandmother!" she said with delight.

Since Finn's birth, people have often asked my mother if she felt bereft or empty following the birth, after carrying Finn in her body for nine months.

"I really didn't," she's always said in response. "I wanted Sara and Bill to have a baby, and to be a grandmother."

My mother and I took turns holding Finn, as I stood flush with the gurney where she lay. I thought of something I'd read years before, by the poet Khalil Gibran—something that having this baby through surrogacy had allowed me to experience:

> *Your children are not your children.*
> *They are the sons and daughters of Life's longing for itself.*
> *They come through you but not from you . . .*
> *You may house their bodies but not their souls . . .*
> *You are the bows from which your children as living arrows are*
> *sent forth.*

"You are the son of Life's longing for itself," I said to Finn, absorbed in the light of his eyes.

My father and Bill appeared in the doorway. They sounded out of breath, as if they'd run the distance from the visitors' lounge.

Bill ran to the baby.

"Oh my god," he said, and started crying.

My father walked to my mother's right side, looking her over for any signs of damage.

"He has your head shape, I think, Grandpa Casey," Bill said, holding the baby up for my father to see.

"And your dad's hands and feet," I said to Bill, running my fingers over Finn's wide palms and long fingers.

"He is everything," Bill said, and stopped. He looked across the room at my mother and began crying again. "You made this possible," he said, choking on the words.

"We did this," my mother said. "We did it as a village."

We carried Finn back across the room toward her so that my father could get a better look.

"Maybe the baby in your dream in England was a boy," I said to Bill. "He has the right hair color."

"This is so much better than the dream," Bill said. "He's real."

Bill tugged the swaddle blanket tighter around Finn's body and held him, feeling his weight, so little and so here.

Before we were released to the postdelivery floor, a lactation consultant arrived and asked if I wanted to nurse. I hadn't expected to have the opportunity to try right away. I struggled to remember the protocol we'd worked out with Jamie Simms. My brain felt overloaded, and it took me a minute to access our plan: to give the baby colostrum (my mother would pump and I would nurse) for the first two days. Then my mother would bind to dry up her milk, the way I did after the twins were born, and I would continue to nurse and hope that milk would come in.

The consultant walked us to a glider chair in the adjoining room and instructed me to sit straight in the chair. I felt afraid then, not having expected to face this moment in front of my family. For the first time since Finn had been placed in my arms, I was afraid that he would reject me.

I slipped my sweater down from my shoulders. Bill handed Finn to the nurse. He lingered a moment before letting him go. The nurse placed Finn in my arm like a football.

"You have to turn him to you, offer the nipple, and push him into the breast," she said, miming the motion she wanted us to make.

How did babies, having just been born, know how to eat? I felt rising pressure, as if this were a test of Finn's recognition of me as his mother.

The nurse positioned Finn and squeezed my breast with a firm grip. He opened his eyes, popped open his mouth, and latched, unassisted, onto my nipple.

The force of his sucking shocked me, and I gasped.

"He's strong," the nurse said. "This one is going to do fine."

Finn's jaw began to move as he swallowed, sucking hard with his jaws. The room was cold, but his mouth was warm on my skin. "Oh, wow," I said. Our baby was nursing. Our baby, a baby who was biologically made from parts of Bill and me, was sucking on my breast. He raised his hand from his side and placed it on my chest. His fingers curled on my skin, and he burrowed into the breast as he sucked.

"He's nursing!" I called to my mother across the room. Tears spilled again down my face; salty drops ran over my cheeks and neck. I couldn't know for sure what the Great Mother would have said, but this moment, with our baby feeding from my breast, felt like an initiation, too.

The nurse showed Bill and me how to feed Finn formula through a small tube called an assisted nursing system, so we could nurse even if I did not get milk.

The rest of the family rotated through the recovery room in shifts of two or three. At 11:20 PM, a resident sent Bill and me up to the fourteenth floor with the baby.

"We'll bring your mother up right behind you," she said.

A nurse with apple cheeks who looked so young I thought she must still be in school delivered us to an odd, octagonal-shaped room at the corner of the hallway.

The room looked like a Holiday Inn. The walls were brown and green. There was a pullout coach, a flat-screen TV, and a wooden cart topped with a clear plastic bassinet for the baby. She handed us some diapers, the assisted nursing kit, two-ounce bottles of formula, and an extra swaddle blanket.

"Push the button if you need anything," she said, gesturing to a remote control mounted on the wall.

"That's it?" Bill and I asked.

"Good night," she said, and closed the door. We placed Finn, who was sleeping now, into the bassinet. I looked around for some kind of equipment. Where was the heart rate monitor to ensure he would continue breathing? Who was overseeing things from the central desk? The hallway was silent. The entire maternity wing seemed hollow, like a cave. The lone light, a dim floor lamp, eked out a stingy yellow glow in the corner. We were on our own.

Bill and I pulled the bed out and perched on the end, eye level with the bassinet. In all our years of waiting, I couldn't have imagined the magnitude of this moment. We could not sleep. All we wanted to do was look at the baby. I was afraid that if I closed my eyes for a moment, he could disappear, like a mirage.

We decided to take turns standing guard, just to make sure. But neither of us was able to sleep while the other kept watch. I'd lie down and start laughing as I thought of Finn's tiny Connell feet, or the look on his face when the nurse had pulled him away from my breast after feeding.

"He looked like he was pissed," Bill said, gazing at Finn's sleeping face. "He wanted more food."

We stayed on our knees like that, watching Finn sleep, from 2:00 until 5:00 AM. When he awoke, hungry again, I nursed, fumblingly changed his diaper, and reswaddled his tiny body, which trembled every hour or so, the way the doctors had said it would, as his nervous system assimilated to his new world.

At 5:00 AM, I went to find my mother's room. If she was awake, I knew she'd want to see Finn. I peeked out into the hallway. The floor looked deserted, the only sound a soft hum from some kind of generator or central heater. It took me a few minutes to find a nurse. She informed me that my mother had never come up from the recovery room. Fear sounded in my head like an alarm. Shoeless, not even sure if my chest was covered, I ran to the elevator and jammed the DOWN button. On the eighth floor, I flashed my ID bracelet and raced through the whitewashed corridors to the room where I'd last seen my mother.

One of the nurses I recognized from our cesarean stopped me near the entrance. I inquired frantically after my mother.

"She's stable," the nurse said.

I searched her expressionless face, my fear rising to a scream.

"*Stable?*" I said. That was a word people used in the ICU. "What happened?"

The nurse gave me some cryptic words about Dr. Gerber's not being happy with my mother's urine content, about needing to monitor her kidney function.

"Can I see her?" I asked, my voice raspy and hoarse.

"Wait until she's been cleared," she said.

I walked back to my room as if I were wading underwater. How could no one have told us something was wrong? Kidney malfunction was serious. My mind swirled.

Back in our room, Finn was awake again and ready to eat. Bill and I set up the assisted nursing system, and I tried to keep calm. "They're probably just being extra careful," Bill said, stroking the top of Finn's head and the side of my arm.

He didn't sound convinced. His brow was furrowed into an arrow, and he moved his jaw back and forth several times, the hinge making a clicking sound. I tried not to imagine catastrophic scenarios. I wondered if the risk we'd taken was too great. I was looking into the chasm of my worst fear: that we could not have this healthy, alive child without some kind of trauma.

I turned to our baby, his wisps of blond hair, a nose that turned up like Bill's. His little hands rolled into balls. He went back to sleep in the bassinet, a feeling of grace emanating from his body. I tried to emulate him.

I asked the nurses to notify me immediately when my mother was cleared. With each hour when we heard nothing, I plummeted several times into terror and despair.

At 9:30 AM, I heard voices in the hallway. I put Finn in the bassinet (a requirement for taking him outside the room) and rolled the cart into the hallway, waving to Bill to follow. A nurse with wide hips and long gray hair, with a badge on her scrubs marking her as HEAD NURSE, greeted us.

"I'm Jane," she said, introducing herself. She balanced a tray of food and a bottle of water in her hands. I asked if she knew anything about Kristine Casey, who was due up from Recovery.

"You're the daughter!" she said, as if she'd met a celebrity. "Brought your mom up thirty minutes ago." Bill caught up to us in the hallway. "This food is for her. She said that she is really, really hungry."

Bill took Finn in the bassinet, and I ran past Jane down the hallway. My mother was sitting in bed, eating breakfast on a large tray. Dr. Gerber came by later and explained that there had actually not been anything wrong with her kidneys; my mother's urine output had simply been very low from dehydration during labor. In the ecstasy of relief, I forgave the staff for not telling us what had been happening all those hours. I wrapped my arms around my mother's shoulders, an awkward motion over the rails of the hospital bed. I put my face in her hair, drawing my cheek down next to hers, reveling in her physical aliveness and the fact that I was right there to touch it.

"I thought—" I said, my heart still stomping in my chest from the terror of the last few hours.

"I'm okay," she said. "Better than okay. The Great Mother brought us through. Jane is treating me like a queen. Do you know I can order room service twenty-four hours a day here? And the food is good."

I laughed as she showed me the menu. My father walked over and put a hand on my head.

"Congratulations, Momma," he said. His eyes looked both joyful and strained. I'd seen the same look on his face the day Bill and I were married.

My mother looked radiant, as if she'd just won a race.

"Now, let me see this grandbaby again," my mother said to Bill, who was pressing Finn against his chest.

By 4:00 PM, my mother had eaten two more meals from room service and slept for several hours. My father slept, too, rolled up in his coat, his eyes covered with a towel, on the pullout couch against the window.

Our visits continued like this all day. As soon as my parents woke up, my mother would have Jane race down the hall to get us. We'd pack the breast pump and clean onesies and swaddle blankets in

Finn's bassinet and roll down the hall to spend the next several hours in their room, until it was time for my mother to rest again. She and I squished ourselves into the hospital bed together so we could hold Finn and marvel at the blue of his eyes, his perfect unlined forehead, his gangly legs.

Jane and her nursing team brought vases of flowers in from the nursing desk, apologizing for the frequent interruptions. I closed my eyes, leaning into the sunlight that trickled into the room through the open blinds. A feeling was working its way to the surface, something important and desirable. I reached for it inside me, my inner fingers feeling as though they were touching air. The sensation caught in my chest, in the center of my heart: the realization that there was no more crisis, that I no longer needed to keep holding my breath. All parties were accounted for. We'd set out on a voyage, and we'd all come back safe. I shuddered as my body released what I had been holding. Finn moved in his blanket. He opened one eye and I smiled at him.

My cell phone screen lit up, and I was startled to see I had seven new messages, several from the same phone number. Dr. Colaum and Tracey had heard about Finn's birth and wanted to visit. They'd already driven into the city from Evanston and were now standing in the lobby at Prentice. I smiled to hear Tracey's voice: "Would it be too intrusive for us to come see you and meet Finn?"

Dr. Colaum hugged and congratulated my mother, held Finn in a practiced embrace, and then encircled me in her arms at the side of the room. Since we'd seen her, Dr. Colaum had had her nineteenth grandchild. She spoke so quietly, I could not hear what she said over the noise in the room. I like to think it was, "I'm proud of you." I leaned into her soft body and let her hold me for a minute. It was like hugging a part of the Great Mother.

Someone in the media had heard about our story, and by noon, reporters from news stations and papers all over the country were bombarding our voicemails with messages. A local station picked up the story for the evening news. International media began to call, asking if we would do radio and television interviews via satellite in Australia, India, and the UK. My mother was identified as the oldest woman in Illinois to give birth. We declined any interviews, saying we wanted to spend this time focusing on being together as a family.

A news station in Ireland called and said the nation was celebrating the birth of Finnean—due to his Celtic name, we guessed. This call impressed my father, who had felt repelled by the media interest up to that point. I'd finished nursing, and he was now rocking Finn in the green glider chair. He whispered, and I could not hear his words, only see his lips moving as he rocked. Finn stared, his eyes riveted on my father's face. The generator in the hallway kicked off then, allowing me to hear my father speak.

"Your birth was heard 'round the world," he said, as he pushed the glider with his foot, holding Finn close as they rocked back and forth.

Epilogue

Three weeks after Finn was born, my mother, Finn, and I were together in the downstairs guest room. My father and Bill were upstairs, watching a basketball game on TV. I could hear the announcers commenting on the game, and an occasional shout from my father when his team scored. We'd been in to see Dr. Gerber that morning, and my mother had been cleared for the drive home to Virginia that my parents would make the next day.

Finn lay next to us, looking like a baby cub on the fur throw that my mother and I had snuggled up under all those days during the pregnancy. He was dressed in a white long-sleeved onesie with hand mitts, and a small blue knitted cap to keep his head warm. It was still February, and cold in the basement. I'd moved our large space heater beside the bed and turned the heat on high, shooting warm air toward our faces. I'd carried Finn downstairs in the red Moby wrap Bill had brought to the hospital. I'd worn it constantly since we'd come home, carrying Finn around as I walked around the house, made phone calls, and folded laundry. Bill worked from home as much as he could, peeking in at Finn on the way to and from phone calls and meetings. He was fascinated by the way Finn curled into a crescent, as if he were still in the womb. When he fell into a deep sleep, he would lift up his head a few times, then drop down, making a sound that Bill swore was a purr.

Finn was now awake on the bed and making smacking sounds with his mouth. He'd freed his arms from the swaddle blanket, and every few minutes he would lift them in unison, holding them over his head in a move we had nicknamed "the maestro."

In the three weeks since Finn's birth, I had not slept more than three hours at a stretch, taken regular showers, or eaten a regular meal. And yet I felt amazing. I remembered talking with Kaitlin once, in the scary days of our miscarriages and my stillbirths: "Won't it be awesome when we call each other to complain about being exhausted because we were up with a baby?" she'd said.

The ecstasy I had felt the night of Finn's birth continued, even intensified, once we were home. In those first days, even months, every maternal task was a joy.

When Bill or my mother took a shift watching him, I would nap. When I woke, I would half-run into the nursery or down to the guest room, still hardly able to believe he was there, that we had a child to burp and feed and dress.

Later, when we weaned Finn to a crib, Bill and I still sometimes raced each other from the bedroom to be the first to arrive in the nursery.

Friends asked if motherhood was everything I had envisioned, perhaps wondering if it would be one of those things that reality tempers a bit. I answered truthfully that it was better than I had imagined—and I had imagined a great deal. "Likely a gift from a seven-year journey," I said to friends who said they'd thought about giving their children back after three months or more of not sleeping.

My mother's milk had stopped enough that she no longer needed to bind her breasts with a sports bra or Ace bandage. At night, she sweated so profusely from postdelivery hormone withdrawal that once or twice she had to wring out her clothes. The night sweats had the advantage of expelling the excess fluid she'd been carrying from the surgery, so that by the third week postbirth, she was no longer wearing maternity clothes. A friend who'd had a cesarean the week before Finn was born said she couldn't believe how quickly my mother had recovered. "You're in better shape than me," she told my mother when she stopped by with her baby to meet Finn.

"It's different when you don't have to take care of a baby all day and night," my mother said. "I feel as if I've been on vacation."

She and my father were leaving the next morning. When I thought of her going, I felt a wrench of sadness in my chest. She would be back in Chicago for her eight-week checkup, and Bill and I planned to take Finn on his first plane trip to D.C. Mother's Day week. I knew that the bond we had forged during the surrogacy could never be undone. Still, the separation felt profound—the cutting of a cord.

My mother confessed to feeling a sense of groundlessness as she approached the return to her life in Alexandria. "Every birth is also a rebirth," I remembered the counselor I spoke with saying after the twins died. The coach my mother had worked with during the pregnancy had given her a homework assignment to journal about what she'd like out of the next chapter of her life.

"I've never liked journaling," my mother said, sighing. I'd told her I could sit with her while she wrote. She kept setting down the pen she'd picked up on top of her leather-bound journal.

The Chinese lamp we'd placed next to the bed cast a pink beam of light onto the blankets.

"We could do a visioning," I suggested. "Like in my workshops."

"Let's!" she said. Her eyes lit up with hope.

We propped Finn between us on a pillow. He blew a bubble out of the side of his mouth. I offered my finger, which he sucked at with his lips, confirming he wanted to eat. I reached to the side of the bed, where I'd placed a warm bottle.

My milk had not come in, which had initially felt disappointing. The lack of it seemed to open a pocket of unfinished grief. But then I'd had the grace to remember that three years ago, in the nadir of our experience, I would have clawed through a jungle naked to have a child and would not have wasted a moment caring whether or not I could breastfeed. "Big picture," Bill had said when I'd cried my few tears about nursing. I'd nodded and smiled. And we surmised, based on the kind of miraculous way Finn had come into the world, that if it was in his best interest to breastfeed, we would have.

We'd continued to read to Finn every day. I would pull out *Harry Potter* or a Shel Silverstein book, and my mother would hold Finn while I read. When I started, he would stop wiggling, widen his eyes into circles, and form his mouth into a big O.

My mother was so impressed by this unusual display of attentiveness that she took photographs and emailed them to her friends. Subject line: "incredible."

My mother did some meditation breaths to prepare for the visioning while I fed and burped Finn. Under her tutelage, I had grown adept at this basic skill and was able to bring up the burps with more forceful claps than Bill or I would ever have been comfortable with on our own.

"Ready to vision?" I asked my mother, once Finn was resting again on the pillows.

"Ready," she answered.

A trickle of afternoon light seeped through the high windows above the bed, and Finn seemed transfixed by the dust particles in the air. I spoke an intention: that we could both hear whatever was useful in the visioning, especially that my mother would receive inspiration for her path.

"Let's vision for you, too," my mother said.

I assumed the next few months for me would entail more of exactly what I was doing now: caring for Finn in the family nest.

I asked the standard visioning questions I used in my practice: "What is the highest vision for our lives now? What must we now release? What must we embody? Anything else?"

When we'd finished writing our answers in silence, we shared.

"Lots of writing," my mother began with what she had seen for me. This tickled me, since in the visioning I'd seen several images of Finn in the Moby wrap while I typed at my computer.

"I saw you speaking to a group and teaching a class," I said to my mother. I spoke quickly, knowing how averse she had been to public presentations.

"Ha," my mother said, without explaining.

"I saw you sharing about following your vision," I continued. "Maybe even leading visionings yourself."

"I saw myself teaching, too," my mother said, "maybe a course at my church. A year ago I wouldn't have considered such a thing."

I lay my hands in my lap. I felt happy thinking about my mother teaching a class.

"I felt one more thing for you," my mother said, breaking the silence. She stopped again before continuing. She picked at the trim on the blanket, not looking at me. "It came like a message, during the last question."

I sat up straighter against the cushions. The skin on my neck pricked.

"I'll just say it," she said. "*Tell Sara: You are chosen, not broken.*"

I looked at my mother. Her eyes were wet and full.

I began to cry.

I'd heard more than once that it is not the events of our lives that upset us; it is the stories we make up about them. And the story I'd made up about my childhood trauma and infertility experiences was that I was a broken mess. I wondered now if the story I'd believed myself was a lie.

Jungien psychologist Caroline Myss told a story once that I never forgot, about a Native American man captured during World War II and held in a POW camp. He was tortured and starved for months, and then, on the brink of his death, he was fed maggots from a dirt floor by one of the guards just before the camp was liberated. When he returned home to his tribe, he wallowed in grief and self-pity and likely a fair amount of PTSD. The tribe left him be for a while and then took him to the edge of a large lake with a stone tied around his neck.

"You can either choose to forgive and live," they said, "or die. There are only two choices."

The man walked into the lake, intending to choose death. He started to sink, when his life force seized him and he began to forgive. As he struggled to the surface, he faced the final situation he'd endured: the guard who had shoved the maggots into his face, moving his jaw so he was forced to swallow, encouraging the other guards to laugh at and humiliate him. It was too much, he felt, to forgive this man. He let go of the rock so he could drown. At the last second, before all his oxygen had gone, a watery light entered his mind and he saw that same man reading a book while the other guards slept, reading about a way to keep someone alive using the protein from bugs in the earth. The soldier had not been tormenting him, it turned out, but saving his life.

Caroline Myss said that before we label a situation, we must consider the possibility that we may not have all the information.

Before you name them as broken and bad, consider that there may be something profound and important—not just for you, but for a greater good—that could not come any other way.

I imagined that, like the soldier in Myss's story, I did not have all the information. I liked the idea of being open to chosen-ness, contemplating how even the broken-seeming parts of my story were and could be a portal for good.

Perhaps I *had* been chosen. Perhaps we all had been.

"Thank you," I said to my mother.

I wiped my face with the back of my hand.

"Thank you," she said.

Finn, who had fallen asleep during our visioning exercise, now stirred. My mother lifted him to her shoulder and patted his back. I made a note in my sketchbook; the visioning had given me an idea for a lecture. I'd been invited to give a talk on Mother's Day at an organization in Lincoln Park. The founder of the organization told me that they had handed out flowers to the mothers in the audience in years past, just like they had at the church I'd attended the previous year. Inspired, I dialed the center's number and reached the office manager. I asked how many people typically attended the talks.

"Three to four hundred," he said.

"Could we give out three to four hundred roses?" I asked.

"We can," he said, without asking for an explanation.

On Mother's Day, I would give a rose to every person who attended the service. I would share the message I felt from the Great Mother—that we are all part of her. And I would ask, no matter what each person had labeled as broken in themselves, that the lie be healed and that they might know that they had been chosen.

That talk was still two months away, though. I put down my

sketchbook and leaned my head back onto the bed. My mother and I had one more afternoon and evening together. The hum of the electric heater lulled me to rest.

I wanted to sit here one more minute without saying anything, locking in the exact shade of cream paint on the walls, the tiny timbre of Finn's voice, my mother's strength next to me, so close I could touch her.

We each put a hand around Finn, our fingers touching. And I felt that the Divine Mother was holding us now, the way she could anytime but was so tangibly, in this moment of initiation, holding us together, where she had brought and would continue to bring us home.

A Conversation with Grandma and Surrogate Kristine Casey

What was it like to read about the experience from Sara's point of view?

I had many emotions in reading the book. I was sad to revisit the struggle and pain in the early portions of the book. I learned things about Sara's perspective on our relationship that were hard. I was struck that even though we were very close throughout the pregnancy, her story, the thoughts and emotions around the facts, are uniquely hers. I've been thinking about that perspective in many of my relationships since then.

My favorite part of the story is seeing Finn's little face when Sara read the end of the *Harry Potter* book. In that moment, I knew that he knew who his mommy was. How beautiful!

Did you ever doubt the pregnancy would happen or turn out successfully?

Yes, from the beginning there was no illusion that I could make this work by anything I could control. Even the very idea of the surrogacy seemed to come from outside and beyond my own mind and will. At each step we just went one step forward and then waited. There seemed to be a lot of waiting, time suspended between hope and resignation. Even as he was being born, I was just praying for him to breathe. It was all such a gift.

What were people's reactions when they saw you pregnant?

Mostly it was winter in Chicago and people really couldn't tell—so I experienced fewer reactions than I might have otherwise. If they did notice, most people kept their reactions to themselves—maybe they thought I carried weight in my middle. People that we did meet in stores, when trying on maternity clothes, for instance, and in the OB waiting room typically looked surprised and then were moved and wanted to hear the story. Most of the people that heard the story seemed to go into themselves to see if they would do the same. Like a chance to stop and smell the roses, many spent a moment connecting with the love they had for their own mothers and daughters.

**Would you encourage others to take on
this kind of surrogacy experience?**

That's a hard question to answer. It was an amazing experience for me. And I'm sure I'm not unique.

I think surrogacy is a beautiful example of the old truth, "It takes a village to raise a child." If a woman has the health to nurture a new life, I think it's such a privilege to do that, even when you are not going to be the mother of that child. But a surrogate needs to be very clear about her motivations and expected outcomes.

What was the most difficult part of the experience for you?

Being away from home, husband, family, friends, activities, and routines for four months was the most difficult part. Contrary to popular belief, it's actually hard to sit around for that long. I was interested to see how much of my identity was wrapped up in what I spent my time doing at home.

Although I could have stayed at home during the pregnancy, I really wanted Sara and Bill to experience as much of that time as normally as possible. I know that they were worried and we were all in foreign emotional territory, so it was well worth it to be able to see, talk, and touch them each day.

What was your husband's very first reaction to the idea?

He listened to the whole idea—my excitement, why I wanted to do it, how the idea had come to me. He said he could see it was a very important calling for me and supported pursuing it from the beginning. I think/wonder, in that first moment, if he thought there was any real possibility I would actually be able to do it.

What were the key differences between having a baby in 2011 and having one in 1975?

So many things were different this time. Medical technology; seeing ultrasound pictures several times along the way; and, of course, being a high-risk pregnancy, I saw the doctors so frequently. This time my relationship with the doctors and staff became personal and supportive. I loved every office visit for the medical wisdom and friendly excitement that things were gong so well.

In 1975, I saw the doctor at four months and then monthly till the end of the pregnancy. I'm not sure he knew my name. I didn't know if the baby was a boy or a girl. No discernible ultrasound photos. And when it came to labor, I was in a city hospital with one communal labor room full of women mostly having natural childbirth; it was loud and extremely low-tech. The dads were in the delivery room but didn't stay overnight with their new families. Our room at Prentice suite was palatial.

**How did you view your relationship with your
daughter before this experience, versus now?**

I would have said that we had a normal mother-daughter relationship. Sara was a really fun kid. She was funny and excited by things and always ready to go and to do. In her teen years and twenties, when we were not as close, I took that as part of normal individualization—Sara was finding herself. Now, I feel very close to Sara. We've shared quite a journey. We don't talk every day, but we can pick up at any point and feel connected and loved.

What's been the response of people hearing about your experience?

Amazement. Amazement that this was medically possible and that when I came home, I was walking around and doing all the things I used to do. Women fall into two camps: those who say they would do the same and those who say absolutely not. Many men are totally perplexed and speechless. Some people love the family story when I can pull out the baby pictures at the end. Others ask questions about the spiritual and psychological journey. There's a lot of food for thought there.

**Do you feel you have a special relationship with Finn,
versus other grandchildren?**

I am delighted to have a second grandchild, born also [in 2011], so
I can actually answer this question: I feel the same kind of grandmother love for both. They light up my life!

However, I will remain forever grateful that Finn turned at
thirty-seven weeks. He was taking care of Grandma on that one.

Would you do it again?

I'm so grateful that I could do this once. If I had an intuition as
strong as the first one, I would never turn it down. But I don't. It's
the furthest thing from my heart right now.

What are you going to do next?

I'm interested in the answer to that question, too. I've been meditating and enjoying the possibilities. Life is good.

Reader's Guide

Questions for Discussion

1. As a young adult, Sara feels distant from her family. By the end of the book, she is experiencing great intimacy with her mother. Have you experienced transformation in a relationship that you thought would never change?

2. Early in the book, Sara references a talk she heard about covenants and their possible power to carry the people that make them through to fulfillment. What do you think of this idea? Is there somewhere in your life where making a covenant to something could give you fortitude?

3. Chapter 6 deals with grief and trauma. What kind of modeling do you think our society gives for dealing with these kinds of experiences—both as the one experiencing and as the one witnessing a traumatic experience?

4. Many women share that they've had a miscarriage or perinatal loss. Do you think it's better for individuals, or society at large, to keep such experiences private?

5. After she loses her twins, Sara shares that she believes healing requires both time and inner healing. Do you agree? What actions does she take to heal from her loss? What would you turn to?

6. At the end of chapter 6, Sara's mother offers to be the surrogate for Sara and Bill's baby. What do you think of this decision? Would you ever take this type of risk with a family member? Would you ever want to take this kind of risk with your own body?

7. Statistics show that losing a child can be devastating to a marriage. What do you think of Sara and Bill's response to their experience? What do you think helped them navigate through and stay committed?

8. Both Sara and her mother speak about calling and vision in this book. What do you think makes something a calling versus a desire? Have you ever experienced being called to something? If so, what was it, and how did it turn out?

9. Heading into the psychological evaluation required for surrogacy, Sara acknowledges that the proposed surrogacy arrangement could be seen as crazy and contemplates the notion of crazy versus inspired ideas. Have you ever been inspired by a "crazy"-sounding idea and followed through on it? What was it like?

10. In the epilogue, Sara receives the idea of being chosen, not broken. Have you told yourself a story that you are broken in some area? If

so, is there any evidence you see of how the situation could have been chosen, or a way in which your situation might be an avenue for some good in your life and others'?

Enhance Your Book Club

1. Sara's mother attends Sara's annual vision workshop twice in the book. Create your own vision workshop: Invite members to bring magazines, catalogs, or old books (along with poster board and glue sticks) to the next meeting and create vision boards of things you'd like to see unfold in your lives. Share the boards with one another and allow fellow members to comment on what they see.

2. Think of an area of life where you'd like guidance. Take a walk in nature or even through city streets, lightly holding the topic in mind but then focusing all your attention on what you see, hear, smell, feel, and sense. Share any insights with book club members.

3. Sara is an active author and life coach in Chicago. To learn more about Sara, and maybe even invite her to your book club, visit www.saraconnell.com.

About the Author

Sara Connell is a writer and life coach with a private practice in Chicago. She lives in the city with her husband, Bill, and son, Finn. Visit Sara at www.saraconnell.com.

I Never made it hrl.
Passport Universe Hanks
UN AUTH FULL LS

Ren. 4/16
GL 6/11

July 31st Food
July 23
July 16 food
July 9
July 4 Food
25 SS
18 food
11 SS
June 4 food

28 SS
21 Food
14 SS
May 7 Food
30 GLJ
Apr 23 Food + pancakes
9
?? SS

$$(x + 10)(x - 8)$$

$$x^2 - 8x + 10x - 80$$

$$x^2 + 2x - 76 = 4$$

$$(x \quad)(x \quad)$$

$$x^2 + 2x - 76 = 4$$
$$ - 4 \quad -4$$
$$\overline{}$$
$$x^2 + 2x \quad - 80$$
$$(x + 10)(x - 8)$$

Selected Titles from Seal Press

For more than thirty years, Seal Press has published groundbreaking books. By women. For women.

Choosing You: Deciding to Have a Baby on My Own, by Alexandra Soiseth. $15.95, 978-1-58005-222-1. The deeply honest memoir of one woman's decision to brave pregnancy and motherhood alone.

I Love Mondays: And Other Confessions from Devoted Working Moms, by Michelle Cove. $16.00, 978-1-58005-435-5. Michelle Cove explores the common difficulties faced by working moms—and provides real-life anecdotes, helpful new perspectives, and mom-tested strategies for dealing with each one.

We Hope You Like This Song: An Overly Honest Story about Friendship, Death, and Mix Tapes, by Bree Housley. $16.00, 978-1-58005-431-7. Bree Housley's sweet, quirky, and hilarious tribute to her lifelong friend, and her chronicle of how she honored her after her premature death.

Deliver This! Make the Childbirth Choice That's Right for You...No Matter What Everyone Else Thinks, by Marisa Cohen. $14.95, 978-1-58005-153-8. A smart, informative book that helps expectant mothers explore traditional and alternative birthing choices.

Rockabye: From Wild to Child, by Rebecca Woolf. $15.95, 978-1-58005-232-0. The coming-of-age story of a rock n' roll party girl who becomes unexpectedly pregnant, decides to keep the baby, and discovers motherhood on her own terms.

Seeing Ezra: A Mother's Story of Autism, Unconditional Love, and the Meaning of Normal, by Kerry Cohen. $16.00, 978-1-58005-433-1. An inspirational chronicle of a mother's struggle to protect her son from a system that seeks to compartmentalize and "fix" his autism, and of her journey toward accepting and valuing him for who he is—just as he is.

Find Seal Press Online

www.SealPress.com
www.Facebook.com/SealPress
Twitter: @SealPress